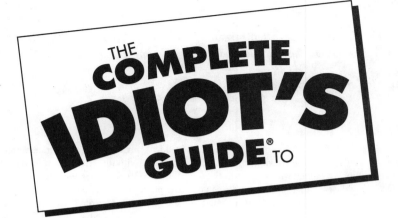

THE COMPLETE **IDIOT'S** GUIDE® TO

Understanding
Mormonism

by Drew Williams

ALPHA

A member of Penguin Group (USA) Inc.

For my wife, Carol, who is my greatest hero; and my adoring children, my favorite fans!
For Thomas Johnson, who was my role model in righteousness; and to Leo and Scott—
the first "Miracles" in my life.
And finally, for anyone who ever wondered about the true meaning of life, and what
the heck we're supposed to do while we're here.

Copyright © 2003 by Drew Williams

International Standard Book Number: 0-02-864491-3
Library of Congress Catalog Card Number: 2003100703

05 04 03   8 7 6 5 4 3 2 1

Interpretation of the printing code: The rightmost number of the first series of numbers is the year of the book's printing; the rightmost number of the second series of numbers is the number of the book's printing. For example, a printing code of 03-1 shows that the first printing occurred in 2003.

Printed in the United States of America

Note: This publication contains the opinions and ideas of its author. It is intended to provide helpful and informative material on the subject matter covered. It is sold with the understanding that the author and publisher are not engaged in rendering professional services in the book. If the reader requires personal assistance or advice, a competent professional should be consulted.

The author and publisher specifically disclaim any responsibility for any liability, loss, or risk, personal or otherwise, which is incurred as a consequence, directly or indirectly, of the use and application of any of the contents of this book.

Most Alpha books are available at special quantity discounts for bulk purchases for sales promotions, premiums, fund-raising, or educational use. Special books, or book excerpts, can also be created to fit specific needs.

For details, write: Special Markets; Alpha Books, 375 Hudson Street, New York, NY 10014.

Publisher: *Marie Butler-Knight*
Product Manager: *Phil Kitchel*
Senior Managing Editor: *Jennifer Chisholm*
Senior Acquisitions Editor: *Randy Ladenheim-Gil*
Development Editor: *Lynn Northrup*
Production Editor: *Billy Fields*
Copy Editor: *Susan Aufheimer*
Illustrator: *Chris Eliopoulos*
Cover/Book Designer: *Trina Wurst*
Indexer: *Tonya Heard*
Layout/Proofreading: *Rebecca Harmon, Mary Hunt*

Contents at a Glance

Contents

Foreword

When I was a high school student, some of my best friends were Mormons (or, as they preferred to be known, "LDS"). I was a life-long Catholic, and proud of it, but my interests were more compatible with the Mormon kids I knew than with some of the rowdier party people. My Mormon friends, Walt Denham, Liz Foley-Johnson, Trey Matson, and Lori Stapley, tolerated me, their "gentile" friend, and made me feel comfortable around them. When they got to know me better, they started to talk to me about their church.

Unfortunately, I wasn't a very good listener at first.

Although I had been raised a staunch Catholic, I knew very little about religion and religious histories. I believed in God, of course, but my conception of God was something I had personally concocted, something in conflict with most of the basic principles I had been taught in Catholic catechism. Unlike my Mormon friends, I had little interest in religion, so their attempts to engage me in religious conversations usually ended in frustration for me and for them.

As I got older and more mature, and as the good example of my Mormon friends began to have a greater influence on me, I was more open to their attempts to talk about their religion and their own faith in it. My willingness, though, didn't make me a good audience. The basic principles of the LDS Church as described by my teenage Mormon friends were too alien to my Catholic brain to be comprehensible. I wasn't always intentionally obtuse in these conversations—although sometimes my stubbornness made me resist their missionary approaches—but even when I wanted to understand their religious explanations, I couldn't. Despite their good intentions, my Mormon friends didn't have the experience or the resources available to them to present Mormon/LDS principles to me in ways that I could understand.

Still, something about these kids, these good-hearted, clean-living kids, made a life-long impression on me. I liked them, and I wanted to learn more about what it was that made them the way they were.

In my senior year in high school, Brigham Young University, the largest private—and Mormon—university in the United States, offered me a football scholarship. On my recruiting visit there, the beautiful campus, nestled at the base of Utah's Wasatch Mountains, and the wholesome environment won me over. I came home and announced that I would go to college at BYU. And not long after that announcement, I began meeting with the Mormon missionaries. Just weeks before I left for college, I was baptized a member of the Church of Jesus Christ of Latter-day Saints. I became a Mormon.

My Mormon friends were influential in my conversion, but I sometimes wonder if our conversations about the LDS Church would have been more fruitful if we could have referred to a basic, easy-to-read guide to their religion. This book probably would have saved us all a lot of time, frustration, and arguing.

The Complete Idiot's Guide to Understanding Mormonism is an accessible and comprehensive overview of Latter-day Saint doctrine and history, mingled with humor, that will be a handy guide to the LDS religion for non-Mormons and Mormons alike, whether or not they're complete idiots.

I enjoyed the logical, clear format of the text that made it easy for me to find the answers I was looking for. In addition to providing an easy-to-understand discussion of basic LDS beliefs and history, Drew Williams has integrated snippets of popular Mormon culture.

I wish I could have read this book 30 years ago.

—Dr. Chris Crowe, English department, Brigham Young University

Introduction

Welcome to *The Complete Idiot's Guide to Understanding Mormonism*. The intent of this book is to provide you with a fundamental understanding of the origins, challenges, and practices of the Church of Jesus Christ of Latter-day Saints. By the way, members of the Church have often been referred to as "Mormons" over the years. Recently, however, Church authorities have suggested moving away from this term, encouraging reference to the "LDS Church" or "LDS people." I try to heed their advice throughout this volume, but you'll still see the term "Mormon" show up at appropriate times.

When I was invited to write this book, I was immediately overtaken by this awesome responsibility. My LDS friends reminded me that I would be representing not only the fastest growing Christian religion in America, but also the nearly 12 million people who are part of the LDS Church worldwide. It has been a great opportunity and honor to be asked to represent the LDS faith on this project, and although I have spent quite a bit of time in research and development of the subjects included, it's impossible to cover everything. This book offers an introduction to Mormonism, from the point of view of someone who has lived on both sides of the baptismal font. If you want to dig deeper into LDS culture, I encourage you to go to the Church's website at www.lds.org, or check out some of the books I list in Appendix B.

There are many reasons for the increased interest in Mormonism—or Latter-day Saint beliefs. The LDS Church has become more visible than ever before over the past five years, especially due to the popularity of current LDS leader Gordon B. Hinckley—a regular on *Larry King Live* (Larry is married to an LDS woman, by the way)—and probably because of the hosting of the 2002 Winter Olympics in Salt Lake City. As well, there are more LDS people living outside the United States than within.

And of course, we still have Donny and Marie!

One reason for the increased interest in LDS beliefs surrounds the Church's focus on the family. Although the LDS lifestyle and family traditions are not new to the world, interest in that lifestyle seems to be increasing proportionate to the impact of negative influences on families throughout the world. This book will spend quite a bit of time discussing LDS family values.

What You'll Find in This Book

Christian views of God, and how we fit into the eternal equation, have varied over the centuries since Jesus walked the earth, and it is still a popular subject of religious debate. Many Christians may believe things that others in their congregations might not agree with or have answers to. This can add to the confusion about who we are as children of an eternal being, where we came from, and why we're all here. In **Part 1, "The Relationship Between God and Man,"** we examine the life of Jesus Christ and God, and the LDS concept of the "Eternal Progression" of man from the origins of our spirits, through mortality, and into the afterlife.

A unique characteristic within the LDS culture is the concept of continued revelation from God. Latter-day Saints believe that God still talks to the children of the world, and that the heavens are not closed. In **Part 2, "The Word of God Revisited,"** we explore important aspects of the Old and New Testaments, as contained in the King James Version of the Holy Bible. We also look at the lives of the early apostles, and how an important tenet of LDS doctrine—the Apostasy—affected the stopping of God's ordained church from existing on the earth for a period of time.

We conclude the second part of the book with a discussion on the Holy Trinity, and a review of a creed that has stood as the foundation on which most of the Christian faiths still stand today. These are important topics for people who want to understand LDS beliefs. The Church grounds itself in being a direct restoration of the church established by Jesus Christ 2,000 years ago, and then re-established in 1830. So the historical info will help explain the "whys" of LDS theology.

You can't discuss Mormonism without spending a fair amount of time examining the life of LDS Church founder Joseph Smith Jr. In **Part 3, "The Prophet from Pennsylvania,"** we look at the other religious influences that brought the 14-year-old Joseph to a grove of trees in upstate New York where he saw God and Jesus Christ, who instructed him to create a religion. In the years that followed, New England society did not take kindly to the ways of Mormonism, and so the trek across America began. We trace the early days of the Latter-day Saints as they wandered through the wilderness of the Midwest, finally settling for a time on the swampy banks of the Mississippi River. It would be the last home for Joseph Smith, who was murdered by a mob in Carthage, Illinois, in 1844.

In **Part 4, "Pioneering a New World Religion,"** we introduce the LDS Church's longest-running leader and most prominent name in Mormonism, Brigham Young. Under his watchful leadership, the trek of his people across the plains begins. We follow the 2,000-mile journey of the LDS pioneers as they make their way to their final home in the Salt Lake Valley. Incidentally, Brigham Young's influence in the world is still part of today's LDS culture. Both the University of Utah and Brigham Young University were founded by Brigham, and today his name is still prominent in the legacy of his great great great grandson, NFL football legend Steve Young.

Part 4 also examines the LDS priesthood, the role of women in the Church, and one of the most controversial topics in Mormonism: polygamy.

The Latter-day Saint culture includes many unique characteristics, which set it apart from the more traditional aspects of Christianity. However, LDS beliefs also include strong feelings about keeping the Sabbath Day holy, paying tithing, and strengthening families. **Part 5, "Modern-Day Revelation,"** explores traditional Christian values. We also examine a couple of the more common identifiers of Mormonism, including LDS doctrine on food and drink choices, and the most common LDS symbol in the world—the missionaries.

We wrap things up with **Part 6, "Latter-day Landscape and Leadership."** This last section looks inside the mystique that often surrounds the LDS Church's sacred temples, of which there are just more than 100 scattered throughout the world. You are also introduced to the 15 prophets of the LDS Church. In most cases, these men spent the most of two or even three career lifetimes in the service of their church work, *prior* to being called to the office of "prophet."

Helpful Hints Along the Way

Throughout this book you'll notice boxes that contain helpful and interesting information to enhance your understanding of Mormonism:

Mormonology

These boxes define religious or LDS concepts and terms that may be unfamiliar to you.

Mormon Myths

Here's where we'll clarify various myths about Mormonism.

Latter-day Laughter

These boxes offer a dose of good-hearted humor, Latter-day style.

And It Came to Pass

Check these boxes for stories, interesting tidbits, and little-known facts about Mormonism.

Words of Wisdom

In these boxes you'll find basic tenets of Mormonism, as quoted by noted sources, from Church authorities to celebrities to business leaders.

Acknowledgements

I'd like to recognize the key spiritual influences in my life, without whom I could have never been prepared to write this book.

I must first acknowledge my Heavenly Father, in whose good favor I am constantly striving to gain. I must also pay homage to the man in whose name the subject of this book is about—even Jesus Christ—who stands at the head of the LDS Church.

Moreover, I wish to pay my most sincere respect and love for my dear wife, Carol Lynch Williams. Although I have read or heard every one of her nearly 20 novels in publication, I never knew how challenging it is to actually *write* a book. Once again, I am amazed at the ability she possesses, to home-school our children, raise her niece and nephew, take care of our home while I travel, manage her church responsibilities, maintain an active life in support of her writing and teaching others to write, and still crank out a novel or two each year. She has always been a role model for humility and integrity.

I'd also like to thank my five wonderful daughters for their patience with an often cranky dad, as he sat for hours—even days—in the shadows of a basement office, reading, writing, and complaining about the noise upstairs. You girls are my world! As well, having the experience of living with the gentle spirit of my niece Maggie and the strong integrity of my nephew Craig has been added inspiration to our family and this book.

To Scott Miracle and his father Leo—their examples as true Christians and men of God have influenced me all of my life.

I must also thank three men who were undaunted in their efforts to introduce and teach me about the LDS Church some 20-plus years ago. Chris Krebs, with whom I proudly served in the U.S. Navy, who introduced me to the Book of Mormon and the House of the Lord. We shared an experience that I will always hold most sacred. LeRoy Welch, another shipmate, from Blackfoot, Idaho. He carried the torch all the way to the night of my baptism. Wherever you are LeRoy, I hope you know that the water did its job! To the late Charles Hansen, who gave his very life in the service of God, as mission president in Oakland, California. He was a great and gentle man.

To two young missionaries, Elders Kent Costner and Rich McClendon. Both of these men found something to finally convince me that, after almost three years of study, I needed to make a decision about my own personal salvation. And by the way, sorry, Kent, about ripping your pants out when slipping through the window at the baptismal font room that Sunday night!

I would not be an honorable son if I did not offer a nod to my parents, Dorothy and Lee Williams. They always tried to make things work, and they never questioned my spiritual judgment. (By the way, Mom and Dad, there's still water in the font!)

I would be remiss in not thanking my dear friend and technical advisor, Erika Wilde. This savvy Latter-day Saint woman is incredibly gifted as a writer and as a woman of godly integrity. As well, she is a stalwart wife and mother who has paid a dear price for her experience. Erika lost her two-week-old daughter, Ruby, during the time this book was being written. Yet despite her profound loss, she has managed to carry on in her life—as a long-distance runner, entrepreneur, and young women's leader in the Church.

I also wish to thank my agent, Jessica Faust, who contacted me about this project in the first place; and my new friends at Penguin Putnam, including Randy Ladenheim-Gil (who received more "Oh-My-Heck!" e-mails and phone calls than she probably cared to); and my development editor Lynn Northrup, to whom I send a warm "Yippee Skippee." In both cases, your patience has been greatly appreciated, and your input made this work much stronger. It has definitely been an all-hands effort.

Trademarks

Part 1

The Relationship Between God and Man

For many people, members of the Church of Jesus Christ of Latter-day Saints (or "Mormons") stand as a peculiar subculture of Christianity. Latter-day Saints do not trace their roots back through Catholicism and the Holy Roman Empire as the rest of the Christian world does. Instead, the origins of Mormon theology date directly to the days of Christ, although the Church itself is only slightly more than 170 years old.

So how does a faith that considers itself "Christian" *not* bare a lineage similar to the rest of the Christian community? How can a religious organization claim to be associated with the restoration of the ancient church of Christ and still be so different from mainstream Christianity?

The Original American Religion

In This Chapter

◆ The beginning of a 170-year journey

◆ How Jesus is the center of Latter-day Saints' beliefs

◆ Mormonism and the gospel of Christ

◆ Early ridicule and misconceptions

◆ The "FUD" factor

Curious about the intriguing and often misunderstood world of Mormonism? You've come to the right place! In this book I give you a peek into the world of the Church of Jesus Christ of Latter-day Saints (commonly referred to as the LDS Church), its culture, and its often peculiar religious beliefs. We'll be spending quite a bit of time discussing not only the core tenets of Mormonism, but also its origins, which predate traditional Christianity. We'll also separate the common myths from the facts. What about all those wives? What's the role of women in the Church? How did the Mormons make the long trek to Utah? And is it true Mormons don't drink coffee, do drugs, or even go to R-rated movies?

These are just a few of the questions this book will address, as I introduce you to the world of the Latter-day Saints and the Mormon faith.

We'll start by heading back in time several thousand years, when religious lifestyles were all the rage in the Middle East. You'll discover that Mormonism itself is linked to the ancient Church of Israel. Then, we'll move to the time of Jesus, when his ministry "fulfilled" the laws of his prophetic predecessors.

I'll also introduce you to Joseph Smith, Jr.—the boy who got Mormonism and the LDS Church off the ground. It's amazing to many people, both inside and outside the Church, how similar *some* of the events in Joseph's life were to those of Jesus. I say "similar," because ultimately (as Latter-day Saints would tell you the world over), nobody lived through more powerful, devastating, or enlightening events than did Jesus Christ.

It's a fascinating journey, so let's get started.

The Journey Begins

According to faithful members of the LDS Church, although the Church itself is slightly more than 170 years old, Mormonism is founded on the principles established by the first "Covenant People" of God—the Israelites.

But it wasn't just the Jews who had a corner on trekking through the wilderness. For nearly 20 years, commencing in 1830 the LDS people—"Mormon Pioneers," as they were called—wandered the wilderness of early America. To the Latter-day Saints of old, their valleys were in Ohio, not Mesopotamia. Their rivers weren't the Tigres, Euphrates, and the great Nile, but the Missouri, North Platte, and the muddy Mississippi. And their plains weren't in the dry lands of Jordan, but rather, the desert prairies of Nebraska and Wyoming.

> **Mormonology**
>
> In recent years, the LDS Church has encouraged use of the term **Latter-day Saints** or **LDS people** in reference to Church members. The leadership believes these terms are more in line with the general focus of the Church. Although I use the reference "Mormon" occasionally—especially during the chapters that discuss the events of the pioneers—I try to follow the Church's advice elsewhere.

Latter-day Saint people followed a belief that would not sit well with the status quo of "civilized" Christianity. Consequently, like the former "Chosen People" of God, the LDS religion and those who claimed a hold to it were persecuted—Church members were even killed—often at the hands of a government-sanctioned militia.

Let's now share a bit of their journey, as we look back at more than 170 years of Mormonism, and stretch even farther back to the days of Adam and Eve, who laid the groundwork for what Latter-day Saints claim to be the "Kingdom of God on Earth."

A Genesis of a Different Kind

In the beginning (I've always wanted to write that!), there was a simple plan to follow: a "Mosiach" (more commonly spelled "Messiah"), as foretold by the Jewish prophets of the Old Testament, would redeem the world from its fallen state.

Then, in a small community near the eastern reaches of the Roman Empire—a nation that forcefully encouraged its citizens to worship a collection of gods—a baby Hebrew boy named Joshua ("Jesus" in the Roman dialect), was born. His life almost immediately began to change the tide of religious thinking throughout the known "civilized" world, and—the way civilization even counted its years. By the time Jesus was about 14, this controversial son of a Jewish carpenter was mingling with the learned men of the community in the sacred halls of Jerusalem, discussing the laws of God, many of which were described as being the fulfillment of the current ideology of that era. They called him a prophet, a missionary—even the Son of God. But within another two decades, Jesus, the man, would be mocked by an angry mob, and killed, his death sanctioned by the local government.

It's amazing that the influence of one person's life—more than 2,000 years ago—could so permanently alter the future perspective of mankind throughout the world. Even the way humanity counts time was changed after the birth of Jesus. This one individual, half mortal, half God, is the single entity on whose arrival balanced the meridian of time itself. For Latter-day Saints, gaining a personal assurance that Jesus Christ is the Savior of the world means distancing themselves from some of the things *in* the world. This idea plays off the notion believed by many LDS people that "man cannot serve two masters."

Mormon Myths

Myth: Latter-day Saints are not Christians. If there is one fallacy that stands out as the most profoundly inaccurate judgment of Mormonism, it's the assumption that Latter-day Saints are not Christians. Many Latter-day Saints find the idea that traditional "Christians" don't consider LDS members as Christians, inconsistent and downright ridiculous. A church that calls itself "The Church of *Jesus Christ* of Latter-day Saints" and whose fundamental principle is that all things are predicated on the atoning sacrifice of Jesus Christ as the Savior of the world, follow the same core principles as the rest of mainstream Christianity. Members of the LDS Church worship God, the Father of all creation, and recognize his Only Begotten Son, Jesus Christ, as the only mediator between God and man.

Jesus Christ stands at the center of the LDS Church. This statue of Christ is featured in the Visitor's Center of the LDS Church in Salt Lake City.

©*Drew Williams (2002)*

Another Young Man Emerges

Let's fast-forward 18 centuries after Jesus' birth, and half way around the earth. During the 1800s, religious talk was all the rage throughout the New England settlements. Former members of the Anglican Church—among them, the Methodists, Presbyterians, and Colonial Baptists—were eager to recruit new followers. But each of the religions shared a common theme, they had all evolved from the one faith that stood for more than a thousand years: Catholicism.

In a small community in the northeastern reaches of an emerging nation—ironically, founded on the idea that its citizens should be free to worship whomever and however they wished—a young man was compelled to find a way to relate to that missionary of so many centuries past. This 14-year-old boy's pursuits would raise controversial new ideas in the way people understood the role of deity, which was not part of the day's religious ideologies.

While his friends were probably milking cows, dusting dirt floors, and chasing chickens, 14-year-old Joseph Smith Jr. was looking for God. Coincidentally, within 20 years, Joseph, the man, would meet his untimely death at the hands of an angry mob, sanctioned by the state. Little did he know that when he stepped into a patch of woods near his home in upstate New York, to hide away in prayer, Joseph Smith Jr. would walk out with a new conviction that has stirred controversy within the Christian community ever since. (You'll learn all about Joseph Smith Jr. in Chapter 11.)

Today, as a result of believing that Joseph stood in the presence of God Himself, the Church of Jesus Christ of Latter-day Saints now claims the position as the fastest growing Christian religion in America.

With more than 11 million members world-wide, and financial assets that rival a small nation, the LDS Church has become a power-ful voice in the Christian community. But the Church's controversial past, and its unique ideologies pertaining to the size of families, watching R-rated movies, drinking coffee, and, of course, polygamy, have often placed it along the fringes of traditional Christian the-ology throughout its peculiar history.

> **Words of Wisdom**
>
> Vital religion has always suf-fered when orthodoxy is more regarded rather than virtue. The scriptures assure me that at the last day we shall not be exam-ined on what we thought but what we did.
>
> —Benjamin Franklin (1738)

So What Exactly Is "Mormonism"?

Mormonism, quite simply, is the unique position that God created mankind in his own image, first in spirit, then in material form, and that under the direction of men whom the LDS community believe to be ordained and led by Jesus Christ himself, faithful followers will be allowed to return into God's presence and live as part of an eternal family—so long as all of the laws of Christ are adhered to.

I'm not big on 70-word sentences, but that, in a nutshell, is the theme of LDS theol-ogy in one burst!

However, the tenets of Mormonism are far more expansive than what I just described. To fully understand the LDS Church and its beliefs, we'll stretch it all out into 28 chapters.

But first, we must go back to the end of Christ's ministry on the earth to start the story.

> **And It Came to Pass**
>
> For many people, the LDS Church is known for the warm and homespun duo of Donny and Marie Osmond—from their 70s variety show and later their talk show. The LDS faith is not a back-room side show of Christianity. Like the Osmond family, there are many successful entertainers, athletes, politicians, and top business executives who are members of the LDS Church, including billionaire chemical mogul John Huntsman, former Senate Judiciary Committee Chairman Orrin Hatch, and golf great Johnny Miller. In fact, even the television itself owes its genesis to a 14-year-old LDS farm boy from central Utah named Philo T. Farnsworth.

LDS belief is largely based on the restoration of the "primitive" church that was established by Jesus and sustained by his chosen apostles, but was subsequently "killed off" with their deaths.

By the end of the first century, LDS theology marks the beginning of the Great Apostasy, which lasted until the restoration of the early church by Joseph Smith in 1830. (We'll examine the history and fate of the apostles of Christ, as well as the Great Apostasy, in Chapter 9.)

Mormonism Ties Directly to the Gospel of Christ

According to Latter-day Saint theology, there are five key components of the gospel, as it was established during Jesus' ministry. So chances are, you know you're a Latter-day Saint, if you ...

- **Believe that Jesus really was the literal Son of God, sent to redeem the world.** The New Testament Apostle Paul wrote that faith is "the substance of things hoped for, the evidence of things not seen." For Latter-day Saints, exercising faith is the principle by which people are allowed to demonstrate not only their understanding of God's plan, but also their willingness to trust him—even when some things might sound somewhat "nontraditional" with the day's teachings.

- **Believe that repenting of sin and transgression, including confession and restitution, is essential to your salvation.** LDS doctrine stresses that there can be no salvation of the soul without first repenting of transgression, and making restitution where possible. According to LDS beliefs, God cannot dwell in the presence of unclean things—or people. Repentance was essential in Adam's time, just as it is now. It is the process by which the human race may begin to prepare to return into the presence of God.

- **Have been baptized, by immersion, by an authorized representative of God.** The concept of baptism is not new to Christianity. Ancient scripture records this ordinance, and in the writings of the prophet Isaiah, there's even mention of John the Baptist coming forth in the future, to "prepare ye the way of the Lord." (Isa. 40:3) For Latter-day Saints the key element of the ordinance of baptism is in the rightful authority of the person performing the ordinance. Latter-day Saints believe that a man holding the Aaronic Priesthood—which is the preparatory priesthood (discussed in Chapter 20)—is the only authorized person who can perform the sacred ordinance of baptism.

◆ **Received the Gift of the Holy Ghost by the laying on of hands, as it was performed by the apostles of the first century A.D., and by one who was authorized to do so.** Baptism by water is part of a two-step ordinance for people entering the LDS Church. For a person to become a member of the Church of Jesus Christ of Latter-day Saints, they must also receive a second ordinance, often referred to as the "baptism by fire." The baptism by fire is receiving the gift of the Holy Ghost, through the laying on of hands by one who is authorized to perform this ordinance. Although the Holy Ghost, also known as the "Comforter" (John 14:26), visits the world and is the testifier of truth in all things, to actually receive the *gift of the Holy Ghost* is a separate issue.

◆ **Are striving to endure to the end in all things commanded by God.** Where baptism is the gate to the path of heaven, the concept of enduring to the end represents the distance of the path itself. Once a person has faith that God lives and Jesus is the redeemer of the world, and he or she accepts baptism and the Comforter in his or her life, the task of walking the path of righteousness begins and never ends until death itself.

> **Latter-day Laughter**
>
> A man who was guilty of wrongdoing throughout his life wanted to make amends with God. Two LDS missionaries taught him about the purpose of baptism. One of the missionaries said, "When you enter the waters of baptism, the ordinance is symbolic of washing away all of your sins." "Well, if that's true," said the man, "I'll need to wear a snorkel—I might be underwater for a long time."

"Horny" Saints?

There are a lot of misconceptions about the people of the LDS Church—some bordering on the absurd. In the early years of the Church, having been created while surrounded by the post-Anglican, highly charged puritanical culture of New England, Latter-day Saints were considered a favorite topic of ridicule. In many cases, rumors were spread about "those evil Mormons." One of the oddest notions was that once someone joined the LDS Church, that person grew a small set of horns on his or her head as part of a pact with the Devil.

Apparently, some people are still slow to reality. My friend Rob, a local television personality in Utah, was recently at a conference in a midwestern state (I won't say which one), where a person who, after learning he was a member of the LDS Church, rubbed the top of Rob's head. Rob asked why the personal intrusion, the man replied, "I'm looking for the horns." Whether serious or in jest, the whole idea was ridiculous to begin with. However, human nature is often hostile as a first reaction to new ways, which brings us to some of the reasons why Mormonism might stir emotions so often.

FUD Often Influences the Uneducated

In the computer security industry in which I work I often see companies use a concept known as "FUD" to take advantage of unsuspecting customers. FUD—fear, uncertainty, and doubt—is a way of preying on those less informed. Hackers and cyber-troublemakers like to prey on the less informed, and so do many of the software manufacturers who market products to protect the market. Conversely, those who may not be completely informed of the truth, also use FUD as a vehicle to spawn discontent.

> ### And It Came to Pass
>
> In the case of Adam and Eve, God walked and talked with the first man and woman up to the point where the infamous forbidden fruit was introduced to Eve. When Adam and Eve chose to partake of the fruit of the Tree of Knowledge of Good and Evil, they had to be separated from God's presence, and thus were "cut off." Consequently, the Garden was taken from the earth, and Adam and Eve were left to struggle through the world as we know it today—in a nonglorified state.

For example, just as in the early days of Mormonism, many people today find satisfaction in generating animosity toward the LDS Church, usually over a misinterpretation of Church doctrine or a misunderstanding about an LDS practice.

Why does Mormonism generate this kind of reaction? Why should people care so much what others believe?

Here's one idea. Many of us are taught the ways of truth from those who influence us the most—usually our parents. Likewise, they learned certain aspects of truth from their parents, and so on. So when a new idea surfaces, which appears as something completely nonconforming to the status quo, the idea might often be inferred as a threat.

In the days of the Israelites, for example, "God's Chosen" were constantly questioned and attacked for their beliefs—usually by people who were afraid, not of the Jews themselves, but of Judaism creeping in and influencing the lives of the stronger culture. The same thing happened when Jesus taught the Jews that he was the answer to the world's troubles, and that they could stop believing in old Jewish traditions. Not a lot of people take well to change.

Mormonism is quite similar. In many ways, the claims made by Latter-day Saints, which are based on LDS doctrine, are outrageous compared to what has been traditionally accepted as "Truth." Such claims often lead many people to question the validity of what they believe versus what they don't know they *don't know*.

Words of Wisdom

Wherefore the Lord said, Forasmuch as this people draw near me with their mouth, and with their lips do honor me, but have removed their heart far from me, and their fear toward me is taught by the precept of men: Therefore behold, I will proceed to do a marvelous work among this people, even a marvelous work and a wonder: for the wisdom of their wise men shall perish, and the understanding of their prudent men shall be hid.
—Isaiah 29:13–14

As we move forward in this book, I'll introduce some of those unique concepts that have raised many eyebrows over the years. Matters concerning women holding the priesthood, abstaining from coffee and tea, and, of course, polygamy, will all be covered in subsequent chapters.

Let's continue by getting an understanding of how Latter-day Saints view deity and the concepts of a pre-earth life.

The Least You Need to Know

- Mormonism has its beginnings even earlier than Christianity.

- Knowing who Jesus was and what he did is essential to understanding the principle beliefs of Mormonism.

- Latter-day Saints believe the ancient Church of Christ was taken from the world.

- The gospel of Jesus was restored to the world in the 1820s.

- Members of the LDS Church have had to deal with much criticism, some bordering on the ridiculous.

Chapter 2

God's Divine Presence

In This Chapter

- ◆ God, the father of all things
- ◆ Understanding the Godhead
- ◆ A week in God's time might be longer than in ours
- ◆ The power of prayer

Latter-day Saints believe that there is a God. He is the divine ruler of the universe. By his direction, all things were created—first in spirit, then in material form. God, called *Elohim*, is central to Mormonism. He is the recipient of our prayers, and the one who LDS people seek to return to when their mortal lives are complete. Latter-day Saints believe that God has a very clear role in the lives of mankind. He is, quite simply and completely, the Father of creation.

By the way, the name "Elohim" is so sacred to Latter-day Saints that the preference in prayer is to address him as "Heavenly Father." In a more casual reference the LDS community also refers to him in the third-person as "the Father." For practical terms, however, I'll use the more common reference of "God" to represent the Father throughout this book.

The scriptures record that God made all of us in his own image. LDS belief is that he is a glorified being who has attained eternal perfection in all things. Though the thought of actually being ever compared to God would send many Christians running for spiritual cover, Latter-day Saints believe that the ultimate gift God can bestow on his children (Latter-day Saints), is to give them all that he has. This, in turn, glorifies him even more. LDS people believe, as Christ pointed out so many times throughout his ministry, that those who follow his commandments may inherit all that Christ and his Father have. It's something Latter-day Saints look forward to.

Who or What Is God?

The inspired words of Genesis states, "God created man in His own image, in the image of God created He him; male and female created He them." If Genesis is to be taken literally, then God is in the image of man, and, therefore is a man himself. That's the Latter-day Saint philosophy in a nutshell: "Man is what God once was, God is what man may become." (Joseph Smith Jr.)

Members of the LDS Church believe they can become like God himself. They believe that God is a glorified man, in whose image man was created. Latter-day Saints believe that man's spiritual progression can include the glorified privilege of having all that the Father has, as Christ promised in Romans 8:17.

> **Words of Wisdom**
>
> All our wisdom comprises basically two things … the knowledge of God and the knowledge of ourselves.
> —Theologian John Calvin

According to LDS belief, Elohim—God—is the creator of everything we see and hear, the ruler of the universe. It was under his direction that Jesus Christ created the universe and the world in which we live. The stars and other heavenly bodies, in their perfect order, testify to God's handiwork.

©*Drew Williams (2002)*

The Latter-day Saint relationship with God is at the center of LDS lives. As all Christians do, Latter-day Saints believe God created everything we see, all matter and all living things throughout the universe. The manner by which he accomplished these tasks is often debated by science, but for Latter-day Saints and the rest of the Christian community, the results are the same: God created the heavens and the earth and everything contained in them.

After the Great Apostasy—the killing or banishment of Jesus' apostles, which I'll discuss in Chapter 9—Christian sects cropped up throughout the Roman Empire, and the concept of God became as diverse as the cultures that were part of the empire. In one case, God was a genderless being, called the "Father-Mother." In others, God was a great spirit who was so big he could fill the universe, yet so small he could pierce our hearts.

According to LDS belief, God is literally the spirit father of all mankind—including Jesus Christ, who is also called "Jehovah" by Latter-day Saints. Of course, the difference between man's elder brother Jesus and everyone else is that God is also Jesus' *literal* father, as discussed in Chapter 1.

The Godhead

Elohim and Jehovah are two different personages, and both are part of a *Godhead* of three divine beings, the third being the Holy Ghost. God, the eternal Father of heaven and earth, presides over all things, including the Godhead. In other Christian philosophies, the Godhead is often referred to as the "Holy Trinity" (also known as "Father, Son, and Holy Ghost").

Latter-day Saints pray to God—Elohim—worshipping him and only him. He is, ultimately, the leader of the divine threesome or Godhead. The concept of three separate persons in the form of deity will be further discussed in Chapter 10, when we look at the evolution of early religious creeds, and discuss the Christian tradition of the Holy Trinity.

According to LDS belief, because God cannot live in the presence of anything unclean or unholy, without Christ and his atonement, it would be "Days of the Living Dead" for everyone. No one would have had the chance to return to God's presence, or live with their families in the next life, or escape the shroud of death itself.

Mormonology

The **Godhead** is the divine council of three separate and distinct personages, often referred to as the Holy Trinity. The Godhead is comprised of Elohim (the Father), Jehovah (Jesus), and the Holy Ghost. Both the Father and Jesus have had physical bodies, the Holy Ghost has not yet descended to a state of mortality.

The Holy Ghost is somewhat of the unseen partner in the Godhead. LDS people know that the Holy Ghost has form, but in spirit only. When the Holy Ghost communicates, it's spirit talking to spirit. For example, you know those times when you look out at a beautiful sunset, or sunrise, or stop to listen to the ocean waves break—or when you experience the birth of a child, and you get that warm feeling telling you that this was God's work? That's the Holy Ghost talking.

And It Came to Pass

Latter-day Saints often refer to the Holy Ghost as the "Comforter" or the "Holy Spirit of Promise." Once a person has been baptized into the Church, he or she receives the Holy Ghost in a special ordinance. This ordinance provides the recipient with the knowledge that as long as he or she lives a righteous and obedient life, the Holy Ghost will be present in spirit to guide, direct, and comfort him or her. For Latter-day Saints in times of

Together, these three divine entities form the Godhead, and act in unison in voice and attributes. Together, God—Elohim—the Father, and Jesus Christ—Jehovah—constitute the governing body of Heaven. The Holy Ghost—a separate and distinct being—testifies to the truth of the Father and Son. In LDS doctrine, it's a perfect triangle of power and stability.

All in a Day's Work

When they're young, my daughters and I take time to discuss the concept of a "day" and its many parts. It's always fun to see their surprise when I explain to them that a day is only 24 hours long when we're here, standing on this earth, but it's different in other places in the solar system. They thought the concept of a day was universal.

It's not even universal for those of us who travel from time zone to time zone here on earth. For example, when a person flies from Los Angeles to Sydney, the longest one-way, nonstop commercial flight in the world, the trip takes about 13 hours—or half of a day. But through the course of that 13-hour flight, a person crosses multiple time zones and the International Dateline. For the traveler, the trip becomes a 16-hour advancement into tomorrow!

Why is this concept important in relation to God? Because we have no idea how long a "day" is in the life of deity. Did it take him and his team of assistants six of our days to make everything we see?

Who cares?

According to scripture, God created the heavens, the earth, and everything in it in six periods of time. The Book of Job, for example, describes a day as a single lifetime of a person: "Now is the time and the day of your salvation."

A "celestial day," or a day in the time of God, has been revealed through modern-day scripture as a span of 1,000 years. That probably doesn't sit well with the evolutionists, but for Latter-day Saints, the inspired word of God offers insight into God's timeframe.

In the end, though, what matters to Latter-day Saints is what people do with those precious few days *they* experience in their brief mortal lives.

Praying to the Man Upstairs

I have sat in many different congregations of Christian faiths, and have observed the diversity in understanding what constitutes "prayer." I have seen people fall to the floor and shake around, claiming to be "slain in the spirit." I have heard people speak in odd garbled syllables, claiming to have the "power of tongues." I have heard people pray to God, to Jesus Christ, and to so-called "saints" who would serve as liaisons of man to deity. "Why all the confusion?" I've thought. And while I was at it, "Does God really listen to what we tell him?"

Let me relate the following story as the turning point when I knew God answered the simple pleadings of an extremely vulnerable teenager.

> **Words of Wisdom**
>
> They say that God is everywhere, and yet we always think of Him as somewhat of a recluse.
>
> —Emily Dickinson, U.S. poet

A Lesson in Prayer

I once made the challenge to some friends to find an action that human beings perform that doesn't fit into one of the four following motivators. I've listed them because the following story demonstrates all four:

- ◆ Natural instinct
- ◆ Fear
- ◆ Duty
- ◆ Love

The closing months of 1979 were difficult times for the world. The Soviet Union had invaded Afghanistan, and the Shah of Iran was deposed and sent into terminal exile. A passive United States government was suffering through double-digit inflation. The world watched live television coverage as American Embassy workers in Iran, who were taken hostage by Islamic radicals. I was thousands of miles away, in the middle of nowhere—getting a front-row seat as another piece of Cold War history unfolded.

I was an apprentice journalist aboard the USS *Coral Sea*, an antique aircraft carrier of post-WWII vintage. This ship was so outdated, there weren't even any combat weapons installed!

In the spring of 1980, I took an opportunity to travel by plane from my ship to the new nuclear carrier USS *Nimitz*, which was with us on-station in the Indian Ocean. My assignment was to get some first-hand advice on how the big ship provided news information and entertainment services to its 6,000-man crew.

While aboard the massive 120,000-ton warship, I had the opportunity to get a behind-the-scenes look at something that I thought was out of place on a Navy vessel. The *Nimitz* was carrying several big Army helicopters. I knew something was in the works—either for Afghanistan or for Iran. My first instinct was to book the next available flight back to my own ship—which I did.

Little did I know that the makings of a historical disaster were well underway.

Several weeks later, on the night of April 24, I couldn't sleep. There was a lot of noise in the cargo holds of the ship, which were just a couple of decks below where I slept. I went up onto one of the catwalks overlooking the flight deck. The deck was washed in red/amber lights, which is how the night crews had to work when at sea.

> **Words of Wisdom**
>
> It is the first principle of the gospel to know for a true certainty the character of God, and to know that we may converse with Him as one man converses with another.

I was shocked at seeing, for the first time, a deck covered with wagonlike carts of bombs—big, green, and gray conventional bombs. But that wasn't what bothered me (after all, this wasn't the *Love Boat* I was sailing on). Most terrifying were the shiny silver bombs that I saw tucked away beside one of the cargo elevators. We all knew what *those* bombs were, because of the rifle-toting Marines that surrounded each of them. I realized it wasn't just the *Nimitz* that was part of the "Nuclear Navy" on that night.

That evening, out of fear, mostly, I offered my first "sincere" prayer (one that actually had a purpose). I hoped he would hear me. I remember asking him not to let our ship or the other 30-plus warships in the vicinity lead us into something that would be devastating to us, or to the world. To this day, I am amazed at the level of courage *anyone* in harm's way must demonstrate to do their jobs under such threatening conditions.

After my prayer, I remember getting the feeling that things would be okay for most of us.

A short while after my visit to the flight deck, the general alarm sounded for everyone to man their battle stations. The ship's crew moved to combat readiness, but the mission failed shortly after it began.

The next day, the fleet on-station throughout the Persian Gulf, were saddened by the news of our troops' failure to accomplish their mission, which resulted in the deaths of many of the commandos chosen. Although it was demoralizing for everyone, we were all grateful that more lives weren't lost in what was close to becoming another twentieth-century military nightmare.

With the exception of our lost comrades, we all returned to the States the following month. It was the first time that the Spirit of God offered comfort to one worried, naïve 19-year-old.

And It Came to Pass

When I was studying the theology of the LDS Church, I met with two missionaries, who told me prayer was like a hamburger. You start with the top bun, which is to open with the address—"Dear Heavenly Father" or some variation—as long as it's to God himself that we're praying. Then we dress it with all that good stuff like pickles and ketchup—represented by the thanks we offer for whatever it is we're grateful for. Then comes the real meat of the sandwich—what we're asking for. Finally, the bottom bun (the closing), which is *always* "in the name of Jesus Christ" (kinda goes along with the top bun), and finally, the "Amen," which, for the sake of this analogy, means, "Let's eat!"

A Turning Point

That single experience, on the eve of the failed attempt to rescue the American hostages in Tehran, forever changed my attitude toward prayer and about God. It was the turning point for my search to find him, and to learn—if I could—where I fit into the equation.

It wasn't something that led me to the LDS Church, because I didn't know it existed at that point. But that experience did lead me to start asking tough questions, such as why am I really here (not on a ship, but alive), and what am I supposed to do while I'm alive? The whole "meaning of life" thing started to grow inside me.

I said earlier that all four motivating factors—natural instinct, fear, duty, love—were at work on that calm April night. My natural instinct was to run and find someplace to hide, not out of any kind of cowardice, just because I hadn't seen a bomb larger than an M-80 before that night. Out of fear, I turned to the only source that I thought could give me an answer or settle any anxiety—God. I felt like a little kid running

Words of Wisdom

If men do not comprehend the character of God, they do not comprehend themselves.

—Prophet Joseph Smith Jr.

into the house to tell my parents of a terrible storm that was approaching. Regardless of the unseen future that faced all of us that early morning in April, everyone knew it was our choice to be where we were—we had done so out of a feeling of duty.

But in the end, it was God's love that told me all would be well.

The Least You Need to Know

- ◆ God is the supreme creator and father of all things.

- ◆ The Godhead (Father, Son, and Holy Ghost) are three divine beings who rule the universe together.

- ◆ God's time and man's time aren't on the same scale.

- ◆ Never underestimate the power of prayer.

Chapter 3

The Pre-Mortal Existence: Our Life Before Earth

In This Chapter

- ◆ God's council in heaven: man's pre-mortal existence
- ◆ Lucifer speaks up
- ◆ Choosing right from wrong: the power of free agency
- ◆ Satan's early beginnings
- ◆ Banished from paradise

There's an old axiom that states you can't make something out of nothing. Latter-day Saints believe that to be especially true when talking about life with God prior to living on earth, which LDS doctrine refers to as the "Pre-mortal Life." Mormonism contends that all things were created in spirit form prior to their existence in material form.

Latter-day Saints are the spiritual children of divine parents, without beginning or end. As such, Mormonism teaches that man's intelligence—the very core of what makes people who they are—was created out of the matter that has always existed, by God, prior to the formation of our world.

Before the World Was

According to the earliest accounts in Genesis, God (or "Elohim," as he is called by LDS people; see Chapter 2), created every little detail (such as rocks, plants, animals, etc.), that now exists in the world, well before those material details showed up here. Their energy, so to speak, was unorganized matter, but formed first in spirit, then embodied in a mortal state. (It sort of makes you wonder what God's plan was for cockroaches and mosquitoes!)

Words of Wisdom

Our birth is but a sleep and a
    forgetting;
The Soul that rises with us,
    our life's Star,
Hath had elsewhere its setting
And cometh from afar;
Not in entire forgetfulness,
And not in utter nakedness,
But trailing clouds of glory do
    we come
From God, who is our home.

—William Wordsworth, U.S. poet

Along with our various multilegged, winged, gilled, scaly and slimy neighbors, we existed in God's presence long before we showed up on the earth.

During the time we walked and talked while in the presence of God, mankind developed characteristics at the individual level. Some spirits rose in stature and responsibility, others focused on their own personal agendas—pretty much the same way man has developed throughout mortal history. However, there is one important difference. As pre-mortal spirits, man was not capable of *experiencing* the actual emotions and choices an unbridled life has to offer. In a way, our pre-earth existence was all about research, and not about hands-on application.

The Lone and Dreary World is the term often used in the LDS community to describe the world in which we live. Mormonism teaches that the big blue planet we call home is actually a world in a fallen or nonglorified state, created as a result of the departure of Adam and Eve from the Garden of Eden.

©*Drew Williams (2002)*

At some point in the progress, as the human race developed various predispositions to certain talents, roles and characteristics, God decided it was time for his children to get a chance to experience life firsthand. It was time to be tested, time to *leave the nest*.

The Grand Council

For this purpose, God assembled everyone together at a Grand Council, at which time he presented his plan for the progression of his children. LDS doctrine teaches that, like any parent, God wanted to provide his offspring with the same opportunities that he had enjoyed. Otherwise, why bring us here in the first place? So I'm going to embellish my storytelling skills a bit, and explain the significance of the Plan of Salvation, and how it came to be created at the foundation of the universe itself.

God's plan would start off simple enough. He would place man in a situation where he would be allowed to make decisions for himself, allowing for certain errors if he made bad decisions. Because God knew man would be immediately vulnerable to making bad choices, he provided a process of redemption, by which man could recover from his bad decisions and be allowed to return into God's presence. As a glorified and exalted being, God cannot dwell in a nonglorified environment, any more than man could survive in the glorified presence of God.

Mormon Myths

Myth: Some people were indecisive in the War in Heaven. Nothing could be further from the truth. The concept that some people who find themselves out of favor with society, due to ethnic background or social status, was the result of not choosing God's side in the Grand Council in Heaven is a fallacy. By the mere fact that we are born into mortality proves which side we chose. Those who chose with Lucifer fell with Lucifer.

And so, the presentation was given. It was one plan—just one. Ultimately, the goal was to undergo a physical trial called mortality, and—after meeting certain requirements which would be provided along the way—God's children would each be rewarded based on their individual level of obedience to his guidelines.

The plan was pretty straightforward, and most everyone agreed with what the Almighty had drafted.

"Whom Shall I Send?"

The time had come to set the plan into motion, and to prepare the way for his children. God needed strong leaders to launch his plan, so he asked for a volunteer to head up this eternal project.

"Here am I, send me," came a voice from the Grand Council. It was the one who God had always known he could depend on—a spirit who had been with him from the beginning, even his first spirit child. The voice was the great Jehovah himself (known on earth as Jesus Christ).

> ### And It Came to Pass
>
> Latter-day revelation teaches that the accounts of "God" given throughout the scriptures, especially in the Old Testament, are actually references to Jehovah, who was born into the world as Jesus of Nazareth. Mormonism teaches that Jesus, in his own pre-mortal state, was not only our elder brother, but also co-creator of the universe and everything in it.

It was Jehovah's position that he should be sent into the world at some given point, to redeem the world from its fallen state, should man fail to remain in the presence of God. As a consequence of his actions, according to Jehovah's strategy, man would not be lost in his transgression, but would be redeemed from death, and given an opportunity to repent and return into God's presence.

The glory for the work, however, would not remain with the Son, but be given entirely back to the Father.

Introducing the Son of the Morning

Another voice spoke up, even though the plan was already accepted (there was no "Plan B"). It was another highly persuasive spirit, a leader among spirits —with a strong presence of influence. It was Lucifer, also known by Latter-day scripture as the "Son of the Morning."

Lucifer's plan was that he would personally ensure all generations of man would go through life, but not permitted to fail, and would be returned into the presence of God. The return on his investment of effort was that Lucifer—not God—would receive the glory and recognition for accomplishing such a noble task.

God reminded Lucifer, along with the rest of us, that he would chose the first, indicating that Jehovah's ideas were in line with God's plan. This didn't sit well with Lucifer, and apparently about a third of our spirit brothers and sisters.

> ### Words of Wisdom
>
> How art thou fallen from heaven, O Lucifer, son of the morning! How art thou cut down to the ground.
>
> —Isaiah 14:12

A rebellion took place, and God banished Lucifer—now called the devil—and his followers from God's kingdom. But their banishment came at a high price. Not only would they not be permitted back into the presence of their maker, they would also never be allowed to experience life as we know it—they would never obtain mortal bodies of their own.

They were damned (meaning their progress through eternal life had been stopped) for all time. It wouldn't be the first time Lucifer would be cast out of God's presence, which we'll learn more about in a moment.

Free Agency: The Right to Choose

The whole argument was about the most basic principle of humanity—the one principle that has always sat at the balance between liberty and oppression: the right to choose.

God's plan, according to LDS doctrine, was designed to empower man with the opportunity to freely choose a path that would result in making the correct decisions necessary to not only enjoy life, but also to endure life's challenges—while not losing sight of the goal: a glorified and eternal life in the presence of God.

The right to enjoy life, it would seem, depended on man's ability to make choices. The two characteristics would be forever balanced and offset by *free agency*.

Ideally, if a person makes bad choices (that is to say, he or she knows in advance what the consequences will be), his or her rights will be affected, and perhaps the person will even lose the ability to make any future choices altogether. Conversely, should a person make correct choices, his or her abilities might be enhanced with even greater opportunities for choosing, according to this principle.

Mormonology

Free agency is the ability to sign up with whatever team an individual wants to play for, without force, but while accepting the consequences for making the choice—whether good or bad. For mankind, the idea is to not worry about whose side God is on, but rather, to pick the team that is always on *God's* side.

However, such is not always the case, and as generations of society and cultures have shown, man has not always been allowed to make independent decisions. But even in such cases, the oppression itself is always caused by somebody being allowed to make choices where his or her influence could overpower those of less influence.

Ultimately, the goal, as God planned, was not to intervene in the natural course of man's decision to choose right from wrong. Divine intervention would be kept at a minimum, and used only when steering the general direction of the human race.

Latter-day revelation supports the concept of a "time and purpose under heaven," as outlined in the Old Testament book of Ecclesiastes. There are many such cases where God has interceded with mankind, but in each situation, divine involvement was for the purpose of progressing God's children through various steps of his divine plan. Here are a few of them:

- Parting the Red Sea to allow the Jews to escape Pharaoh

- Directing Columbus to the New World

- Inspiring the authors of the Declaration of Independence

- Freezing the Mississippi River, to allow the early Saints to walk across, escaping the pursuing mobs

- Raising up important influences among world leaders

There are countless stories of divinely inspired intellects, artists, musicians, and leaders of great nations. In each case, their talents were shown to exist early in life. In some cases, those talents of great influence or great knowledge produced results of terrible consequence (such as in the mastery of the atom, or in the persuasiveness of strong leaders such as Hitler and Stalin). But in all cases, the individuals were free to choose how they would exercise their abilities.

No Sympathy for the Devil

Many people believe that Lucifer, who became "Satan" when he fell from the presence of God, got what he deserved. But there are a few people who speculate that the head of hell's army got a bad deal—that he was goaded into falling by a resentful God.

Latter-day revelation teaches that the concept of free agency was offered to *all* of God's children, with no exceptions. It was Lucifer's choice, ultimately, that led to his own demise, just as it was the choice of each individual who followed with what would obviously be called a bad decision. Lucifer and his minions did not choose wisely.

The idea that there was a pre-earth life for the human race, and that a great war ensued between the forces of good and evil is not unique to the Latter-day Saint culture. For centuries, civilizations have documented the idea that mankind lived in a spiritual state in God's presence, prior to our natural births. The following is an excerpt from John Milton's great seventeenth-century epic poem, *Paradise Lost*, which calls reference to the downfall of Lucifer:

> Who first seduced them to that foul revolt?
> The infernal Serpent; he it was, whose guile
> Stirred up with Envy and Revenge, deceived
> The Mother of Mankind, what time his Pride
> Had cast him out from Heav'n, with all his Host

Of Rebel Angels, by whose aid aspiring
To set himself in Glory above his Peers,
He trusted to have equaled the most High,
If he opposed; and with ambitious aim
Against the Throne and Monarchy of God
Raised impious War in Heav'n and Battle proud
With vain attempt.

Fallen Cherub to be weak is miserable
Doing or Suffering: but of this be sure,
To do ought good never will be our task,
But ever to do ill our sole delight,
As being the contrary to his high will
Whom we resist.

Paradise: Not Lost, Just Left Behind

For the human race to reach our full potential, according to tenets of Mormonism, we had to pass through a state of mortality to experience the good with the bad. To experience this, we would have to leave God's presence, and venture into the world, to learn for ourselves what was right and wrong.

Our lot in life, it would seem, was to face each challenge as one that would strengthen and build our spiritual character, or sink us into despair and long-term failure.

And although we might not always be in control of our circumstances, the choice, regardless of difficulty, would still be ours on how to manage the experience.

The good news, however, was that man would not be left to his own devices on a long-term basis. There would be times when God would remove his presence from our midst (which I'll discuss in Chapter 9), but he would not let us fail as a race. It wasn't part of the plan.

Words of Wisdom

What a piece of work is man!
How noble in reason!
How infinite in faculty!
In form and moving how express and admirable!
In action, how like an angel!
In apprehension, how like a god!

—Shakespeare (from *Hamlet*)

The Least You Need to Know

- We lived with God before we were born as mortals.
- During God's Grand Council, Lucifer let it be known that he wanted God's job.
- With free agency we accept consequences of our actions, good or bad.
- God's plan for mankind included learning what is right and wrong.

Chapter 4

Trapped in a Mortal's Body

In This Chapter

◆ Adam and Eve make a choice—and experience the consequences

◆ The beginning of mankind's fallen state

◆ How Christianity and Mormonism measure mortality

◆ The road to immortality

After the spiritual dust settled following Satan's banishment from God's presence, God moved forward with his plan to prepare an environment in which his children could progress through the next phase of spiritual growth. This world would provide mankind with a place to be tested in all matters concerning man's willingness to follow God's instructions—a state of existence we refer to as "mortality." Mortal life is something that those who followed Satan will never have the opportunity to enjoy, as pointed out in the previous chapter.

According to LDS teaching, if you can read this, you chose God's side in the great battle between Jesus and Lucifer. This means you, me, and everyone who has ever walked the earth or will do so, gets an opportunity to experience life firsthand.

That's the good news.

The bad news is that, being cast down from the presence of God, Satan and his followers are among the inhabitants of the world, but in spirit form only. Knowing they chose the losing side, these lost souls are forever miserable, and make every effort to deny mortal man the opportunities that come with enjoying life.

But then there's the great news: Christ told us that God would not allow Satan to ever tempt man beyond his ability to endure.

The World's First Fall Guy

According to LDS teaching, as part of an eternal plan, God created a world for his children to experience the joys and trials that come from life's experiences. However, for those experiences to become real to his children God gave them the new concept of choice, which would allow them to decide for themselves what is right and wrong (as discussed in Chapter 3).

> **And It Came to Pass**
>
> According to LDS revelation, Adam and Eve were selected for the job of "first parents" before the world was created. Latter-day Saints believe Adam (who was the archangel Michael in his pre-mortal state) and Eve were extremely righteous leaders in the spirit world.

Adam and Eve were the first couple of mankind to walk and talk with God on a glorified earth. But at some time in their evolution within the Garden of Eden, Adam and Eve would eventually come to a crossroad that would forever change the human race. They would have to choose between following God or pursuing their own self-interest.

Adam and Eve Make a Choice

Traditional Christianity teaches the concept of "original sin," which implies that the human race exists in a fallen state—that all people are born with the stain of sin, thanks to Eve and her appetite, and Adam's acquiescence. However, according to modern-day clarity offered by LDS revelation, making the decision to disobey God was clearly the necessary choice to bring to pass the mortality of man.

Let's present the case, and you can decide:

◆ God brought Adam and Eve into his presence in the Garden of Eden, where they could safely exist, but without experiencing right and wrong. Simply, they would remain as two emotionally hollow eternal creations of God, with limited capability for learning.

◆ They did not know joy or sorrow, happiness or sadness—they knew nothing other than what God had revealed to them (things like, "that's a tree ... that's a bird ... that's a fish," etc.).

◆ God commanded the First Couple to take care of his garden, but also to "Be fruitful and multiply and replenish the earth."

◆ LDS scripture, as recorded in the Book of Mormon, states that Adam and Eve were eternal beings, without the ability to do the very thing God instructed them to do, which was reproduce.

◆ God gave Adam and Eve the opportunity to partake of anything in the garden, with the exception of the fruit of the tree of knowledge of good and evil. Partaking of that forbidden fruit would bring death to the couple.

◆ They would gain knowledge of the world's goodness and its pitfalls, but they would also sacrifice their immortal state for the price of that knowledge of good and evil.

To mix things up, God allowed an old acquaintance—the fallen Lucifer—to make a cameo appearance in the Garden of Eden. No doubt, God knew that Satan's desire would be to corrupt his father's plans for man, and so he was allowed to tempt the couple with a good old-fashioned dose of excuse-making and self-justification. "You won't die," their fallen brother boasted, "but you'll know what our Father knows." Frankly, Satan reasoned, how could anyone mindlessly walk around through the Garden of Eden, when there was a *whole world* just waiting to be discovered?

And then came Satan's final argument: How could Adam and Eve possibly do the very thing God had commanded them to do, which was multiply and replenish the earth, without knowing *how* to accomplish this strange commandment?

Mormonism teaches that it was Eve who understood the necessity of reason on the matter presented by Satan—while also immediately recognizing him as the great deceiver that he was. And like many of us male folks today, Adam wasn't about to ask for directions anyway.

Thank goodness for Eve's persistence.

Latter-day Laughter
Adam blamed Eve. Eve blamed the snake. The snake didn't have a leg to stand on. —Anonymous

So the situation was clear. Adam and Eve had made a *choice*. It was probably the first, most important choice they made since defending God's plan while at the Grand Council (see Chapter 3).

But with all choices come consequences. God was bound by the decision his son and daughter had made, and had to remove them from their glorified surroundings. They no longer walked in purity, and thus had to leave the Garden of Eden.

Words of Wisdom

Just why the Lord would say to Adam that he forbade him to partake of the fruit of the tree is not made clear in the Bible account, but in the original [account] as it comes to us in the book of Moses it is made definitely clear. It is that the Lord said to Adam that if he wished to remain as he was in the garden, then he was not to eat fruit, but if he desired to eat it and partake of death he was at liberty to do so. It was not in the true sense a transgression of a divine commandment. Adam made a wise decision … the only decision that he could make.

—LDS Prophet Joseph Fielding Smith

Welcome to the World

Mormonism teaches that with the fall of Adam, the advent of the human race entered its mortal condition as we now know it. It was also the beginning of the world's existence in its nonglorified or *fallen* state, where it will remain until the return of Christ.

The whole matter concerning the fall of Adam brought to his posterity the ability to live and die. However, Mormonism teaches that it was only through the atonement of a perfect being—Jesus Christ—that the human race could reunite spirit with body and return into the presence of God.

As part of the plan, man would be allowed to fall into a mortal and imperfect state, so that he could experience self-government. It was the price each of us would pay for the privilege of making choices as our consciences dictate. However, knowing us like a father knows all of his children, God knew we would not always follow the way *his* conscience would recommend. So he would eventually have to send a "redeemer," who was above reproach, to even the balance between required justice and provisional mercy.

So that's how it all happened—from the LDS point of view, anyway.

Latter-day Saints don't buy into the notion that man is born with the innate ability to be evil, any more than in the belief that infants require baptism to save them from eternal wrath, should they meet an untimely, premature demise. LDS doctrine teaches that children are born pure in the sight of God, and lack the ability to reason between good and evil until an accountable age—which was revealed to be eight years. Thus, Adam's decision has nothing to do with your neighbor's kid being a bully!

What Is Death?

And so we are born to die. Well, that's not *all* we were born to do. In fact, that's where things (pardon the expression) get *heated up*.

As I discussed in Chapter 2, the whole purpose for life itself is for mankind—the children of God—to be tested, to experience choices, to endure trials, to enrich our knowledge. When God believes we have had sufficient time to accomplish these objectives, we leave (die). It's that simple.

But before anybody writes to me with words of admonition and rebuke over such matters as unexpected deaths, or the unwitting demise of somebody (or a group of people), at the hands of someone else, let me just say that it's important to remember that we might not fully understand the Lord's motives for things. I certainly don't. But he does.

For Latter-day Saints, death is just as real and just as difficult to cope with as it is for anyone else. The loss of a loved one or any tragedy that strikes human life is just that—a tragedy. Moreover, Latter-day Saints would defend life to the very last, as was often the case in the many accounts of enduring both the elements of uncharted wilderness and the ongoing persecution of the early Saints. But in the LDS culture, many people find a greater level of solace in knowing that death is part of God's eternal plan for the progression and redemption of mankind.

Having suffered the recent loss of a new baby, this Latter-day Saint family knows that death has no grasp over mortality, because of their belief in the sacrifice of Jesus Christ. LDS people believe that families are given the opportunity to be together for all eternity, and that young children who die return into the presence of a loving, waiting God.

©Drew Williams (2002)

For traditional Christianity, most of the concepts surrounding death and the afterlife are based on the many interpretations and opinions of the early leaders of the Catholic Church.

Here are the basics of traditional Christianity:

◆ You're born in sin (because of Adam's transgression).

◆ You live your life, always in the shadow of the fear of God and eternal damnation.

◆ You die and go to a spirit paradise called heaven, if you were good and accepted Christ as your Savior during your mortal life. If you didn't, you'd go to hell—that endless lake of fire and brimstone, where your soul spends eternity tossing and toiling among the flames.

Without prematurely revealing the LDS concept on resurrection and judgment, which are the subjects of Chapter 6, let me point out here several subtle differences in the LDS version of mortality:

◆ You're born without sin, but will inevitably mess up your perfect record.

◆ You live your life under the watchful eye of a loving Heavenly Father, who has prepared a process for you to return into his presence.

◆ You learn and accept the divine guidelines as they were established by Christ during his mortal ministry.

◆ You eventually die, and your spirit dwells in a state of rest or turmoil, depending on those choices you made during mortality.

◆ Jesus returns to the world (something many revivalists refer to as the "Rapture"), and sets his government in order.

◆ There comes a time when, while in spirit form, every person is brought before the bar of judgment.

◆ You are resurrected (meaning your physical body is reunited with your spirit).

◆ You're permitted to obtain a level of eternal paradise that is concurrent with your obedience to God.

◆ Nobody's swimming in lakes of fire, but some of the more hard-core evildoers will find it very cold. In Mormonism, hell definitely freezes over.

Okay, so that's the short version. We'll explore all of this in greater detail in the next chapter.

A Roadmap to Spiritual Success

The road to immortality requires all of us to walk through "the valley of the shadow of death" at some point in our lives. On the eternal pathway, mortality is the proving ground, and the place where mankind embraces the very passions of life itself.

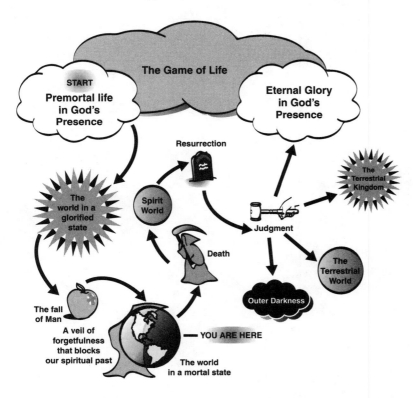

Unlike the cycles of business, professions, careers, or technologies, man's life cycle is only one-way, and not really a "cycle" at all.

©Drew Williams (2002)

In the end, however, no matter how difficult or challenging the death of a loved one might be to those left behind, Latter-day Saints believe that a reunion with the dearly departed is as inevitable as the sun coming up tomorrow.

The Least You Need to Know

- ◆ Adam fell so that mankind might enjoy mortality.
- ◆ The world in which we live exists in a fallen state.
- ◆ Death is part of God's eternal plan.
- ◆ The pathway of life is only one-way.

The Second Coming of Christ

In This Chapter

- ◆ Events that will precede the Second Coming
- ◆ Reuniting the lost tribes of Israel
- ◆ Baptism by fire: nowhere to run, nowhere to hide
- ◆ What will you be doing during the final millennium?
- ◆ Conditions that apply to the Lord's return

At the end of his brief visit back on earth, after his resurrection, Jesus assembled his Apostles one final time. He told them that he would leave them for awhile, and that he would return at the appropriate time, after the world had the chance to grow up a bit. Now, almost 2,000 years since Jesus' departure, the Christian world still looks to the day when Jesus will return.

Mormonism teaches that the Second Coming of Christ opens the final chapter of the mortal probation of mankind. Jesus' return has been the subject of extensive discussion since he left. His return has been called the "Great and Dreadful Day," "Rapture," and "End of Days." Although many cultures today and throughout history claimed to know when the Lord will return, the scriptures record that even Christ himself does not know the day God will send him back to us. But according to LDS teaching, one thing is for sure—he's coming soon. Will we be ready?

When the Party's Over, We Pay the Bill

Everybody seems to have an insider track on the ultimate Christian events corresponding with the Second Coming of Christ. There have been books written about it, songs sung, and plenty of wailing and gnashing of teeth over false alarms throughout history. The term "apocalypse" is often used to describe the events surrounding the last days of mortal man on the earth, just prior to the return of Christ.

Around the end of the first millennium, religious fanatics of Medieval Europe were so convinced that the Lord would soon appear, some hurled themselves from mountaintops, thinking their offering would compensate for any misdeeds in their lives. Others walled themselves into caves—even stopped talking and eating for as long as they could before succumbing to exhaustion, madness, or death.

> **Mormon Myths** _____
>
> *Myth: The apocalypse is the end of the world.* Many religious cultures consider the return of Jesus as heralding the apocalypse (in this context meaning the end of the world). However, the word "apocalypse" is a Greek word that means "revelation," and the term actually means anything that is revealed about future events. For example, if someone were to profess that the Utah Jazz will actually win an NBA championship, that would be considered an apocalyptic statement. And by the way, such an event would in no way coincide with hell freezing over (which would be another apocalyptic statement).

When Christ finally does return, Christianity teaches that there will be a reckoning of souls, meaning that the righteous will be united with Jesus at his coming, being spared God's wrath upon the world. For those who have chosen wickedness as a way of life, there'll be hell to pay—literally.

Mormonism teaches that for the people who followed in the path of righteousness—which implies those who have followed God—the return of the Lord will not come as a surprise.

Let's look at what Mormonism teaches about some of the important events that will take place prior to the Second Coming.

Grand Teton National Park. According to apocalyptic scriptures such as the Book of Revelation and prophesies by the Old Testament Prophet Isaiah, the mountains will "be made low" at the coming of Christ in the last days.

©Drew Williams (2002)

Falling Away (Great Apostasy)

We get into the topic of the Great Apostasy in Chapter 9. Briefly, though, the Great Apostasy represents a time when there is a separation of communications between God and man. For example, throughout the time before Christ, God always had a representative on the earth. Men like Adam, Moses, Solomon, and David all served as the Lord's spokesmen.

However, following the life, ministry, and death of Jesus, and after the elimination of the apostles who followed him, the world was without a direct line to God, according to LDS teachings and modern-day revelation. Civilizations were left to secular interpretation for their religious guidance. Consequently, the world remained in a state of spiritual floundering until around the middle of the nineteenth century. This event of a "Great Apostasy" has already come and gone. It began at the end of the ministry of Christ's last living Apostles, and ended when God and Jesus appeared to Joseph Smith Jr. in Palmyra, New York, in 1820 (see Chapter 11).

Latter-day Laughter

The leader of a world religion got a phone call from the Lord one day. "I want you to assemble leaders of all the popular faiths of the world," the Lord instructs. The man did as he was instructed.

Then by conference call, the Savior spoke to the assembled crowd: "I have some good news and some bad news for you."

"What's the good news?" one prominent leader asked.

"I have returned as promised," Jesus said.

The crowd of faithful followers burst into shouts of hosannas and hallelujahs. "What could possibly be the bad news?" asked another.

The Lord replied: "I'm calling from Salt Lake City."

Restoration of the Original Laws of Christ

Also referred to in Mormonism as the "Restoration of the Gospel," this important feature of a pre-second-coming era was also fulfilled—as anticipated in Revelation 14:6, in which John writes: "And I saw another angel fly in the midst of heaven, having the everlasting gospel to preach unto them that dwell on the earth, and to every nation, kindred, tongue and people."

Latter-day Saints believe Restoration of the Gospel began with the widespread influence of Mormonism, primarily through the extensive missionary program of the LDS Church.

Revelation of the "Stick of Joseph"

Throughout the Old Testament—especially in Isaiah and Ezekial—the Lord talks of a "Stick of Judah," which is the record of the Jews, represented by the Old Testament, and a "Stick of Joseph," which the LDS faith teaches to be the Book of Mormon, as translated by Joseph Smith.

LDS thinking holds that these two "sticks," or volumes of holy writ, will be combined to offer a single body of work before the return of the Lord.

Once again, according to Latter-day scripture comprised in the Book of Mormon, Doctrine and Covenants, and the Pearl of Great Price (see Chapter 10), combined with the King James Version of the Holy Bible, this event has come to pass.

Wars and Rumors of Wars

Anyone who picks up a copy of a newspaper can see that rumors of wars have been cast, assessed, analyzed, and documented for generations. There wars and rumors of wars ever-present in the world. In fact, according to scripture, the presence of conflict will continue to increase up to the time of Jesus' return.

No doubt, this prophesy is a work in progress.

Armageddon

I have left out much of the forecast regarding the days preceding the Lord's return. However, to not include reference of the Battle of Armageddon would be like explaining the value of a birthday cake without mentioning the candles. Armageddon will be the ultimate fireworks display.

There have been many references to "Great Wars." In fact, the American Civil War was often referred to as the "Great War between the North and South." World War I has historically been called the "Great War." And I'm sure anyone who was involved in the Second World War would never doubt the great impact of its effects on the human race.

"Armageddon" refers to the *last* Great War, according to accounts in the books of Joel and Isaiah in the Old Testament, and Revelation in the New Testament. Armageddon, which has been prophesied as occurring in the lands in and around ancient Israel, is to take place between two massive armies. The battle includes armies called "Gog" and "Magog," from countries north of Israel. This final battle, according to Christian tradition, marks the beginning of the end-of-the-world conflict. Events preceding the battle of Armageddon are forecast to resemble much of what we are currently seeing in the Middle East.

But although it might seem like we're living in a world similar to what has been prophesied, according to the prophecies, this is a picnic to what's coming. Things will get a lot worse. Nations will collapse, evil will reach an all-time high, and the world will pretty much be caught up in a total meltdown.

Whatever they're called, or whoever this last great battle will include, you don't want to be around when the shooting starts!

> **And It Came to Pass**
>
> Mormonism teaches that after the return of Jesus, the world will be returned into a state of glorified existence, necessary to accommodate those eternal beings (the righteous souls who walked the earth throughout time), who will eventually visit and ultimately inhabit the earth. This state of existence is the same condition the world was in when God walked with Adam and Eve in the Garden of Eden.

Gathering of Israel

Several pre-apocryphal events need a bit more attention. For one, the nation of Israel has to be reunited, as described in the books of Isaiah and Jeremiah:

> For a small moment have I forsaken thee [Israel]; but with great mercies will I gather thee. —(Isa. 54:7)

> The children of Israel shall come, they and the children of Judah together. ... They shall ask the way to Zion with their faces thitherward, saying, Come, and let us join ourselves to the Lord. —(Jer. 50:4–5)

Many religious scholars question the so-called "Israelization" of the LDS Church—referring to the Church's intimate interest and alleged desire to align itself with the original church of God.

Mormonism could not exist without a close, well-established tie to Judaism, because in the earliest days of mankind, it was the Jews who possessed the laws and covenants of God. They were his first Chosen People. Any religious organization that claims a direct tie to divinity without acknowledging the children of Israel, denies its own heritage.

As accounts from the Old Testament reveal—particularly in the books of Leviticus and Deuteronomy—God's covenant people eventually rejected his covenants. Israel fell into a state of captivity and persecution, problems that still haunt the Jewish culture today. The greatest consequence for their disobedience, according to scripture, was the scattering of the original nation of Israel among all of the early nations, and the sacrifice of their lands.

Words of Wisdom

And he shall set up an ensign for the nations, and shall assemble the outcasts of Israel, and gather together the dispersed of Judah from the four corners of the earth.
—Isaiah 11:12

One of God's revealed requirements for the world, according to Mormonism, is that the original tribes of Israel will be reunited, and all of their land restored. According to LDS belief, Israel's many family branches may be obscure in the eyes of man, but they are *not* lost or hidden from God.

The gathering of Israel has already begun. It has been restored to a portion of its original land, and is recognized as a nation, all of which have come at a high price for the people who live there. However, according to modern-day revelation, the literal gathering of Israel isn't just about reuniting the lost tribes, or peacefully restoring them to their former prominence and territories.

The revelation also includes blending Jewish doctrine with the restored truth of Christ, as he taught during his mortal ministry. That's when God's modern word will be united with his ancient people. It's a time that many LDS people see has begun, and will continue to take place until the Savior's return.

A Hot Time in the Old Town

The old war philosophy of "scorched earth policy" (meaning the burning of an enemy's town and its resources), is also part of the events marking the Second Coming. Christian belief—one that agrees with Mormonism—is that upon his return, Jesus will use fire to consume the wicked, the prideful, and anyone who chose not to follow his commandments.

This "baptism by fire"—referring to the fire by which the earth will be cleansed this second time around (the first was by flood)—follows the pattern of people being first baptized by water (as in the case of the flood at the time of Noah), following which the person received the Holy Ghost—also referred to as the baptism by fire. To God, the world itself and all who live here is alive. As such, it too required cleansing after the fall of man. This cleansing, as in the case of total immersion into water, must now be followed with a cleansing by fire. Although the term "baptism by fire" is symbolic in the way man receives the gift of the Holy Ghost, it has literal meaning where the world is concerned. (See Chapters 20 and 25 for more information on the nature of missionary work in the LDS Church.)

Those who were righteous throughout their lives, referring to those who chose to follow godliness over worldliness, will be "taken up" to be protected from the wrath of God, prior to this event.

That's when things really get cooking.

The Final Millennium

The children of the earth have already passed through nearly six millennia (depending on whose calendar you're looking at). At present, we're closing out the final days of the last millennium prior to the beginning of the seventh and final, thousand-year period—hence the reference "Latter days."

Many Christian faiths teach of a "rapture," in which those who accepted Christ as their savior will immediately vanish from the world when he returns. Although Mormonism does teach of a time when the righteous will be called up to meet Jesus before he cleanses the world with fire, LDS people learn that there's more to getting that spiritual ticket to ride with Christ than just admitting that he's the Messiah. This time is often referred to in the LDS Church as "the Millennium" (not to be mistaken for the new millennium that began January 1, 2000).

"The Millennium" is the period of time that represents the 1,000 years following the return of Christ, and is what Latter-day doctrine refers to as the final period before the last judgment. LDS doctrine teaches that the millennium is a time to catch up on any unfinished business from world history, such as teaching the gospel to those who never had a chance to hear it during mortality.

> **Mormonology**
>
> The **First Resurrection,** which began with the resurrection of Christ, is a time during which the righteous dead will be restored to their resurrected form, as they participate in the activities pertaining to this restoration process. This period of time will continue until all of those souls who were righteous are brought forth from death.

During the final millennium, LDS doctrine teaches that Jesus will personally preside over his church here on earth. During this sort of transitional period, Jesus and those who followed him throughout the ages will be working to establish divine order throughout the world. This period of time is when the earth will be prepared for its eventual transition back into a glorified world (as it was when Adam and Eve walked with God in the Garden of Eden), prior to the end of the *First Resurrection*.

When Will Jesus Return?

We've already discussed a few of the events that have been and are part of the prophesies of the Second Coming of Christ. LDS doctrine also teaches that certain conditions apply to the Lord's return. Here are a few:

- ♦ God knows exactly when Christ will return. No effort on the part of mankind can expedite or postpone the day when Jesus returns. It's pretty much set in stone, so to speak.

- ♦ Righteous efforts on our parts will not speed things up. God will not wait for the world to get its act together before he sends in the troops. But LDS doctrine teaches that it's probably a good idea for us to get things in order sooner than later.

- ♦ Wickedness and carnal chaos will be commonplace. One way we can check the eternal clocks is against the moral condition of the civilizations of the world. And as if the world isn't already in enough turmoil, Latter-day revelation found in the Doctrine and Covenants teaches that Christ will return during a time of worldwide strife, corruption, and evil, more widespread than has yet to be seen.

♦ The world will be ripe with iniquity. Once the world is about as bad as it can get, conditions will be ready for outside help. Think of it as one of those video games where you get one "smart bomb" to use, which wipes all the bad guys off the screen in one shot. That's what we can expect on that "Great and Dreadful Day."

Mormon Myths

Myth: Latter-day Saints claim a superior position over Christianity. When it comes to claiming "insider knowledge" about the life and activities of the Messiah, Christians who are not of the LDS faith believe Latter-day Saints think of themselves as having the corner on the market. Although the LDS Church does believe its very organization was directed by the Lord himself, nobody—LDS or otherwise—can know the will of God without the direction of Jesus, and without being duly ordained and authorized to represent him to the world.

If the reassurance of a devastated world, succumbed by raining fire and damnation doesn't pose enough incentive for mortal man to get his spiritual self in order, LDS doctrine also teaches that there will be no second chances. If people don't prepare to meet God in this life, according to Mormonism, it will be too late in the next life.

But for the righteous many who followed God's law, the afterlife won't all be about sitting on clouds, playing with our harps and halos. There will be much work to do for those who were obedient, which I'll discuss in the next chapter.

The Least You Need to Know

♦ At the return of Christ, man will be held eternally accountable for his actions.

♦ Jews will flock to God's Kingdom in the last days.

♦ The world will burn when Christ returns.

♦ The earth will be transformed into a celestial home.

♦ It's better to plan whose side we want to be on, rather than ponder when Christ will return.

Chapter 6

The Afterlife

In This Chapter

- ◆ What awaits in the afterlife
- ◆ Matching eternal reward with mortal obedience
- ◆ The spirit world on earth
- ◆ Everybody gets a wake-up call
- ◆ Judging the masses
- ◆ Home in the heavens

In the previous chapter, we discussed what Latter-day Saints believe to be the events that will take place during the Second Coming of Christ. Following this thousand-year period, in which Jesus himself presides over the world's religious affairs, LDS doctrine teaches that there will be one last battle between Satan and the followers of Christ. According to modern-day revelation, in this final, decisive, and epic confrontation, the good guys win, with Satan and his minions finally being cast out of man's presence—forever. Sounds like the makings of a great movie!

With Satan out of the picture and the righteous followers of God finding divine refuge, the world will be transformed into a glorified state—as it was when God walked with Adam and Eve. Mormonism teaches that after this time, all people who have ever lived on the earth will be resurrected and judged. Each individual will be granted an eternal reward, based on his or her obedience to God during mortality.

But here's another point where LDS belief differs from traditional Christian thought: In the afterlife, "one size fits all" doesn't work when it comes to spiritual rewards and punishments. Not everybody lives at the same level of obedience and will not receive the same rewards in heaven. Let's now look at how LDS doctrine positions the afterlife.

Life in the Afterlife

Once we have lived out our days on the earth, we die. According to LDS belief, when we leave this world, we will appear in a glorified spirit form, in our peak physical and mental condition—unadulterated by mortal restrictions, limitations, and the physical maladies that may have plagued us in life.

Many people have wondered what *age* we'll be during the afterlife. Since there's no concept of time there, age is irrelevant. However, as far as our physical appearance goes, most people agree that our physical condition will match the peak of our lives during mortality.

Furthermore, we will be allowed to take a few things with us into the afterlife. Not only will we have memories of our mortality, our individual characteristics and personalities will also be part of our spirits, as we developed them throughout our mortal lives. Unfortunately, we'll also be tormented by any earthly vices we might have developed. (I sure hope there are golf courses!) So any bad habits that we might have had (such as smoking, alcohol, drug abuse, liking reality television), will be even more tormenting to us, because—although we won't have physical bodies with which to experience those habits—our somewhat glorified mental capacity will remember those cravings. Sort of an eternal "cold turkey."

Mormonism differs from traditional Christian beliefs in the way it considers the disposition of spirits in the afterlife.

> **Mormon Myths** _____
>
> *Myth: We all get wings when we die.* "Clarence Oddbody" could ring all the bells he wanted to, but nobody is getting any wings in the next life. If that were the case, my wife—who's terrified of flying *anything*—would have to make other arrangements, like trading in the wings for a good set of running shoes. By the way, harps aren't on the list either!

Michelangelo's painting of the Last Judgment in Rome's Sistine Chapel depicts the Lord dispensing justice and mercy to the resurrected souls of mankind. LDS doctrine teaches that each individual will be judged by his or her actions. Those who were righteous and obeyed God's laws will inherit a celestial glory. Those who chose the ways of the world will be granted lesser states of glory and won't be allowed to return into the presence of God.

©*Drew Williams (2002)*

Post-Mortal Waiting Rooms

Following our death, we will find ourselves in either a state of rest or misery—depending on the decisions we made and how we lived our lives during mortality.

For example, if we were righteous and chose to follow the will of God, abstaining from wrongdoing, selfishness, and all of those devilish deeds, we will dwell in a state of spiritual rest, a relief from our worries and sorrows—a paradise of sorts. We will still be, however, somewhat "imprisoned" by the fact that we're not yet glorified as resurrected beings.

Mormonism also teaches that the organization of God's church reaches into the spirit world as well. Those righteous souls who performed tasks under the direction of God's priesthood, for example (see Chapter 20), will be called to serve as ministers to the souls of all of those who were not given the chance to hear the Gospel during mortality.

Words of Wisdom

Death is the starlit strip between the companionship of yesterday and the reunion of tomorrow.

—Mark Twain, U.S. writer and humorist

And that's where temple work comes in (see Chapter 26). Once people who dwell in the spirit world have been informed of God's plan, should they accept that plan, they must rely on the living to perform their baptism, and saving ordinances (which are described in the chapter on temple work).

So the missionary work will continue in full swing while in the spirit world. Of course, we won't be wearing dark suits or riding bicycles!

No Second Chances After Death

But before anybody gets the idea that they can put off their salvation until the afterlife, let me break the bad news: It's now or never.

LDS doctrine explains that the only people who will be offered the chance to participate in learning about the Gospel are those who never really got a chance to hear it in the first place, those who never knew anything about Jesus, and those who were too foolish to pay attention to God's warnings throughout history, when his appointed leaders were here to give them direction.

Still, the choice will be theirs.

Then there's the other side of the spiritual tracks, so to speak. For those who chose to follow any degree of evil, they will find the afterlife a place of continual discomfort and anguish. This is a far different type of place than what awaits the righteous. Hell, as it is often referred, is a place completely removed from even the spirit of the Lord. It is a place of darkness, a cold place in which the wicked are abandoned to be tormented by their own grief and anguish for their terrible actions during mortality.

Conversely, traditional Christian hell originates from Dark Age-era misinterpretations of scriptural reference to a place of anguish, where souls are forever consumed by fire. It's all symbolic. The bottom line is, hell is a place where God never goes and man should never want to be left.

That whole "weeping, wailing and gnashing of teeth" should come to mind when you think of hell.

Both spiritual estates, however, are only temporary holding places. It's not until our bodies are resurrected and reunited with our spirits that we receive our final judgment.

Take King David, as an example of being left in a spiritual prison until he is resurrected, judged, and finally sentenced to his eternal dwelling place. David had everything going for him. He had the big house, lots of influence, and a few thousand people at his command. He also had the favor of the Almighty himself. But the boy-king developed one giant problem. He had a libido the size of Goliath.

David enjoyed the company of many women. And commanding a congregation of concubines and wagons full of wives wasn't enough to satiate his desires. David had a man killed so he could add another bride to his bedroom (see the account in Second Samuel in the Old Testament).

The king of Israel committed that one unpardonable sin—the shedding of innocent blood. For David, the party was over. He was forever banished from God's presence, and after he died, would be left in hell for a time, to pay his own way for the death of Uriah. But David was also promised that his soul would not linger in anguish forever, because of his otherwise righteous life and obedience to God. According to passages in both the Old and New Testaments, David will eventually be resurrected and judged, but will be given a *lesser* eternal rest than that of a celestial glory. (I'll cover those lesser kingdoms later in this chapter.)

David will enjoy God's mercy for the many great things he accomplished in the name of the Lord, but still suffer justice for his murderous deed. In a true sense, although he will experience a portion of paradise, David's eternal progress will cease to continue until the final judgment—David will still suffer a "damning" of sorts.

By the way, if you ever want to hear the voice of a man pleading for mercy, the book of Psalms is loaded with David's cries for forgiveness—along with memorable passages of praise.

Side-by-Side with Spirits

Many people ask where the spirit world exists. LDS doctrine teaches that the spirit world is actually right here on earth—but sort of in a different dimension. Here's another one of those "unexplainable" phenomena many people experience: A loved one passes away, yet for a time, those who were closest to that person, often claim that they can *feel* his or her presence nearby.

You won't get much argument from the LDS community on this matter. Mormonism teaches that, not only does the spirit world dwell on the earth, the veil that separates us mortals from those "on the other side" can often become very thin—especially right after death. Eventually, we will be reunited with our loved ones in the afterlife, as long as we live righteously.

But even after death, we're going to eventually have to face our actions on a long-term basis. We will be resurrected to be judged and rewarded accordingly.

The First and Second Resurrections

Three days after Christ was crucified, he was resurrected, reuniting a glorified body with his eternal spirit. Christianity teaches that until that time, no one had ever escaped the bonds of death. That event marked the beginning of what LDS doctrine refers to as the "First Resurrection."

When Christ was resurrected, many other righteous spirits came forth from the grave, according to ancient scripture: "And the graves were opened; and many bodies of the saints which slept arose, and came out of the graves after his resurrection, and went into the holy city, and appeared unto many." (Matt. 27:52–53)

Mormonism teaches that mortal man is now living during the First Resurrection, which started with Jesus himself, and will yet continue after his return, until all of the righteous souls are brought forth from the grave.

Mormon Myths _____

Myth: Only Mormons will be in Heaven. The Church of Jesus Christ of Latter-day Saints holds to the belief that there was one holy order of government established by God. The idea that Latter-day Saints will be the only inhabitants of heaven is an *almost* inaccurate statement. Anybody who follows God's commandments, obeys the principles of the Gospel of Jesus Christ, and lives a righteous life, will find a place in the presence of God. What those people are called isn't important. The path they took to achieve that goal, however, is.

The scriptures teach that all people who ever lived on the earth are entitled to the resurrection. However, the scriptures also note that not all people receive the same reward, and as such, are not brought up at the same time. The First Resurrection is the time when the most righteous of souls will be raised up to join Christ during his millennial reign on the earth.

After the end of the First Resurrection, LDS belief is that the Lord will call forth a Second Resurrection, which is probably not the invitation list you want to find yourself on. The Second Resurrection is designated for those who were not the best of people throughout the history of the world. Their judgment will come by those righteous men who were called during their mortal lives to assist Christ as "Judges in Israel." The eternal reward for those late sleepers will match their mortal behavior.

But don't look to me for judgment on who gets the first-round draft pick where resurrections are concerned. If you want to get a good idea of who will be included in the "good people" category, look up the Beatitudes from Jesus' Sermon on the Mount in the New Testament.

As for the bad examples, well, who cares as long as we're focused on the good side?

 **Words of Wisdom**

Blessed and holy is he that hath part in the first resurrection. … They shall be priests of God and of Christ and shall reign with him a thousand years.

—Revelation 20:5,6

Judgment

According to LDS belief, once everyone is reunited, spirit-to-glorified body, we will find ourselves under spiritual scrutiny by the hosts of heaven. Think of your entire life playing out on a huge screen—the "uncut version"—complete with the ultimate in sound clarity. That's what we can expect following our resurrection.

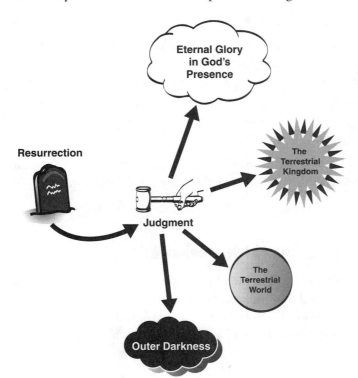

Although the Judgment of God comes to all people throughout history, a person's final resting place will vary depending on his or her level of obedience to God's laws.

©Drew Williams (2002)

And after experiencing the horror or delight in seeing the history of our lives being played out before us and the rest of God's kingdom, we will find ourselves given a reward to match our ability to live God's commandments.

Four Eternal Retirement Communities

Imagine yourself in the best shape of your life, being given a choice between sharing an exclusive resort with your family, being invited to an eternal singles party at the best theme park, shacking up at the local "Y" with a bunch of strangers, or being left naked at the South Pole in June (the sun doesn't shine at the South Pole in June). That's sort of analogous to what we can all expect as our "final resting place" after we are resurrected.

The scriptures describe "many mansions" within the kingdoms of God. Because each individual will be judged according to his or her works during mortality, the final residence will depend on those actions.

Mormonism teaches that there will be three communities of glorified souls, and one place where only the very dregs of humanity will be left to mingle with the unborn spirits who were cast out of God's presence.

Celestial Glory: The Place Where God Lives

Those fortunate spirits who are found worthy to live in the Celestial Kingdom, are those who gained not only a strong understanding of the life of Christ, but also a personal conviction to follow his teachings throughout their lives. The Celestial Kingdom is God's own personal community. It is also the place where Latter-day Saint families know they can be together forever as a family unit, and can continue to grow as an eternal family (see Chapter 24).

Mormonism teaches that celestial beings walk and talk with God and Jesus, accomplishing what God had established as his plan during the Grand Council.

Celestial glory is the grand prize for obedient living and long suffering.

Second and Third Place: Less Than Stellar Behavior

There are two other levels of glory, which God provided for a final resting place of those who lived to some level of goodness, but not to the point where they could be considered "perfect" enough to dwell in God's presence. In a way, these lesser kingdoms might be considered heavenly—and are certainly much more glorious than the world in which we currently find ourselves—but they still limit those who dwell there from ever walking in God's presence again. There will be no further progress for these inhabitants, and family units will not exist there. So there will still be a measure of misery in knowing what they *could* have enjoyed, had they lived more worthily.

Mormonism teaches that people who lived honorable lives while on the earth, but rejected the word of God, will be given limited access to deity. The *Terrestrial Kingdom* will be the everlasting place of residence for these glorified spirits, and the spirits of those who accepted the Gospel of Christ during mortality, but chose not to live up to its precepts. These souls will know of the greatness of God's plan, but will be prohibited from living as part of a family unit. They may live and walk among other glorified souls and will even have the privilege of Jesus in their midst from time to time. But these souls will nonetheless, walk alone forever.

If there was a bottom wrung on the spiritual ladder of glory, the *Telestial World* would be the place. Although it could still be considered a far greater place than the world in which we currently find ourselves, the Telestial World is reserved for those who chose not to receive the Gospel in both mortality and in the spirit world. These are the spirits who suffered through hell, paying their own way for their actions, until called forth *after* the end of the First Resurrection. It figures that even for a loving father who couldn't bare to lose even one of his children, a portion of mercy would be poured out to just about everyone. Although barely a "glorified" kingdom, the Telestial World is full of souls who could be classified as "liars," "thieves," "whoremongers," "adulterers," etc. Not a pretty place.

And let me say a special note about "murderers": As I mentioned earlier, although David did have a man killed, he was promised some form of glory for his obedience. Mormonism teaches that David's ultimate residence will be among the wicked of the Telestial World. But as for the *really* bad guys, it's hard to anticipate what judgment they will receive. I'm glad I don't have that responsibility, so I won't waste time speculating where they will or should go.

Outer Darkness: No Rest for the Wicked

Latter-day revelation notes that, having meted out all of the glory and mercy to even the lowliest of souls, God still needed a place for the most wicked of spirits, such as those who chose to follow Satan in defiance of the plan presented at the Grand Council.

If you can actually think of "hell freezing over," you'll have a fragment of understanding the place LDS doctrine calls Outer Darkness. No spirit of God dwells in this place, and consequently, no light of Christ exists. Outer Darkness is the ultimate exile.

For those *Sons of Perdition* who actually knew Jesus Christ as the Messiah, or had the truth of him validated by the Holy Ghost, yet denied the truth of what they knew, there will be no forgiveness. These condemned souls will be left without any connection to eternal grace, and will suffer in eternal darkness and torment forever.

These lost souls would rather have never been born.

Mormonology

Individuals who had a personal understanding of the role of Jesus Christ as the Messiah, and had received the Holy Ghost as a companion, or knew of him by personal experience—but denied the truth of these eternal principles—are called the **Sons of Perdition**. Their eternal justice will be shared by the lost spirits who followed Satan.

The Least You Need to Know

- ◆ We will be restored to perfect health after the Resurrection.
- ◆ The spirit world is a temporary resort/prison.
- ◆ Spiritual rewards will match a person's obedience.
- ◆ There will be no mercy for the wicked.

Part 2

The Word of God Revisited

In the beginning was the word, and the word was with God and the word was God. (John 1:1)

So what is the "Word of God"? The "Word" was a reference to Jesus himself, as both the messenger *and* the message from God. But it also represents the written and spoken words of God's appointed messengers throughout the ages.

This part focuses on four fundamental elements of divine revelation, which include the Old and New Testaments of the King James Version of the Bible, the state of prophecy in the days of Christ (and how communications between God and man were severed for a time), and a brief discussion on the evolution of early Christian scripture.

The Old Testament

In This Chapter

- ◆ Words of God, old but not outdated
- ◆ Moses manages the masses
- ◆ Jerusalem falls
- ◆ Sparing the rod means not reading God's words
- ◆ The 12 tribes assimilated
- ◆ The prophecies of Isaiah

The Holy Bible provides an early record of not only the "children of God," but also foreshadows and testifies of the life and times of Jesus Christ. The Bible has influenced the Christian world for hundreds of generations. Its many historical accounts span from the beginning of man, through the life of Christ, and into our future. In this chapter and the next, we will concentrate on important aspects found within the Old and New Testaments, which serve as spiritual pointers to what Latter-day Saints believe to be indications of the need for a restoration of God's kingdom on earth.

The Old Testament includes the body of religious work used by the Jews of ancient times, which was also later accepted by the followers of Christ. The actual contents of the Bible, however, have varied through the ages, as many interpretations have been made, negotiated, and even fought over.

Books contained in the Old Testament were written over centuries by many authors. In contrast, the contents of the New Testament came from a few sources, and were written during a small period of time, probably within the first 100 years following the life of Jesus.

Ancient Covenants Made Manifest

The Old Testament is a collection of books that were written prior to the birth of Jesus, by people who were designated as God's mouthpieces throughout the earliest years of civilized man. These books include testimonials, songs, poems, prophecies, and words of instruction. The Old Testament also comprises core doctrine for the original church of God. Latter-day Saints, along with most Christian faiths, consider the Old Testament a critical collection of early views into church government, and prophesy of the coming of the Messiah.

The word "testament" means two different things, depending on which section of the Bible you're talking about. For the Old Testament, the general Hebrew equivalent means "covenant." In the case of the New Testament, which was written primarily in Greek, the loose translation would refer to an "arrangement."

Words of Wisdom

The Bible is a book of faith, and a book of doctrine, and a book of morals, and a book of religion, of especial revelation from God.

—Daniel Webster, U.S. statesman and orator

Mormonology

A **covenant** is an agreement between two or more individuals or parties. The scriptural reference connotes a spiritual agreement between God and man. In this case, God sets the guidelines and man accepts them.

The Old Testament includes many significant points of Mormonism. For example, within the first lines of Genesis, God says, "Let us make man in our own image." This scriptural reference to "our," indicating that God was not alone at the time of the creation of man, has particular meaning in the LDS Church.

Mormonism teaches that it was "Jehovah"—the pre-earth life name of Jesus Christ—who created the world under the direction of his father, "Elohim" (see Chapters 1 and 2). Traditional Christianity strays from the belief that God and Jesus are separate and distinct beings, which is part of the discussion in Chapter 10.

From a spiritual perspective, the Old Testament denotes the ancient *covenant* of Moses, the laws given by God, for the children of Israel. These laws are considered by LDS doctrine as the lesser laws, because Israel was not spiritually prepared for God's higher laws (see Chapter 20 for more information about the lesser and higher priesthoods of God).

The Old Testament provides the earliest accepted history of God's kingdom on earth. Moses was God's chosen leader around 1500 B.C., and was the author of the earliest books found in the Old Testament.

©Drew Williams (2002)

Traditional Christian theology holds that the sacred passages within the Old and New Testaments are literal translations out of the mouth of God himself. However, Mormonism contends that a lot of the verses, although inspired and definitely directed by God, in many aspects fall short of being a complete body of divine revelation.

Context is also an important differentiator between LDS and traditional Christian beliefs. Latter-day Saints believe that the Bible is only one small but important volume of canon. Its stories, passages, and directions were specifically authored to address the ancient church, while prophesying the fulfillment of the laws of Moses, in a higher form of spiritual government, which would be established by the coming Messiah.

Christian belief is that Jesus fulfilled those prophesies of a "higher law" described throughout the Old Testament, by giving up his own life. Mormonism extends that principle, believing in a uniting—or fullness—of the Gospel of Jesus Christ, as foretold in the Old Testament, fulfilled by the Lord during his earthly ministry.

And It Came to Pass

Many members of the LDS Church—especially the missionaries—are often confronted by people with hard-line Christian beliefs, arguing that the Bible contains the last Word of God, and that nothing else of divine authorship exists. But even the books found in both the Old and New Testaments talk of other books, which are no longer part of the collection of writings found in the King James Version. This discrepancy begs the question: Prior to 1611, before the councils of James I assembled what we have today, did Christians believe they had a full volume of holy writ—such as in the case of early Bibles like the Vulgate and Tindale versions? Probably.

It's human nature to want to learn more about where we came from, why we are here, and where we will go when life ends. But it's also been shown throughout the history of man that change is painful. Naturally, what becomes accepted as a common belief offers a certain level of comfort, which has historically lulled societies to believe one way or another. That's the neat thing about us humans. We're always discovering something new that, prior to that discovery, would have been considered fiction—or even heresy.

Mormonism teaches that our ability to progress to greater levels of knowledge and understanding is enhanced by our willingness to accept the possibility that we don't know everything. LDS doctrine stresses that this principle was just as true in the days of Moses as it is in modern society, and that once the fundamentals are in place, everything else is just day-by-day "maintenance" so to speak.

The Law of Moses

The term "Law of Moses" is used in LDS doctrine to describe the entire body of rules and covenants collected and written by Moses. Such laws included directives on how to conduct business, both temporal and spiritual, among the children of Israel. These laws provided clear guidelines—sort of a "user's manual" for life.

The Law of Moses also included the law of "Carnal Commandments," (worldly commandments that include directions essential to living by the edicts of the day). From a symbolic perspective, these carnal laws could be mapped to the fundamental principles of the Gospel of Jesus, which are faith, repentance, baptism by immersion, and receiving the Holy Ghost by one who was authorized to perform this ordinance (further discussed in Chapter 23).

Words of Wisdom

For it is evident that our Lord sprang out of Judah; of which tribe Moses spake nothing concerning priesthood. And it is yet far more evident: for that after the similitude of Melchisedec there ariseth another priest, who is made, not after the law of a carnal commandment, but after the power of an endless life.

—Hebrews 7:14–17

Jerusalem's Downfall

Moses was tipped off by God (actually, Jehovah), that while the two of them were spending quality time in the mountains, the children of Israel had turned their desert settlement into a den of iniquity. When Moses returned from Mount Sinai, having the tablets with the Word of God inscribed on them, he threw them down, breaking them at the base of the golden calf that Aaron was forced to make by the wayward Jews (read chapter 34 of Exodus for the full story).

But contrary to what Cecil B. DeMille depicted in his epic film *The Ten Commandments*, there is no scriptural account of the earth opening up and swallowing Edward G. Robinson or anyone else. In fact, a modern-day version of the film would more likely follow the account in Exodus, in which Moses, after looking out at the naked campers, instructs the sons of Levi to use their swords and kill all of the infidels (about 3,000 of them) in the encampment.

"Thy Rod and Thy Staff"

LDS families believe that children are gifts from God, and should be raised with an abundance of love and gentleness. But there's an old and somewhat inaccurate adage that says, "Spare the rod, spoil the child." The notion here is that kids need an occasional whack to keep things straight. That's what the "Good Book" says, right?

Nope. Nowhere in the Bible does it say to hit kids. This is one of those interpretive and very delicate topics where lots of opinions exist.

The Latter-day viewpoint considers the reference to "rod" that appears throughout the Bible as a metaphor to mean the Word of God itself—the scriptures. In the case of the New Testament, the "Word" also serves as a symbolic reference to Jesus Christ. (I touch on this again in Chapter 24.)

And then there's that "staff" reference. According to traditional definitions, the "staff," most commonly recognized from the twenty-third Psalm, was a stick used by a shepherd to *gently* direct his sheep.

Thus, "thy rod [meaning the Word of God] and thy staff [referring to the gentle promptings, commandments, and spiritual guidelines found in the word of God], they comfort me" is more in context to what the original authors probably implied.

As with any religion, however, the final decision on what an individual believes will be somewhat based on his or her own interpretation of what *sounds* reasonable, rather than on what somebody tells him or her is accurate. For the LDS community, however, the leading voice of spiritual reason rests with the current prophet of the Church. The fundamental driver behind believing what was written in the scriptures—regardless of which standard work—is based on principles of faith.

And It Came to Pass

In the LDS adult Sunday school program called "Gospel Doctrine," the scriptures are part of a four-year cycle. Each year, the Old or New Testament, the Book of Mormon, or the Doctrine and Covenants become part of a year-long course in scripture study and discussion. This focus on a single portion of the standard works enables Latter-day Saints time to become more intimately aware of the scriptures and how they can guide the lives of LDS individuals and families.

Why bring this up now? Because as we look at the contents and context of the Old and New Testaments, much of what was written then has changed over time through different languages, cultures, and word of mouth. In some cases, as in the Psalms and portions of Isaiah, the works were written in a way to be memorized. Not many people outside the high priests of the temple were even allowed to possess holy works. Whether out of affordability or mandate, this limited the ability for misinterpretations to surface and kept everyone on the same page, in a futile sort of way.

But all that ended when the separation of the nations of Israel (meaning the 12 original tribes, who each followed a son of Jacob), when Assyria carried 10 of the 12 tribes into captivity. Consequently, new records were written and new concepts pertaining to religion were introduced.

Twelve Tribes Assimilated

For nearly 500 years, concluding about 600 B.C., the mighty Assyrian Empire ruled most of the regions north of the Caspian Sea and east of the Mediterranean. This powerful nation was the original melting pot of civilization.

After conquering a people, the Assyrians would relocate their captives far away from their native lands, forcing them to blend into Assyrian society. Eventually, the conquered cultures would become so diluted throughout the Assyrian empire that they would cease to exist.

The LDS belief, one that applies more to our future than our past, is that one of the important signs of the return of Christ will take place when the 10 lost tribes of Israel are again reunited with their cousins.

Latter-day Laughter

A father was upset to hear of his daughter's involvement in toilet-papering a neighbor's house. "But Daddy," she said, "I was merely demonstrating that the Old Testament promotes toilet-papering houses." "How's that?" the father asked, bewildered. The girl opened her scriptures to Zechariah and began to read: "I turned, and lifted up mine eyes, and looked, and beheld a flying roll."

—Anonymous

Isaiah's Prophecies

Isaiah was the political and spiritual advisor to Jewish King Hezekiah during the middle of the eighth century B.C. No other prophet is more quoted throughout LDS canon than Isaiah. Future apostles in both the Bible and the Book of Mormon—even Jesus himself—quoted from Isaiah's prophecies.

Isaiah's prophecies not only point to the coming of such great men as John the Baptist, but also prophesy of the coming of the Messiah: "For unto us a child is born, unto us a son is given: and the government shall be upon his shoulder: and his name shall be called Wonderful, Counselor, the mighty God, the everlasting Father, the Prince of Peace." (Isa. 9:6)

LDS scripture, as found in 2 Nephi in the Book of Mormon, heavily reference Isaiah's words. But for many people, Isaiah's writings are often considered complex and difficult to understand. That's partially due to the extensive symbolism used throughout the book, as well as Isaiah's routine style of mixing local prophesy with future predictions.

For example, throughout Isaiah: 44, Isaiah refers to a man, named "Cyrus," who will restore Israel to its proper place. Persian king Cyrus I, who lived 140 years later, did in fact free the Jews and allowed them to reclaim their land and even rebuild their temple.

If you go back four chapters, however, Isaiah refers to a voice that "crieth in the wilderness," who Latter-day revelation believes to be John the Baptist.

Isaiah's writings are very important to Latter-day Saints. Throughout his words are references to the rise of great nations, the coming of the Messiah, and the discovery of the Book of Mormon, as in the following account:

> And the vision of all is become unto you as the words of a book that is sealed, which men deliver to one that is learned, saying, read this, I pray thee: and he saith, I cannot; for it is sealed: And the book is delivered to him that is not learned, saying, read this, I pray thee: and he saith, I am not learned. (Isa. 29:11–12)

The Book of Mormon, which I discuss in Chapters 12 and 13, was partially sealed when Joseph Smith recovered it from under a rock on a hillside in upstate New York. LDS people believe that Smith, who was not an educated man, was tasked with translating the Book of Mormon into English by the power of inspiration and faith.

Understanding Isaiah's prophecies, many of which are included in the Book of Mormon, LDS people gain further insight into the fulfillment of the Gospel of Christ, his Second Coming, and the general state of mankind throughout the ages.

Later in the Old Testament, in Malachi, there is reference to the concept of a pre-earth life (discussed in this book in Chapter 3).

Written more than four centuries prior to the birth of Christ, the Malachi includes references to John the Baptist (Malachi: 3) as well as the second coming of the Lord (Malachi: 4). No matter which book we read in the Old Testament, those many authors consistently delivered a message that proclaimed two great events: the fall of Israel and the fulfillment of the law by the coming of the Lord.

The Least You Need to Know

- ◆ The Old Testament contains the ancient covenants of God's first "Chosen People."

- ◆ The Law of Moses was the user manual of life for the children of Israel.

- ◆ Jerusalem was destroyed because it was unwilling to remain obedient to God's laws.

- ◆ The Bible does *not* condone physical abuse of children.

- ◆ Israel's pride cost its people their heritage.

- ◆ Isaiah offered insight for both his time and ours.

Chapter 8

The New Testament

In This Chapter

- Four points of view into Christ's ministry
- One sent forth: being called to the ministry
- Praying in the Garden of Gethsemane
- The Holy Ghost arrives on earth
- Prophesying the last days

The New Testament is the Christian equivalent to the Book of Law in the Old Jewish tradition (The Old Testament). The contents and order of the books collected in the New Testament were first assembled by the first Holy Roman Emperor Constantine, during the fourth century A.D. Our modern-day version of the New Testament comes from the work performed by the councils of James I in 1611. The New Testament contains a collection of testimonials about the life and ministry of Jesus and his apostles, a collection of letters or "epistles" that were used to teach the various branches of the early Christian church, and the revelation of John the Beloved.

Although scholars over the past century have since revised and offered simpler versions of the New Testament, the LDS Church holds that the 27 books found in the King James Version are the most accurate to the original context. The founder of the LDS Church, Joseph Smith Jr., provided further interpretations into some of the passages of the Bible, which are part of the reference material included in the Church's Standard Works.

Proclaiming the "Good News"

The Gospel or "good news" is a reference to the life, ministry, and *atonement* of Jesus Christ. The term has stood as a reference to the government of God since the early days of the Christian church. For Latter-day Saints, the principles of the Gospel (faith in the Lord Jesus Christ, repentance, baptism by immersion, and receiving the Holy Ghost), are the core precepts of the LDS religion.

> **Mormonology**
>
> **Atonement** is the divine reconciliation for transgressions against God. In the days prior to Christ, the atonement was an animal sacrifice of blood offering made on the altars of the temple to purge the individual or group of sins. Part of Jesus' ministry was to provide a single blood atonement by committing himself to be sacrificed for the human race to fulfill the law of sacrifice to God.

> **Words of Wisdom**
>
> And for this cause he is the mediator of the new testament, that by means of death, for the redemption of the transgressions that were under the first testament, they which are called might receive the promise of eternal inheritance.
>
> —Hebrews 9:15

The first four books of the New Testament offer points of view by the Apostles Matthew, Mark, Luke, and John. Although we know that other personal witnesses of the life of Christ were recorded, these were the four men whose works, known as the Gospels, were chosen to represent an accounting of the actual life of Jesus.

But the four Gospels provide more than biographical sketches of Jesus and his disciples. Each book contains segments about the ministry of Christ and what he taught—but more importantly—what he lived and died for.

Latter-day Saints, like the rest of the Christian world, focus on those principles and teachings found in the sacred works of these four books, as providing relevant information on how to live more in tune with what the Lord would expect. Consequently, LDS belief is that each member of the human race can become a disciple of Christ by following his example, and by understanding what it takes to be one of his disciples.

Harmony in the Four Gospels

The accounts in each of the four Gospels share a common theme: the fulfillment of the Laws of Moses through the ministry of Jesus. However, the Gospel of Matthew is more specifically directed at the nation of Israel, often referencing events and passages occurring in the Old Testament.

The Gospel of Mark appears to target the Gentile nations, as it offers greater explanation of the purpose of Jesus' life, and offers further information about the political and logistical landscape.

When many think of the Gospel of Luke, thoughts of the story of the birth of Jesus come to mind (or in my family's case, Linus's famous reading of the true meaning of Christmas in the holiday classic, *Merry Christmas Charlie Brown*). The Gospel of Luke includes perhaps the greatest level of detail into the teachings of Christ.

The Gospel of John runs somewhat tangent from the typical chronologies offered by the other three Gospel accounts. According to LDS doctrine, John's writings are more targeted toward people who had converted from Judaism to Christianity. John's efforts were to help the new converts to remain focused on what Jesus taught, rather than on the chronology of Jesus' life.

The four witnesses of the life of Christ, it would seem, each bore a unique point of reference to the "good news." For Latter-day Saints, the harmony of the Gospels is in proclaiming the ministry, atonement, and the government of God, which the LDS community claims to have been restored in 1832.

Apostolic Callings

Speaking of the disciples of Christ, there is a distinct separation between a disciple—or "student" of Christ—and an apostle. "Apostle" is a Greek word meaning "one sent forth." These men were special witnesses of Christ, set apart as a quorum of leadership to assist in the proclamation of the Gospel throughout the people of the world.

And It Came to Pass

To be called as an apostle was considered the most high and holy appointment by God on the earth. LDS belief is that these men were ministers and witnesses appointed by God himself, not just to preach Christianity to the Romans and Jews, but to bare witness of the life and principles of the government of Jesus Christ (which we learn later was to be considered treasonous and criminal). In fact, even Jesus himself held the position as apostle, as referenced in the third chapter of Hebrews. Christ was the one sent forth by his father to provide the way back for the human race.

According to the accounts in the New Testament, the original Twelve Apostles were often instructed by Jesus to minister to both Jew and Gentile. Following his act of betrayal and death, Judas Iscariot was replaced by the Apostle Matthias. Other apostles also followed, including another apostle named James—who was the brother of Christ, and the first bishop of Rome (under the direction of the Prophet Peter), and the great New Testament apostle, Paul (see the next section).

The Twelve Apostles continued their ministry until all of them were ultimately killed or banished.

As in the organized church during the time of Jesus, the LDS Church government is comprised of a council of Twelve Apostles, who are called and ordained to the office by the prophet of the Church—who is, himself, the senior apostle (see Chapter 20 for more information on modern-day apostles).

Paul's Letters

Another great New Testament apostle was Paul of Tarsus. From many of the accounts throughout the New Testament, Paul appeared on the scene as the man with the responsibility for keeping consistent the doctrine and procedures of the early Christian church—sort of the apostle at large. For this purpose, Paul authored the many letters—or "epistles"—which comprise the bulk of the New Testament.

One interesting bit of trivia: Many people think that the books in the New Testament appear in order of creation, that Matthew, Mark, Luke, and John were actually written first, following the Acts and the various letters to the nations and cities. This is not true. In the case of the various epistles written by Paul, for example, with the exception of Hebrews, the books were arranged by order of length, not timeline. In fact, according to many biblical scholars, the four Gospels were actually written between 10 and 25 years after the death of Jesus.

Paul's epistles were letters of instruction, often written at the request of local church teachers and leaders, whose congregations had begun to divert from the fundamental principles of the Gospel.

For example, the book of Colossians was a letter written by Paul to members of the Christian congregation in that city after he was asked to do so by the local evangelist, Epaphras. The problem, which was common among the early Christian followers of Christ, was that new ideas and cultural philosophies were creeping into the core doctrine of the church. In the case of the Colossians, they began to worship angels and withdraw themselves from certain accepted practices (such as eating meat).

This is a very important issue. In the case of the LDS Church, consistency rules worldwide. Any time there is a change made by the governing body of the Church in Salt Lake City, it is immediately conveyed to all local church leaders throughout the world, usually in letter form—much like what was done in Paul's time.

Words of Wisdom

And this I say, lest any man should beguile you with enticing words. For though I be absent in the flesh, yet am I with you in the spirit, joying and beholding your order, and the steadfastness of your faith in Christ. As ye have therefore received Christ Jesus the Lord, so walk ye in him: Rooted and built up in him, and established in the faith, as ye have been taught, abounding therein with thanksgiving. Beware lest any man spoil you through philosophy and vain deceit, after the tradition of men, after the rudiments of the world, and not after Christ.

—Apostle Paul to the Christians in Colosse

Through his epistle to the Colossians, Paul's efforts were to steer the congregation back onto the correct path of doctrinal order, as originally defined by Christ. This type of problem began to infect the church almost immediately after the death of Christ, and is written about throughout the New Testament.

Consequently, as I discuss in Chapter 9, the trappings of society and influences of the dominant cultures throughout Rome eventually overtook the church of Christ, which resulted in a complete falling away of its original organization.

Ancient Rome was the pinnacle of power during the final years of the apostles' ministry before God's word fell into corruption.

©Drew Williams (2002)

In the year A.D. 70, the Roman army marched into Jerusalem and conquered the Holy City. This relief from the Arch of Titus in the Roman Forum shows the Roman soldiers sacking temple ornaments and the Ark of the Covenant.

©Drew Williams (2002)

John's Last Request

Many Latter-day Saints believe that, although Paul was probably considered the greatest voice of the New Testament—save Jesus himself—it was the Apostle John the Beloved who was rewarded by Christ with one of the greatest responsibilities ever bestowed upon a man.

In the account given in John 21:21–23, Peter asks what will become of the Apostle John, who Christ often referred to as his "beloved." Jesus answered somewhat rebuking Peter's curiosity:

> Jesus saith unto him, If I will that he tarry till I come, what is that to thee? Follow thou me. Then went this saying abroad among the brethren, that that disciple should not die: yet Jesus said not unto him, He shall not die; but, If I will that he tarry till I come, what is that to thee?

John was given the opportunity to remain on the earth, without having to age unto death, and work on behalf of the Lord until his return. By all accounts, that makes John something in the area of about 2,010 years old. Not bad for a man who's had to survive countless wars, plagues, political struggles, and centuries without plumbing and toilet paper!

Latter-day Saints believe that John's gift would allow him to remain on the earth, which meant keeping the priesthood intact, and the Holy Ghost present with mankind, until the return of the Lord's kingdom. It was probably the only saving grace left in the world, after the eventual dissolution of the church in about A.D. 96.

One Evening in the Garden

For the traditional Christian world, the impact of Jesus' life was in his death upon the cross, as recorded in the New Testament Gospels. Granted, it's not every day that a man is born into the world, endures years of poverty (by his own choice), and then suffers torture and death—again by his own choice. To think that such a man would freely die, while also having the power to raise up his own life and restore it, all for the sake of humanity, such was the purpose for Jesus.

But for Latter-day Saints, the most significant aspect of Jesus' life wasn't his death on the cross. It was in those few hours he spent praying in the Garden of Gethsemane. This focus is a distinctive difference between the LDS and traditional Christian cultures.

Latter-day Saints target the atonement itself as the single most important event in the life of Christ. During his time in Gethsemane, Jesus pleaded with God to consider taking away his burden. In the end, however, even Jesus accepted the will of his father as being sufficient for the task. Consequently, the pressure and strain of bearing the literal burden of all mankind was so intense, Jesus sweat drops of blood.

In LDS circles, it was during this period in Gethsemane that Jesus became the savior of mankind, which he sealed soon after when giving up his mortality on Calvary Hill.

> **And It Came to Pass**
>
> Many Christians wear a crucifix as a symbol of their faith in Christ. Although Latter-day Saints do wear religious jewelry, such as pendants recognizing the achievements of women, they do not wear the sign of the cross, nor does it appear anywhere in the LDS Church. Traditional LDS thought focuses more on the life and atonement of Christ, rather than on the instrument of his death.

Day of Pentecost

According to accounts in the New Testament, following his death and resurrection, Jesus walked and talked with a select few of his congregation for about six weeks. At the end of this period, he ascended into heaven, leaving behind two things:

◆ He let everyone know that there were other sheep in his fold to which he would go to attend, and that he would return to the world some day, to reign over his government across the land.

◆ He left a gift with those who were anointed to receive it—the Holy Ghost.

Mormonism has ties to both of these events. In the case of the former, LDS doctrine supports that Jesus went to the people of the Americas—specifically those native Americans living in South and Central America—to preach his Gospel. This information was recorded by the community leaders, and included in what was later found and translated into the Book of Mormon (see Chapters 12 and 13).

However, in the case of the second event, the gift of the Holy Ghost, this sacred promise from Christ to mankind assured that a member of the Godhead (see Chapter 2) would forever be on the earth—despite what might happen to the government of God. Although the church eventually fell into a state of apostasy (see Chapter 9), the presence of the Holy Ghost remained on the earth.

This issue is key to understanding the principles behind LDS authority, which claims to have received not only the gift of the Holy Ghost, but also the keys of ministry and leadership for God's church, by direct authority of the resurrected Christ.

> ### And It Came to Pass
>
> The Pentecost was originally a feast, which took place 50 days after Passover, to celebrate the first fruits of the harvest. The Christian Day of Pentecost remembers that Jesus bestowed the gift of the Holy Ghost onto the heads of each of his apostles. With the power of the Holy Ghost, Christ commissioned his followers to go forth into the world and testify of his Gospel. During the opening days after Pentecost, one scripture account reports that Peter's ministry resulted in more than 3,000 Christian converts.

Revelations

You can't reference the New Testament without giving the last book, Revelation, its own bit of the spotlight. The Revelation or "Apocalypse" of John was written while he was banished to the island of Patmos, following the deaths and disbandment of the apostles. The Book of Revelation, although containing words of instruction to several church congregations in and around the Roman Empire, mostly contains prophetic writings relating to the last days of the human race.

> ### Latter-day Laughter
>
> You might be a Mormon if:
>
> You received a personal revelation that it would be okay to watch football or golf on Sunday, as long as Steve Young was playing or Johnny Miller was announcing.
>
> —Anonymous

Mormonism teaches that the book is not a group of multiple revelations; it is a single revelation, given to John by Jesus. Through this recording of events, John was allowed to describe his witness of the world's history, from start to finish. John focused more on the end, which, in his best efforts, was to assure the varying believers of Christianity, that all supposition would end with the restoration of God's kingdom on the earth—at the Second Coming of Jesus.

Many Christians, following the notion that the whole New Testament was designed in some type of chronological series, take offense to the LDS philosophy of "Living Revelation," often citing the closing verses of the last chapter of Revelation as their defense:

> For I testify unto every man that heareth the words of the prophecy of this book, if any man shall add unto these things, God shall add unto him the plagues that are written in this book: And if any man shall take away from the words of the book of this prophecy, God shall take away his part out of the book of life, and out of the holy city, and from the things which are written in this book.

For Christians, on a scale of 1 to 10, with 10 being absolute damnation into the deepest lake of the hottest fires of hell, and one being tarring and feathering, the idea that somebody or some group of people would actually be so bold as to consider *additional* books as part of holy writ, would rate about a 12.

But Latter-day Saints tend to look at the body of text found in the Holy Bible in more practical terms. From a scholarly point of view, the books comprising the Bible are simply that: a compendium of books—a lexicon of liturgy. However, as we have already discussed, the Bible was brought together by councils, under the direction of a mortal king in a mortal kingdom. There have been many interpretations of both Old and New Testament passages.

The Revelation of John is no different, and, as a fundamental LDS philosophy, should not be considered out of context from the other books found in the New Testament of the Bible itself. Reference to words being added or taken away pertains, most likely, to the individual revelation John received from God, and refers only to that revelation.

Otherwise, the collection of holy works—many of which were gathered and assembled long after John's revelation was recorded—would not otherwise have been able to be included as part of the body of early scripture. But conjecture about what is and isn't scripture has always been subject of debate. Latter-day Saints rely on the faith and inspiration of the Church's living prophets to decide what we should pay attention to and what we should ignore.

The Least You Need to Know

- ◆ The four Gospels by the Apostles Matthew, Mark, Luke, and John carry distinct but harmonious messages.

- ◆ Many were called, but only 12 apostles were chosen.

- ◆ For Latter-day Saints, the most significant aspect of Jesus' life was the time he spent praying in the Garden of Gethsemane.

- ◆ The Day of Pentecost brought the Holy Ghost into the world.

- ◆ The Book of Revelation was one complete visual experience for John to record.

The Great Apostasy

In This Chapter

- A nation threatens Church beliefs
- The birth of the Dark Ages
- The fate of the original Twelve Apostles
- Fragmentation replaces God's government
- Constantine's conquests
- The vision of a righteous nation: Mormonism is born

In LDS doctrine, "apostasy" is the term used to describe the abandoning or denouncement of divine authority. Although the concept of an apostasy might sound unfamiliar to many people, the cycle of apostate civilizations has been repeated throughout history. For example, the people in Noah's age had forsaken the laws that were established for them, and they were wiped from the earth. In the generations since, there have been periods of apostasy in the world in which God's word was so abandoned that divine order was removed from mankind.

LDS doctrine is founded on the principle that there was one "church" established by Christ, and that church was destroyed within the first 100 years after his death. This chapter examines the evolution of the Lord's church, and the facts that led to its disappearing from the world, which began the Great Apostasy.

Two Thousand Years of Wandering

Mormonism claims that the *Great Apostasy* took place following the death of the last of the apostles of Christ's era. By the end of the first century A.D. the rightful order of the holy priesthood was eliminated from the church, and without ordained church leadership, the people were left to their own interpretations as to what and who to believe, regarding the Word and will of the Almighty. Unfortunately, in the case of the "who," it was usually the strongest or most prominent voice that gained the believers.

Mormonology

The **Great Apostasy** marks a time in the history of mankind when the presence of God, through his established church, was removed from the world.

According to LDS beliefs, for nearly 2,000 years, the world was without direct guidance from God, and his people wandered through generations of confusion. This became well illustrated with the division of Christian sects that began to appear throughout the Roman Empire, beginning almost immediately after the death of Jesus in A.D. 34.

Latter-day Saints believe the priesthood was restored to the earth in 1829, on the banks of the Susquehanna River in Pennsylvania, and has since remained as a "light unto the world."

But to understand Mormonism, and its unique position within the confines of Christianity, we must go back to the early days of a post-Christ Christianity (between A.D. 40 and 340).

When in Rome ...

Under the Caesars, Rome took less than a century to finally destroy God's anointed leaders. Subsequently, scores of thousands of people—mostly Christian factionalists—were slaughtered at the games in the Flavian Amphitheater, more commonly known as the Colosseum.

The Colosseum was commissioned by the emperor Vespasian in A.D. 69. It was later completed by his son Titus, and according to statistics, during its first full year of operation, an average of one person was killed every five minutes around the clock as part of the festivities, usually from mock battles and executions. The killings spanned nearly four centuries, from A.D. 70 to 438.

Rome went through a difficult time during the early years of the first century. Its borders covered virtually all of the Mediterranean, from the shores of the Caspian Sea in the East, to Brittania in the Northwest, and Egypt in the South. Maintaining not only an empire, but such a vast cross-cultural community, grew more challenging for the Senate and Caesar.

The Colosseum, where thousands of Christians were killed.

©Drew Williams (2002)

Adding to the confusion of the day, a religious faction was arising out of the Middle East, which threatened to topple even Jupiter himself—the supreme deity of the ancient Romans—and shake the empire to its core. This did not sit well in the courts of Rome. It was one thing to manage the traditional Jewish subculture, who had been complaining about their oppression for generations. But it was another to consider that a wandering man from the deserts of Galilee could sway even the Jews to rethink their religious position. And thus, the Christian persecution began. Both Jew and Gentile began to follow the words of Jesus, as taught by his appointed apostles.

Mormonism follows Christian tradition, recognizing that, after the ministry, death, and resurrection of Jesus, he *conferred* upon his apostles the power of the Holy Ghost, which, according to the New Testament account, took

Mormonology

To **confer** means to grant, by right of authority, certain rights and privileges associated with receiving a divine anointing, such as conferring the Holy Ghost as a gift and constant companion, or conferring the priesthood. This is not the same as being "confirmed," which implies appointment to membership in the Church or positioning within a particular office.

place on the Day of Pentecost. With the Holy Ghost conferred upon them, and their ordinance to the holy apostleship, which was ordained by Christ himself, the apostles were instructed to carry the Gospel message to all nations. According to the early accounts, Christ also set apart missionaries, called "Seventies," to proceed out into the world in pairs, as described in Luke 10:1–6.

None of this sat well with the local governments of the Roman Empire, or the traditional Jews of the Sanhedrin (the supreme legislative council of the ancient Jews). While the empire was tossing Caesars like a salad (it saw more than a dozen within 60 years), the spreading tides of Jesus' Gospel began to extend even beyond its borders.

Within 30 years of the death of their leader, the apostles of Christ had established Christian churches throughout the empire, including Corinth, Galatia, Ephesus, and Philippi. Christian splinter groups had even begun to crop up in the catacombs under Rome itself.

Then came a turn for the worse. Around A.D. 50, Caesar Claudius decided that Rome should be cleared of non-Roman traditions, and Jews were banished to their own lands.

Christians were systematically rounded up and executed throughout the 300 years that followed. Many people who claimed Christianity over Roman customs found themselves entertaining the empire's senators and citizens from inside the Colosseum walls.

Christians had become an endangered species.

Open Season on the Apostles

For the Roman leaders, the catch of the day was the life of an apostle. The following table illustrates the fate of the original Twelve Apostles of Jesus. Each of the original 12 men called by Jesus, with the exception of Judas Iscariot and John the Beloved, was summarily hunted down throughout the empire, and either murdered on the spot, or made part of a public execution. There are many variations on the actual method of death. What's important is that these men all died for their holy cause. (John the Beloved, who authored several books in the New Testament, was not killed, but banished to the island of Patmos in A.D. 96.)

It's important to note, the information in this table is based on a collection of historical research (Flavius Josephus's *Jewish Antiquities* and other accounts from the period following the apostles).

Apostle	Cause of Death	Approx. Year
Judas Iscariot	Driven by guilt, committed suicide by hanging	34
Bartholomew	Beaten, crucified, and beheaded	52
Phillip	Crucified at Heirapole Phryga	52
Thomas	Impaled by lance while preaching in the East Indies (some accounts say he was in India)	52
Matthew	Killed by sword in Ethiopia	60
James (son of Alphaeus)	Crucified in Egypt	60
James (brother of John)	Beheaded by command of Herod	64
Simon Peter	Crucified head down on a hill outside Rome	66
Thaddaeus	Shot in Arafat by Roman soldiers	72
Andrew	Bound and crucified in Greece by order of the Governor	74
Simon Zelotes	Crucified in Persia	74
John the Beloved	Banished to the island of Patmos	96

Passing of the Keys

The church continued under the authority of Peter, who was given the keys of authority by Jesus, prior to Christ's ascension. Peter held those keys until his death in Rome in A.D. 66. Subsequent apostles including Andronicus, Steven, Barnabas, and even the great Apostle Paul, served as special witnesses of Christ's teaching, under the direction of Peter.

A fundamental aspect of Mormonism is that it follows the same traditions as those established in the ancient church—having apostles, evangelists, and bishops. The ancient church of Christ was established by hierarchy, and included various roles, including evangelists, ministers, and other religious leaders, who were called into specific positions for the administration of the church. James, the brother of Christ, although not one of the original Twelve Apostles, was called to the apostleship after the resurrection, and eventually served as the first Bishop of Rome under the direction of Peter.

And It Came to Pass

There were at least three major references to different men named "James" in the New Testament. "James the Just," who was the brother of Jesus, wrote the Epistle of James in the New Testament, and was said to have been the first Bishop of Rome—under the direction of Peter, who was the presiding apostle following Christ's death. James, the son of Zebedee, was one of the Lord's closest personal assistants, along with the other son of Zebedee—John—and Peter. The LDS community generally assumes that these three men comprised the first "First Presidency" of the Church, after the ascension of Christ. James, the son of Alphaeus, was also one of Jesus' original Twelve.

With the close of the first century A.D., the holy apostleship, under the divine authority granted to them by Christ, vanished from the earth.

How does this history lesson apply to Mormonism? The history of the life and death of the apostles speaks to the very core of LDS belief. According to LDS doctrine, when the last apostles were killed, their authority to act in behalf of God, as it was conferred upon them, died with them. The result of their demise was an immediate departure from church guidelines, which were largely replaced with the secular theology of the day's intellects. As LDS doctrine records, the world was thrust into a state of blindness between man and God—the Great Apostasy.

God's Government Disappears

The Roman Empire was not completely without civility. The three major cities of Rome, Alexandria (in Egypt), and Antioch (in Syria), were social hotspots during the early centuries of the first millennium. They were also large centers of Jewish culture, which had become highly influential in maintaining self-governing control over their territory.

Words of Wisdom

James, the brother of the Lord, succeeded to the government of the Church in conjunction with the apostles. … And they began to stone him. … He became a true witness, both to Jews and Greeks, that Jesus is the Christ. And immediately Vespasian besieged them.

—Hegesippus (Roman historian about A.D. 150)

But the Caesars always had their noses in things, which was the case when the Sanhedrin ordered James the Just thrown from the pinnacle of the temple and clubbed to death. Rome's reaction was swift and firm, resulting in a total occupation of Jerusalem. Roman leadership, it seemed, didn't like uprisings from anyone—even if it was between heretical religious factions opposed to the state religion.

With the last apostles rounded up and executed, the church no longer had direct leadership, and many men became self-appointed leaders. Consequently, religious chapters that were organized by the likes of Steven, James, Timothy, and Paul were left to their own designs and influences of the local cultures.

Greek philosophies and other local customs became stronger influences among the Christian factions. By the close of the second century, there were house churches and Christian spin-offs covering almost every major region of the empire. Some efforts were made to keep the foundation of the church intact, the most notable being that of Ignatius of Antioch in about A.D. 110, but even his efforts were made while he was on his way to his own execution in Rome.

The church of God, as it was organized by Christ and further established by the apostles throughout the lands, was gone from its original state, and so was its authority. Over the course of the next several centuries, religious factionalism began to creep into the Roman government, and secularism infiltrated the pure church of God.

Constantine's Rise to Power

I could spend another gazillion chapters on the history and evolution of Christianity, which has been a favorite subject of mine for the past 30 years. But that's another book—and many have already been written on the subject. For the sake of time and focus, let's spin the clock ahead about three centuries.

The Roman Empire was stretched like a balloon throughout the known Western world. But like a balloon, it would withstand only so many pokes from outsiders before it would burst. And sharp things were coming at the empire from both sides of the border.

By the beginning of the fourth century, Rome was so large it was the edict of the emperor Diocletian that four lesser kings (two Augustuses and two Caesars) assisted in leadership to fend off the barbarian enemies from the North (the Goths, Vandals, etc.). The tetrachy, as it was known, was not very successful, and within a few years, everybody wanted to sit in the big chair.

One of these leaders, Constantine, was the son of a Roman senator. Constantine became a powerful military leader, and eventually rose to become the Western Caesar.

By the beginning of the fourth century, the conquests of Constantine—the first Roman emperor to convert to Christianity—resulted in reunifying Rome under one leader. But when he chose to shift the seat of the empire to a port town near the mouth of the Black Sea, where traditional Eastern Europe meets West, it planted the seeds of the destruction of the secular empire of the day, to be replaced by what became a religious empire throughout the world by the close of the first millennium.

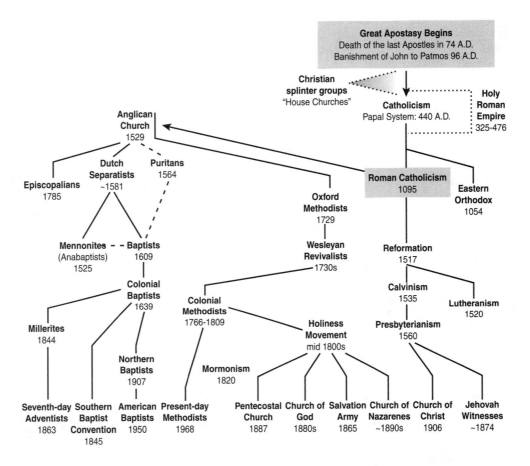

This illustration shows the date of origin and lineage of many of today's Christian faiths. With the exception of Mormonism, all major Christian religions can be traced to the Catholic Church. However, LDS doctrine shows a gap in the authorized priesthood of God, from the death of the last apostle around A.D. 96, until the restoration of the priesthood in 1829—a period called the Great Apostasy.

©Drew Williams (2002)

Words of Wisdom

It is the nature and disposition of almost all men, as soon as they get a little authority, as they suppose, they will immediately begin to exercise unrighteous dominion.

—Doctrine and Covenants 121:39

Constantine's changing the central capital of the empire from Rome to what is now Istanbul, had a significant impact on the religion of the day. It created a religious center in the eastern portion of the region, which was highly influenced by Greek tradition, while the city of Rome was left to the devices of local Christian leaders, who claimed to be the official headquarters of the legacy church of Christ.

In 476, when Rome was taken by the Goths, any remote traces of the original Christian faith were permanently altered.

The Birth of a Nation (with the Soul of a Church)

Looking ahead 600 years, long after the battle between Leo and John (the respective bishops of Rome and Constantinople in 588), to 1074, the Roman Catholic Church was fully established as the religious backbone throughout Europe and the known world. The irony of religious domination was again in full swing, when, under the direction of Pope Gregory and the Roman Catholic Church, the first Crusades began, with a focus on ridding the Holy Land of the many religious "infidels" who inhabited it—namely, those who were not Christian (or Catholic).

> **And It Came to Pass**
>
> For a good understanding of the history of Catholicism, see *The Complete Idiot's Guide to Understanding Catholicism* by Bob O'Gorman and Mary Faulkner (Alpha Books, 2003).

America: New Religions for a New World

By the beginning of the seventeenth century, the Roman Catholic Church was the governing body over virtually all of the Christian world. The Vatican's position, strengthened through the Crusades, would ensure a strong religious hold on political and religious heads of state throughout Europe.

But a new era of enlightenment, which focused on secular independence and religious interpretation on the freedoms of worship, began to spread, largely as a result of Martin Luther's disenchantment with his Catholic leaders.

By the mid-1700s, a third generation of religious persecution was underway, as American colonists began to embrace new philosophies on prayer, baptism, and the role of religion in day-to-day life. The Church of England (having itself being formed after splitting from Catholicism), was not pleased with the influx of new religious ideas spawning in America, thanks mostly to the efforts of evangelists such as Jonathan Edwards and George Whitfield.

> **Words of Wisdom**
>
> We have staked the whole future of American civilization not upon the power of the government—far from it. We have staked the future of all of our political institutions upon the capacity of each and all of us to govern ourselves according to the Ten Commandments of God.
>
> —U.S. President James Madison

But the damage was done, and with the "Great Awakening" that was spreading throughout New England, the stage was set for the coming forth of a new religion, which did not descend from any of the existing faiths: Mormonism.

In the lineage of LDS thought, the notion is that, since God's true and ordained church vanished from the world, it would take the right combination of religious, political, and cultural conditions to allow the original church to be reestablished. Moreover, there arose no better place than the colonial states of early America, or better time than in the early stages of a new nation, free from religious and political tyranny.

Mormonism teaches that America truly was God's chosen land, and the land on which he could reestablish a fullness of his Gospel. In the next chapter we're going to explore the written word, and how, based on LDS revelation, America was established as a place from which written revelation would come forth, as part of the reestablishment of divine enterprise.

The Least You Need to Know

- Christians wandered in ambivalence for nearly 2,000 years.
- Rome had little patience for those who would upset its political or religious landscape.
- Christ's followers were systematically hunted down and killed for their beliefs.
- Rome went from persecuting Christian beliefs to enforcing them.
- The "New World" provided the perfect place to establish a new religious following.

Chapter 10

Which Scriptures Are Scripture?

In This Chapter

- ◆ Revisiting scripture vs. interpretation of canon
- ◆ The Word of God becomes diffused and confusing
- ◆ Adapting God's Word (again and again)
- ◆ Three divine beings, one God to rule them all
- ◆ The creeds of man add to the confusion of the Gospel
- ◆ Rome volleys between love and hate for Christians

One of the most compelling characteristics of Mormonism lies in the idea that God still talks to the world. For many in the Christian community, the notion that the Word of God continues to be revealed is as difficult to believe as it is for LDS people to think that a living, loving God would *not* speak to us.

For most Christian faiths, it's enough just getting through a good dose of the Holy Bible on a daily basis. Latter-day Saints, however, consider "scripture" to include works beyond those assembled by the councils of England's King James I in 1608. This chapter explains the history of canon, and discusses the significance of ongoing revelation, which is a core belief of Mormonism.

What Is the Word of God?

In the LDS Church, "scripture" is defined as doctrine that was inspired, revealed, or directed by the Holy Ghost, and ratified by authorized Church leadership. The term "canon" is used to describe the sacred text considered to be *Standard Works*. These works include the King James Version of the Bible, the Book of Mormon, the Doctrine and Covenants, and the Pearl of Great Price. The last three works are considered "Latter-day revelation," restored as part of the founding of the LDS Church.

I'll be discussing these various works throughout this book, but for now let's take a brief look at each of the volumes considered to be "Standard Works" of Mormonism.

Mormonology

The **Standard Works** is the sacred canon of the LDS Church and includes the Old and New Testaments, as recorded in the King James Version of the Bible; the Book of Mormon, a record of a Mesoamerican civilization; the Doctrine and Covenants, which outline many aspects of LDS government; and the Pearl of Great Price, a collection of inspired writings published in the early days of the LDS Church.

Holy Bible

The collection of books found in the traditional King James Version of the Holy Bible is considered by the entire Christian world as canon. However, for the LDS community, God had plenty more to say than what King James decreed in the early seventeenth century as the end-all to God's conversations with mankind. (More on that later in this chapter.)

The Book of Mormon

As described by the Thirteen Articles of Faith discussed in Chapter 23, LDS people believe the Bible to be the Word of God (as far as it has been translated, revised, retranslated, re-edited, and so on). However, Latter-day Saints also believe the Book of Mormon to be another testament of the life of Jesus Christ.

The Book of Mormon, which is discussed in Chapter 13, contains the record of a civilization that existed in Mesoamerica from the fourth century B.C. through about the second century A.D. The Book of Mormon is the cornerstone of LDS faith.

Doctrine and Covenants

The Doctrine and Covenants contains many inspired revelations by early Church Prophets—most notably, Joseph Smith Jr. This volume, which is divided into 138 sections, includes a history of revelations and significant events dealing with the Restoration of the Gospel and the government of the LDS Church.

The Pearl of Great Price

The Pearl of Great Price is a collection of inspired writings published in the early days of the LDS Church. It contains important doctrine about the origins of man, and the early leaders of God's kingdom, including Adam, Abraham, and Moses. The Pearl of Great Price was added as canon in 1880.

Because Latter-day Saints consider all the works revealed through the official channels of Church leadership as "inspired," other material is considered as spiritual guidelines for God's government. However, in the purest sense of what is considered "canon," these four works comprise the body of focus.

Words of Wisdom

Scripture is the school of the Holy Spirit, in which, as nothing is omitted that is both necessary and useful to know, so nothing is taught but what is expedient to know. Therefore we must guard against depriving believers of anything disclosed about predestination in Scripture, lest we seem either wickedly to defraud them of the blessing of their God or to accuse and scoff at the Holy Spirit for having published what it is in any way profitable to suppress.

—John Calvin, French theologian

But to leave the matter of Latter-day revelation without reflecting on the evolutionary aspects of Christian canon would be to miss a key factor in why the LDS Church includes additional works as part of its practice. In Chapter 9, we looked at the evolution of Christianity, and how America was founded as a direct result of religious influence, something Mormonism teaches as laying the groundwork to restore divine intercession with the human race.

Let's go back a couple millennia to see where the debate of God's word began.

In the Beginning, There Was One Word ...

Up until Jesus, the known population of "God's Children" held to the first five books of the Old Testament as the single volume of divine revelation.

But then Jesus showed up in Jerusalem, and the whole God-fearing world was turned upside down. With the onset of Jesus' ministry, and the subsequent witnesses and admonitions by his apostles, the children of God found new words of inspiration—even a new set of commandments. Such words, which Jesus left behind upon his ascension into heaven, were always revealed under the direction of one of the Lord's authorized witnesses and inspired by the Holy Ghost.

After about A.D. 100, however, Mormonism contends that the heavens were closed to mankind, resulting in a separation, which is described in Chapter 9 as the Great Apostasy. Then, following more than 17 centuries of spiritual floundering, the world was once again prepared to receive God's word, which continues to be revealed today.

Although we could dig deeper into the annals of history to address matters concerning holy writ, this book was designed to *introduce* the reader to Mormonism and its concepts—not to provide a comprehensive history of scripture.

However, it's important to note that throughout the generations of mankind's relationship with the one true God (we're not talking about mythologies based on polytheistic themes, here), there have always been two components of religious dogma: intercession with deity by anointed (not appointed) leaders, and divinely inspired writings.

> **Latter-day Laughter**
>
> Why is it when we talk to God, we're said to be praying—but when God talks to us, we're schizophrenic?
>
> —Lily Tomlin, comedian

Anatomy of God's Written Word

Based on the traditions of God's revealed word to man, we can group holy writings into four categories:

- **Chronological events.** These include accounts such as those found in Old Testament Books like Exodus and Numbers, and the experiences of the civilizations documented largely in the Book of Mormon.

- **Commandments.** These go beyond the 10 given in Exodus 34. The scriptures contain many "words to live by," as outlined in the books of Leviticus and Deuteronomy in the Old Testament, and certain sections of the Doctrine and Covenants.

- **Witnesses.** These were the testimonials, offered by prophets and apostles, which claimed the divinity of Jesus (or Jehovah). Such witnesses appear in Isaiah in the Old Testament, and the traditional "Gospels" found in Matthew, Mark, Luke, and John in the New Testament. Other witnesses appear throughout the Bible and other standard works. I also cluster words of praise into this category, like those many psalms of David and songs of Solomon. Given in the tradition of uplifting testimony, words of praise also bear witness of a loving God.

- **Business affairs (epistles).** The classic "epistle," as those found in the writings of Paul to the various church branches throughout the empire, provided the "official" standard guidelines of operation for the extended congregations.

These were essential to ensuring ongoing consistency, as established during Jesus' ministry. Unfortunately, with the demise of the last apostles, no more epistles were provided, and congregations were left to interpret doctrine on their own.

These four elements of divine writing have always provided the necessary balance of direction, rebuke, and inspiration for man to live life under the watchful eye of the Creator.

Mormonism teaches that these principles haven't changed. The idea that God still talks to the human race often forces people to question their own understanding of what they believe "scripture" to be. Throughout history, ruling nations have had to dictate to their subjects, how they should worship God, and what may and may not be accepted as holy writ.

The pattern goes something like this:

1. An individual rises to power within a political infrastructure (usually by force).

2. The nation adopts that person's personal philosophies about God and government as its own.

3. A subculture forms within the nation, which holds to a different standard of belief.

4. The nation suppresses that subculture, usually forcing it to form its own autonomous community.

5. An individual of influence rises within that community and the cycle begins all over again.

This process can be seen throughout the history of man, such as in the case of the Egyptian empire, Rome (and the subsequent rise of the Holy Roman Empire out of the Catholic Church), the United Kingdom (and the subsequent division from Catholicism by an adulterous king), and even in the United States, as seen in the early days of Puritanism in the New England Colonies.

In every case of the cycle, two elements have always been present: an inspired way of thinking about the relationship between divinity and man, and a definition and acceptance of what constitutes the written word God.

Words of Wisdom

The Church says the Earth is flat. But I know that it is round. For I have seen the shadow on the Moon. And I have more faith in a shadow than in the Church.

—Ferdinand Magellan, Portuguese navigator

Unity in the Godhead and the Holy Trinity

Perhaps one of the most debated topics of all generations since the days of Christ is the issue of the Godhead—or the Holy Trinity.

When he was kneeling in the grove of trees in Palmyra, New York, in 1820, Joseph Smith Jr. testified that he saw two male personages descend from the heavens. One of the two said, while pointing to the other, "This is my beloved son, hear him." From this account, Latter-day Saints gain a personal witness of two separate and distinct beings.

The idea that God was all one person came under great speculation from early leaders of the post-apostolic church in Rome. The topic was the subject of much debate for more than three centuries, until about A.D. 325, when a new, "Christian" emperor made it the point of a general conference of religious leaders.

The Councils of Nicaea

At the beginning of the fourth century A.D., Rome was replete with people claiming to have a portion of the original church of Christ (discussed in Chapter 9). There were many other interpretations of who and what Jesus was—in one case, a bishop from northern Africa actually believed that Jesus was sent to rescue mankind from a blind, crazed fallen angel, who had made the earth without authorization.

After his conquest and reunification of the empire under one leader, Constantine turned his focus on matters concerning these disparate ideologies and also on deciding on what date the empire should celebrate Easter.

The emperor decided that, at the expense of the government and under his personal supervision, all of the leaders of the various Christian sects would be gathered in Nicaea. Their purpose was to define once and for all, the nature of Jesus and his role in deity.

> **And It Came to Pass**
>
> Probably in response to the spread of Christianity through the Roman culture—even though still heavily persecuted by the Pharisees and the Roman government—the Jewish leaders held their own council to discuss Jewish canon, near Joppa in about A.D. 90.

Arius, a Christian leader from Alexandria, argued that Christ was a divine being who was created by God (because of the consistent scriptural reference to him as the "Son of God") prior to laying the foundation of the world. Alexander, the current bishop of Rome, disagreed, arguing that Arius's position implied Jesus as being less than God the Father. Alexander believed Christ and God were of the same "essence."

Under the so-called "objective" guidance of Constantine himself, a vote was taken, and Arius's views were designated as heretical. Arius, by the way, was not only out-voted at the council, he was thrown out of the church. (His views would have been well-received in Mormon theology.)

The Nicene Creed, which was the result of the council held by Constantine, would define the nature of God and his relationship to Christ and the Holy Ghost for the next 1,400 years.

Let's look at what the Creed actually says:

> We believe in one God, the Father, the Almighty, maker of heaven and earth, of all that is, seen and unseen.
>
> We believe in one Lord, Jesus Christ, the only Son of God, eternally begotten of the Father, God from God, Light from Light, true God from true God, begotten, not made, of one Being with the Father. Through him all things were made.
>
> For us and for our salvation he came down from heaven: by the power of the Holy Spirit he became incarnate from the Virgin Mary, and was made man. For our sake he was crucified under Pontius Pilate; he suffered death and was buried.
>
> On the third day he rose again in accordance with the Scriptures; he ascended into heaven and is seated at the right hand of the Father. He will come again in glory to judge the living and the dead, and his kingdom will have no end.
>
> We believe in the Holy Spirit, the Lord, the giver of life, who proceeds from the Father and the Son. With the Father and the Son he is worshiped and glorified. He has spoken through the Prophets. We believe in one holy catholic and apostolic Church. We acknowledge one baptism for the forgiveness of sins. We look for the resurrection of the dead, and the life of the world to come.

Although the original form of the Nicene Creed refers to one religion—Catholicism—many Protestant faiths have revised some aspect of the creed to accommodate their specific flavor of worship, and have subsequently adopted it as their own. Still, the actual interpretation of the creed has been subject to debate for as long as it has been in existence.

And It Came to Pass

In a follow-up project, from the Nicaean Council, Constantine financed the writing and publishing of 50 volumes of authorized scripture, which would contain the first version of what is now called the "New Testament." These volumes were distributed to the "authorized" congregations spread throughout the Roman Empire, and provided the only allowed religious canon of the day.

Same "Congregation," Different Empire

More than 1,200 years after the first councils at Nicaea, and following centuries of religious bloodshed, conquests, and religious crusades, James VI of Scotland ascended to the throne of England, and forever unified the two nations as King James I of Great Britain.

A pattern of enforced religious consistency and interpretation was about to resurface—same God, different empire, different philosophy.

The problem: too many religious factions within the new English Empire (which was not under Catholic rule, but under Calvinist influence), with too many versions of scripture. Those who would publicly interpret the canon of the day often found themselves in the Tower of London (or worse, in pieces scattered throughout the land).

Moreover, only religious leaders were permitted to read, interpret, and in many cases, own scriptures. As had been done throughout the history of man, the curious and the dedicated still found a way to gain a foothold on religious interpretation, and found a way to grow amidst the tyranny.

Consequently, it was once again time for the leader of an empire to define what the *authorized* Word of God would include.

St. Andrews Cathedral in Scotland.

©*Drew Williams (2002)*

King James Unifies Religious Factions

In 1604, shortly after his ascension to the throne, James I outlined what he expected to become the "authorized" version of the bible. To achieve this mandate, the king convened a spiritual think tank of six committees who would provide research into the collection of religious documents that had comprised the current "Bishop's Bible" of the state church, with the warning not to alter the context or its original doctrine.

Four years later, the "Authorized Bible" was produced and published. Today, the Christian world refers to this work as the King James Version (KJV), of the Holy Bible.

> **Words of Wisdom**
>
> The King James translation has been described as the only great work of art ever created by a committee. ... The authors of several boring translations that have followed over the last fifty years mumble that the KJV is "difficult," filled with long words.... Over the past several centuries it's been the single book in most households, an enormous force in shaping the development of the English language.
>
> —Charlton Heston, actor

New World, New Government, Old Challenges

Few scholars in the Christian world would question the inspiration of James I. Not only did he encourage and finance the monumental task of standardizing the Word of God, he also undertook one of the most critically recognized experiments in the history of Western civilization: the independent colonization of a religious community, called "Virginia."

It was from those early seeds that the Age of Enlightenment was born—both in England and in the new colonies. By the close of the eighteenth century, a new nation was formed, which laid the groundwork for what LDS philosophy says is an inspired writing (the Book of Mormon), given to an inspired leader (Joseph Smith Jr.), in an inspired nation (America).

The Least You Need to Know

+ The Word of God has always been left to the interpretations of men.
+ The early Christian Church frequently revised and added new canon as it became available.
+ God's written word includes events, witnesses, and warnings.
+ Essentially, the Godhead and the Holy Trinity refer to the same three people.
+ The Nicene Creed has been modified to fit just about any religion of the day.

Part 3

The Prophet from Pennsylvania

This part begins with a focus on the life of the Smith family and Joseph Smith's role in Mormonism. Also, we'll take a brief look at the LDS body of scripture called the Book of Mormon, which Latter-day Saints believe to be another testament of Jesus' life and ministry.

The chapters in this part should offer you enough objective information to understand where the early Mormon settlers came from and what motivated their leaders to create yet another Christian religion. For the members of the LDS Church, however, it wasn't a matter of creating a religion—it was a matter of restoring one.

11

The Prophet Joseph Smith

In This Chapter

- ◆ The early years of the Smith family
- ◆ A child's determination to find the truth
- ◆ First Vision: Joseph's encounter with the divine
- ◆ Establishing a church for the latter days of mankind

There were many religious leaders throughout the history of civilization who posed remarkable zeal in the face of adversity. Mormonism's Joseph Smith Jr. was among those controversial religious leaders who both founded and was murdered for a philosophy that wasn't part of the day's favored faiths. And with Smith's death, the cycle of religious persecution by a government toward a minority culture was once again in full swing.

However, until the birth of Mormonism and its founder, the roots to ancient Christianity were lost for more than 18 centuries. If you recall from the illustration that appears in the latter part of Chapter 9, Mormonism is the only major Christian religion that has neither a legacy tied to Catholicism, nor is predicated on the extension of any other organization. This is due, in large, to the founder, Joseph Smith, and his uncanny desire to move away from the traditional bickering and spiritual gerrymandering of the times in his search for the pure religion of God.

Early Indicators of Righteous Pursuits

Joseph Smith Jr. was born in Sharon, Vermont, in December 1805. He was the fifth of 11 children of Joseph and Lucy Mack Smith. And as in many of the households today, it was the wife who tended to the spiritual welfare of the children. Lucy embraced Christianity early in her married life, and was the more spiritually outspoken of the two parents on matters concerning religion.

The Smith family constantly moved during Joseph's early years, in pursuit of work and good land to farm. Around 1812, young Joseph was struck with typhoid fever and suffered a serious bone infection in his left leg. His doctors recommended amputation, but Joseph's mother pleaded with them to find another way to solve the problem.

> **And It Came to Pass**
>
> In the 1890s, long after the LDS pioneers had settled the west, William Smith, younger brother to the Prophet Joseph, recalled the happy times of growing up in a Christian home: "I well remember Father used to carry his spectacles in his vest pocket, and whenever we boys saw him feel for his specs, we knew that was a signal to get ready for prayer."

Many accounts record that when it was time for the seven-year-old boy to have corrective surgery on the infectious leg (which required removing a piece of infected bone), even at a young age, Joseph's pattern for making choices of moral conservatism began to show. He refused to drink the brandy offered him to dull the senses before the doctor began, and insisted that his mother leave the room so his father could hold him throughout the operation.

Over time, Joseph's leg healed, and after five more years of unsuccessful farming and business ventures, the Smith family settled in Palmyra, New York, in the Finger Lakes region. His family shared strong Christian beliefs, a love for the Bible, and regularly participated in family prayer services.

Shuffling Through Religious Confusion

During the mid-1800s, New England saw something of a religious revival. Mostly founded upon old-world Calvinistic ideals, some of the religions—particularly the Methodists and Baptists—employed traveling evangelists, who conducted town-to-town revivals. Church leaders, almost to the degree of political lobbying, were setting up tents and pulpits anywhere they could gather a crowd. In some cases, grassy fields became Sabbath day variety shows, with religious leaders working in sort of a tag-team style. As soon as one finished, another began.

Through the frenzy of faith-promoting and bible-thumping testimonies, the Smiths found themselves looking for answers to their own personal problems. Whether from consistent cases of bad health, economic despair, or something deeper, they, too, were turning to God to provide clarity and understanding.

Two particular religious faiths persuaded the young Smith family into different directions. While mother Lucy, a sister, and two brothers decided to follow Presbyterianism, the young Joseph leaned toward the Methodists. Although somewhat of a religious man, Joseph Sr. remained independent on church preference.

But Joseph Jr. soon discovered that with the varying degrees of religious philosophies, so came greater tension between the respective leaders. According to Joseph's early writings, the Methodists didn't like the Baptists, Baptists didn't like the Methodists, and neither group liked the Presbyterians.

Consequently, Joseph could not decide between the churches, and took the matter to God: "While I was laboring under the extreme difficulties caused by the contests of these parties of religionists, I was one day reading the epistle of James, which reads, 'If any of you lack wisdom, let him ask of God, that giveth to all men liberally, and upbraideth not; and it shall be given him.'"

Joseph was concerned about which church to join, and after reading a passage in the New Testament book of James, he took his concerns to a small grove of trees near his home and asked God for guidance. From his writings: "After I retired to the place where I had previously designed to go, having looked around and finding myself alone, I knelt down and began to offer up the desires of my heart to God."

Joseph believed so strongly in the matter of which religious philosophy he should follow, that he took the challenge given by James and hid away in a grove of trees to ponder and pray over the issue. What followed has been acclaimed by many Latter-day Saints as the most significant event of modern times, which the LDS Church refers to as the "First Vision," which we'll discuss in a moment.

What comes next in the history of the Smith family ignites the spark that runs the very engine of Mormonism. And there's no way to fluff the story, so I'll warn you now, some of this might sound like part of a B-movie. But according to Joseph Smith Jr. and nearly 12 million other members of the LDS Church living throughout the world today, these events really happened.

Close Encounters of a Divine Kind

In the middle of one afternoon, while his family was working their fields and Mom was back at the Smith home, young Joseph walked into the forest with a personal agenda not common for a 14-year-old boy. LDS history records that after he found a spot in a grove of trees, Joseph knelt in prayer. For a short time, according to his account, he felt seized upon by a power of darkness that overwhelmed him. However, the darkness was soon replaced by the feeling of peace.

In what the LDS Church has come to refer to as the First Vision, Joseph reported that he saw a pillar of light descend through the trees, out of the sky. In the center of that light, he saw two personages, which by his account, spoke to him. Both men were dressed in white robes, and their countenance defied all glory and description. One of the men pointed to the other, saying that he was the beloved son of the one speaking. According to Joseph's claims, the man who first spoke was God the father (Elohim), and the second man was the resurrected Jesus.

A brief conversation between the 14-year-old and the Messiah ensued, in which Joseph asked the Lord which church he should join. Many of the churches shared portions of the true Gospel of Christ, according to the Lord's reply, "But their hearts are far from me." Joseph was told that it was worldly corruption that had taken the church and destroyed Jesus' apostles, and nothing had changed over the past 18 centuries.

After strict instructions from the Lord that Joseph should not join *any* of the existing religious groups, the architects of heaven and earth departed.

Words of Wisdom

And now, after the many testimonies which have been given of him, this is the testimony, last of all, which we give of him: That he lives!

—LDS Founder Joseph Smith

Mormon Myths

Myth: *Joseph Smith is worshipped in the LDS Church.* While Latter-day Saints believe that Joseph Smith was the great prophet of the restoration of God's kingdom on earth, the LDS Church does not revere him as deity. LDS people believe (and always have) that Jesus Christ stands alone as head of the Church.

At this point, the Lord didn't firm up any long-term plans for the restoration of his own church, but he did caution Joseph not to join any of the current sects.

Several days later, the young and still very naive Joseph approached one of the traveling ministers—a Methodist—and asked for help to understand what it was he had experienced in the woods the few days before. Not only did the preacher scoff at the idea that a boy had seen God, he went out of his way to make an example of the boy by ridiculing him in front of other preachers and adults.

Most card-carrying Latter-day Saints would probably admit that the events that followed Joseph after he entered that grove of trees would be nothing short of preposterous to accept. Belief in Joseph's talk with God is contingent on the LDS mantra: *having faith* that it did happen. Followers of Mormonism have had to gain their own personal conviction of Joseph's encounters with divinity. Without Latter-day Saints' own personal testimony of the Joseph Smith story, they would merely be believing in just another faction of Christianity.

Mormonism's first leader, the Prophet Joseph Smith Jr., founded the LDS Church, based on what he believed to be direct instruction from God.

©Drew Williams (2002)

Regardless of the observer's position the young Smith went forth with boldness and conviction as extraordinary as his purported events of divine intervention. He never wavered on his accounts of the spiritual visitations, and ultimately died for what he believed to be God's work.

Preparation for a New Church

Many more events took place in the life of Joseph Smith and in the lives of his family and closest friends, which LDS people believe furthered the development of Mormonism. According to LDS doctrine, each of these events held a purpose in restoring the original church of Christ. Let's take a closer look at some of those events.

Discovery of an Ancient Record

LDS Doctrine claims that seven years after his First Vision, Joseph Smith was directed by an angel to a stone box under a rock on a hillside near Palmyra, New York. Inside that box, Joseph found a series of gold plates on which were inscribed various symbols that vaguely resembled Egyptian characters. According to the LDS Church, the information inscribed on those plates became the Book of Mormon. I'll focus more attention on the Book of Mormon in Chapter 13.

Authorized Baptism by Immersion

Nearly two years later, Joseph and his friend Oliver Cowdery were praying alongside the banks of the Susquehanna River for direction over the matter of baptism. The matter, from the revival days of Joseph's youth, had left them both curious over the ancient Christian principle. According to Joseph and Oliver's accounts, John the Baptist appeared to them and placed his hands upon each of their heads, restoring the priesthood power—the power and authority to act in the name of God—necessary to perform the ordinance of baptism. As a matter of note, John explained to the two men that there would be others who would follow who would provide the ordinations relating to the higher priesthood (that is, who would restore the higher priesthood to the two men).

Afterward, both men were baptized by the other. Although no church was still formally organized, the principle of baptism by immersion—by an authorized agent of God—had been brought back into proper practice.

Restoration of the Higher Priesthood

Shortly after their experience with John the Baptist, Joseph and Oliver were visited by the glorified apostles, Peter, James, and John. Acting on behalf of Jesus, the apostles' purpose in visiting the two men was to restore the keys of the higher priesthood to mortal man on the earth. Although John the Baptist had provided the men with the priesthood authority to baptize, the complete restoration of the church was predicated upon having the authority given by Jesus himself (Hebrews 7:14–17). Once they had received the necessary authority to conduct spiritual business on the earth, the Joseph and Oliver set about the task of organizing the new church as the Lord had instructed Joseph to do through subsequent visitations.

What's in a Name?

The Church of Jesus Christ ("of Latter-day Saints" came later, as directed by Section 115 of the Doctrine and Covenants) was organized on Tuesday, April 6, 1830. Nearly 10 years had passed since the young Joseph had his religious discussion with God. Now, while he and a few of his friends—converts to the new religion—met in a small house in upstate New York, the matter of naming the church had been based on a commandment from the Lord, which LDS doctrine notes that Joseph received earlier.

After their prayer service, the group voted each man into various positions, with Joseph's brother Samuel being called as the first missionary in the Church. Carrying a bag of freshly printed copies of the Book of Mormon, Samuel set out to neighboring communities. No companion, no name tag, no bicycle. Samuel was responsible for bringing many of the original Church leaders into the fold, including Parley Pratt, who was himself a minister, and Dr. Willard Richards, who was with Joseph Smith when he was killed in Illinois.

By the end of 1830, Joseph's vision had led to several hundred conversions. The Latter-day Saints were becoming something of both success and controversy among the settlers of the upper Pennsylvania Valley and surrounding areas.

But controversy would follow the "Mormons," as they were nicknamed, which would not only lead to major conflicts with regional militia, but also the death of their leader some 14 years later. For Joseph and his Mormons, the road would be full of challenges, but there would be no turning back.

Incidentally, the term "Mormons" was coined as a slang word for the followers of Joseph Smith by those who weren't particularly fond of the following. Eventually, the LDS Church accepted the term as an informal name of reference, but recently made the request to be referred to as "Latter-day Saints" instead of "Mormons."

> **And It Came to Pass**
>
> Originally, the church did not include "of Latter-day Saints" in its name. That came later to indicate it was the Lord's church as established in "the latter day" of mankind. The addition was made in 1838, based on a revelation given to Joseph Smith.

> **Words of Wisdom**
>
> I had actually seen a light, and in the midst of that light I saw two personages, and they did in reality speak to me; and although I was hated and persecuted for saying that I had seen a vision, yet it was true.
>
> —LDS Founder Joseph Smith

The Least You Need to Know

- Even as a child Joseph Smith displayed moral conservatism.

- When Joseph could not decide which church he should join, he asked for God's guidance.

- Joseph's First Vision sparked the LDS movement.

- Many events took place that furthered the development of Mormonism, including Joseph's discovery of ancient gold plates that became the basis for the Book of Mormon.

- The Church of Jesus Christ was organized in 1830 and attracted a new generation of followers called "Latter-day Saints."

Chapter 12

Guess What I Found: The Origin of the Book of Mormon

In This Chapter

- The angel Moroni appears to Joseph
- Making sense of the inscriptions
- The consequences of sharing
- "Testimony of Three Witnesses"
- Joseph's persecution

Once Joseph Smith told people that he was seeing God, Jesus, and all sorts of resurrected beings, the rumor mill went into action. His life and those who followed him would be continuously challenged by naysayers, self-proclaimed "realists," and other religious groups. It seemed, from society's point of view that Joseph had become celebrated for all the wrong reasons. Today, Joseph Smith is revered by Latter-day Saints as the man who restored the kingdom of God to the earth; but back then, he was called a mystic, a charlatan, and a treasure hunter.

Perhaps one of the most controversial matters pertaining to the new religion was in Joseph's account of discovering an ancient record inscribed on gold plates in Palmyra, New York. The Book of Mormon, as it came to be known, has been surrounded by controversy since its discovery in 1827.

A Visit from the Angel Moroni

In the years to come, Joseph remained true to his faith and loyal to his story of how the book was found and translated. But he soon found that, although he might have been the man called by God to restore his church, Joseph would have to wait on the Lord's timetable to get things done. He also learned that if he did not do what the Lord commanded, even he would be subject to the consequences.

Three years passed since Joseph's sylvan experience with deity. The 17-year-old was struggling with what he had seen, which resulted in continued ridicule.

One evening, according to his account, shortly after Joseph had gone to bed, he was visited three times. However, contrary to the story of Dickens's Scrooge, all three of Joseph's visitors would be the same spirit, and Christmas wasn't the subject—but Christ was.

According to the visitor, named "Moroni" (pronounced *more-OH-nye*), an ancient record existed that contained the history of a nation of people who had left Jerusalem for the lands that are now Central and South America. This record also included an account of a visit by the resurrected Christ, which also took place among these people, following his resurrection in the Middle East.

During the three visits, Moroni also warned Joseph that after receiving this record, he should not show it to anybody other than those designated by the Lord. Joseph was advised of what his task would be, but would not be permitted to retrieve the records for another four years. Moreover, if Joseph did show the record to others, the angel said, Joseph would die. The one exception, however, was that Joseph could share the events with his father.

And It Came to Pass

Joseph Smith was warned by God on numerous occasions that if he showed the gold plates or its contents to anyone not endorsed by God, he would suffer dire consequences. Joseph was jailed many times and ultimately was killed in his early 30s.

Words of Wisdom

And other sheep I have, which are not of this fold: them also I must bring, and they shall hear my voice; and there shall be one fold, and one shepherd.

—John 10:16

The following day, Joseph traveled to the place where the angel Moroni instructed—a large hill called Cumorah, about four miles south of Palmyra, New York. On one side of the hill, Joseph discovered a large round stone. After some effort, he moved the stone aside to find a crude box, hewn and assembled from other stones.

Inside the box, Joseph found the gold plates described to him by the angel, which were bound together in three places, like a notebook would be today. However, he was not permitted to take the primitive book out the box for four more years. Under Moroni's direction, Joseph was to leave the book in its location, replace the stone cover, and wait for further instruction.

On the first day of autumn, in 1827, four years later, Joseph was instructed by Moroni to return to the stone vault and obtain the records inscribed on gold plates. Almost immediately, word escaped that Joseph had discovered a treasure of gold. People chased him, tried to find where he later hid the records, and even shot at him. For the sake of his family's safety (and in pursuit of his future wife, Emma), the Smiths moved from Palmyra to Harmony, Pennsylvania.

> **And It Came to Pass**
>
> Each summer in Palmyra, the LDS Church holds an event called the Hill Cumorah Pageant in which actors portray the discovery by Joseph Smith of the ancient record. Although the event doesn't muster an off-Broadway production quality, LDS and non-LDS people alike have been entertained and informed by the showy presentation over the years.

Translating the Book

Once the Smith clan was relocated to what started out as safe surroundings, Joseph began the process of studying the inscriptions found on the plates. With the plates was a pair of jeweled stones, fastened together like spectacles, attached to a breastplate. Joseph called them Urim and Thummim, which means "to give light and completeness." These "seer stones," as they are also known, were the tools he used to translate the Book of Mormon. However, their history goes back even further, to the days of Abraham, who, along with other high priests and prophets, wore these stones while communicating with God.

Joseph began his translation by first copying the characters onto paper. Part of the record, however, was sealed, and Joseph was instructed not to open the sealed portion.

Share Not

Rumors continued to spread that the Smiths were involved in the interpretation of some type of inscribed record. Word of these events brought to the Smith home a wealthy farmer named Martin Harris, who was curious about Joseph's project. After getting to know the young interpreter, Harris asked Joseph if he would be willing to spare a few pages of the recorded characters, along with Joseph's translations.

Under pressure, Joseph acquiesced and handed over a large portion of translated text to Harris, who wanted to show them to his wife and friends. This was a no-no under divine decree to Joseph, but he let Harris get away with 116 pages of translated text, after bowing to pressure.

Almost immediately upon taking possession of the manuscript, Harris let the documents get into the wrong hands, and they were gone forever.

And It Came to Pass

Martin Harris had sought out Joseph's translated text several times. On one occasion, Harris asked an acquaintance in New York City—a professor of interpreted literature—to validate Joseph's translations. Professor Charles Anthon met with Harris and validated in writing the interpretations that Joseph had made. However, once Harris had revealed the story of how Joseph had obtained the records in the first place, Anthon tore up his validation, saying that there was no such thing as ministering angels. Martin Harris returned to Harmony, Pennsylvania, with only his good word that Anthon had accepted Joseph's interpretations.

News of the "Mysterious Golden Book" Spreads

In the spring of 1829, Joseph met a man named Oliver Cowdery. Oliver, a school teacher, had heard of the legendary Smith family and their gold-plated book. Within a couple of days, Joseph and Oliver struck a unique relationship that would later serve as the founding leadership of the LDS Church.

Oliver became Joseph's scribe. While Joseph, who sat on one side of a table, read and interpreted the pages from the gold plates, Oliver sat behind a partition, on the other side of the table, writing what Joseph recited. The two worked throughout many nights, discovering that the record was a story of a family that had left Jerusalem about 600 B.C.

The book, which we now know to be the Book of Mormon, explained that a man named Lehi was instructed by God to leave Jerusalem before it was destroyed. We'll talk more about the characters and events of the Book of Mormon in Chapter 13.

Soon after Joseph and Oliver began their efforts, another man, David Whitmer, took an interest in the Cowdery-Smith translation project. When the need arose to bear witness that the gold plates existed, the three men, along with Martin Harris, shared the experience.

Upon examining the gold plates, Joseph's three friends wrote and signed a declaration, validating what they had seen and held. That declaration is known in Mormonism as the "Testimony of Three Witnesses."

> **And It Came to Pass**
>
> Interestingly, there are many archeological accounts of ancient records being recorded on plates of brass, gold, and other metals. So from a historical perspective, the media used by the authors of the Book of Mormon is justified.

Here's an excerpt from that declaration:

> We, through the grace of God … have seen the plates which contain this record. … And we also know that they have been translated by the gift and power of God, for his voice hath declared it unto us; wherefore we know of a surety that this work is true.

Whitmer, Cowdery, and Harris signed the declaration, which still appears in the front section of the Book of Mormon.

Joseph Smith later showed the gold plates to eight other men, who also wrote and signed a declaration that bore witness to what they saw, as in the excerpt from that testimony:

> And this we bear record with words of soberness, that the said Smith has shown unto us, for we have seen and hefted, and know for a surety that the said Smith has got the plates of which we have spoken. And we give our names unto the world that which we have seen. And we lie not.

Even though some of the men later left the LDS Church, none of them ever denied what they had seen.

Both Martin Harris and Oliver Cowdery left the LDS Church later in life. However, even though they no longer belonged to the Church, whenever they were asked whether they had actually seen the plates of gold, both men undeniably answered, "yes."

After translation, the plates were again taken by the angel Moroni who will keep them until further use of them is required. Whether those records were actually given to Joseph Smith and then taken away by an angel, or whether he found them on his own, is a principle of faith for the Latter-day Saint community.

In the spring of 1830, about the time the LDS Church was formally organized, 5,000 copies of the Book of Mormon were printed at the cost of $3,000. In contrast, a single, original Book of Mormon would fetch between three and ten times that amount on today's auction blocks.

It's Not Easy Being a Smith

By the middle of 1830, Joseph, his brothers Samuel and Hyrum, and Oliver Cowdery, were all engaged in sharing their discovery with the rest of the world. But their missionary work was soon interrupted when Joseph was arrested for unruly conduct. It would not be the first time Joseph was arrested. Throughout the history of the early LDS settlers, wherever they went, local religious leaders raised concerns about the LDS movement and its impact on their parishioners.

Throughout the remaining 14 years of his life, Joseph was jailed numerous times— often without being formally charged—was shot at, and was even tarred and feathered on one occasion by members of a community he had befriended.

Almost immediately after a court ruling of not guilty in his first arrest in Chenango County, Pennsylvania, Joseph was arrested and detained 15 miles away in Broome County. The three judges spent only several minutes deliberating over his case and then dismissed it, saying that they could find nothing to either charge or condemn in his conduct. Only a few days later, Joseph and his brother Samuel were again threatened by mobs that chased the Smiths for miles.

The early challenges for the new prophet were to not only share the Word of God with the people around him, but in some cases merely to survive.

The Least You Need to Know

- An angel called Moroni testified to Joseph of an ancient record inscribed on gold plates.

- Joseph would have to wait for years before being allowed to translate the Book of Mormon.

- Joseph's discovery could not be shared with just anyone, or it could mean death to Joseph.

- Rumors quickly spread about a book of golden plates.

- Angry mobs began taunting and threatening the Smiths for what they claimed to be divine discoveries.

13

The Book of Mormon

In This Chapter

- ◆ The importance of the Book of Mormon in LDS culture
- ◆ Out of Jerusalem, into the New World
- ◆ Stories from the Book of Mormon
- ◆ The Book of Mormon compared to the Old Testament
- ◆ Moroni's promise: A challenge for all people

Talk to any active member of the Church of Jesus Christ of Latter-day Saints and that person will tell you that the Book of Mormon is the most important piece of scripture in the LDS culture. To Latter-day Saints, the Book of Mormon is the keystone to the entire Church. According to LDS beliefs, there is no better way to draw closer to the word of God than by reading the Book of Mormon.

So what's between the covers of the book that reads "Another Testament of Jesus Christ"? Why do Latter Day Saints feel so strongly about this book? And who is this LDS guy with the horn anyway?

In this chapter, we'll look at some of the highlights from the pages of the Book of Mormon, starting with how it all ties into the people of old Jerusalem and how they fled a captive nation, to build up a new civilization across the ocean.

Lehi Who?

At the time Zedekiah was king of Judah, which was about 600 years before the birth of Christ (you can find him throughout the Book of Jeremiah in the Old Testament), Jerusalem had fallen away from God's fundamental principles as they were established by Moses. But there were many people in Jerusalem who were preaching repentance to the Jews, trying their best to keep the town worthy of God's protection.

One of these was a man named Lehi.

Lehi (pronounced *LEE-high*), who is the father of all of the civilizations tracked by the records in the Book of Mormon, was a wealthy head of a righteous family. As was the case with many of God's chosen spokesmen, Lehi had a vision in which he saw many things. Unfortunately, the highlight of what Lehi saw was the total collapse of his beloved city, brought about by the crosstown rivals of Babylon under the leadership of King Nebuchadnezzar.

Lehi spent much of his time preaching repentance to the people of Jerusalem, but they paid no attention to Lehi and continued in their wicked ways. In fact, conversely to his message, the locals decided that even Lehi's wealth would be better served among them, so they plotted to kill the evangelist and plunder his house.

Lehi was warned in a dream to leave all of his earthly possessions and riches behind, and take his family out of Jerusalem. So Lehi, along with his wife, Sariah, their four sons, Laman, Lemuel, Sam, and Nephi, their daughters, and a few other people, fled into the wilderness.

Words of Wisdom

The Book of Mormon [is] the most correct of any book on earth … a man would get nearer to God by abiding by its precepts, than any other book
—Prophet Joseph Smith

And so this group did what they were told, with only a few setbacks (such as whether or not they would actually build a boat to leave the Old Country and whether they would starve) that were cleared up by angelic visitations. They traveled all the way to a great ocean, guided by a compass given to them by God. When they arrived at what we know to be the Mediterranean Sea, they built ships and continued to travel west until they arrived in a land that was promised by God to be choice above all other lands: the Americas.

A Divine Shepherd in the New World

Just as the Bible is a record of the children of God in the Old World, the Book of Mormon is believed by Latter-day Saints to be a record of God's people on the

American continent. It's a book full of stories about both the righteous and not-so-righteous of societies. Its individual books describe wars and miracles and great conversions.

And Latter-day Saints believe that the Book of Mormon is a record that testifies over and over again of the coming of Jesus Christ.

Prior to ascending into heaven, Jesus mentioned to his apostles that he had to leave to "tend other sheep, which were not of this fold: them also I must bring, and they shall hear my voice." (John 10:16) Members of the Church of Jesus Christ of Latter-day Saints believe that Jesus was talking about Lehi's descendents and other people who were spread throughout the world and not in the vicinity of Christ's mortal ministry.

The Book of Mormon tells of Christ's visit to the Americas after his crucifixion and resurrection. During his short stay among the descendants of Lehi, he blessed the children in the New World as he had in the Old, taught the beatitudes as he did before with his twelve disciples, and loved this people as he had the Jews of Jerusalem.

Latter-day Saints believe Jesus cared about all of the people the world over, and not just the people of Jerusalem. He visited the islands of the sea, the Americas, and Jerusalem. He promised he would return.

So now you know a little about Lehi, and how he is the link between the people of the Old Testament and the ancient civilizations of the New World, and how Christ fits into the picture.

But who was this man for whom the LDS scriptures are named? And why do Latter-day Saints believe this set of scripture to be the word of God?

> **And It Came to Pass**
>
> In many of the cultures in South and Central America and throughout the Polynesian Islands, the early inhabitants often spoke of someone who would one day return to them. During the fifteenth and sixteenth centuries when European explorers (and conquerors) first landed on these shores, the natives welcomed them and in many cases looked to them as the God who promised to return.

The Book of Mormon: A Cast of Thousands

The Book of Mormon is replete with characters of both good and bad intentions. Within its chapters, readers will discover suspenseful stories of espionage, war, a few romances, and a lot of teachings that reinforce those offered by Isaiah and Jesus.

Let's look at some of the characters from the Book of Mormon, whom Latter-day Saints consider to be some of the more influential. You might find their names unfamiliar—but hey, it was a New World, it's a new book, why not a few new names?

Laman and Lemuel

What would a good story be without some bad guys? Laman and Lemuel, sons of Lehi, were the perfect evildoers to get things started. These brothers took "wicked" to new heights. They had a taste for the finer things in life, and were never happy about leaving their worldly possessions behind in Jerusalem. All along the trip to the New World, Laman and Lemuel complained, murmured their discontent, fought, and were downright disobedient. These two brothers set the precedent in the Book of Mormon for generations of complainers and unrighteous people. Laman and Lemuel talked about their father as if he was a senile, visionary old man, and they even threatened to kill their younger brothers for going along with him.

All in all, they caused trouble the whole trip—and even more trouble once the family finally arrived on the American continent. Over time, all of Lehi's children established their own families. The descendants of Laman and Lemuel were called Lamanites, and as the old saying goes, the apple doesn't fall far from the tree. The Lamanites became accustomed to practicing the wicked and disobedient traditions of their wicked forefathers.

> **Latter-day Laughter**
>
> Little boy to Sunday school teacher: "I have a riddle about Laman and Lemuel for you."
>
> Sunday school teacher: "Oh? What is it?"
>
> Boy: "If they were here today, what would their favorite TV show be?"
>
> Teacher: "I give up."
>
> Boy: "Diagnosis Murmur."

The ancient Americas were populated by once powerful civilizations, one of which, the Lamanites, spread across the islands of the South Pacific.

©*Drew Williams (2002)*

Nephi

But where there is the naughty, there is the nice. Nephi (pronounced *NEE-fye*), was Lehi's youngest son when they began their journey out of Jerusalem. And even Nephi questioned his father's wisdom in leaving the city, but only until he prayed for direction.

Nephi was told by the spirit that he needed to obey his father and do the things that God expected of him. So Nephi did what he was commanded and became a strength to the whole traveling group.

Nephi is the first great hero of the Book of Mormon. He prayed often and understood God's will for his family, believing that God would always prepare a way for those who would choose to do his will. When Lehi's family couldn't find food, Nephi rescued them all (even his older brothers, who whined and complained even louder).

Korihor

If Laman and Lemuel were bad, then Korihor (pronounced *KOR-ih-hor*), took evil to even greater depths. He first appears in the book of Alma (named after a really good guy, whom I'll tell you about in a moment). Korihor had discovered that by preaching certain things to the descendants of Nephi (called Nephites), he would become wealthy. He led many people away from God.

Eventually, though, it all caught up with him and Korihor found himself face to face with Alma, who was the religious leader of the time.

While confronting Alma, Korihor asked for a sign, challenging the prophet in front of everybody. Korihor soon learned an important but fatal lesson: Don't dare God to do something. Korihor got what he demanded and was struck dumb. Consequently, he remained that way until he was trampled to death by the many unhappy people who believed him.

> **And It Came to Pass**
>
> Members of the LDS Church often refer to each other not as Mr. and Mrs., but Brother and Sister (for example, "Sister Williams" and "Brother Johnson"). As children of God, we are all brothers and sisters, and this style of communication just reminds us of that fact.

Abinadi

Pronounced *ah-BIN-ah-die*, this man was also one of God's prophets. In one Book of Mormon story, Abinadi confronts the wicked King Noah, who was leading the people away from God's teachings. King Noah became angry with the prophet because he didn't like being told he was going to hell.

Despite his powerful words of repentance, Abinadi was burned to death by King Noah—still preaching to the king as the flames engulfed him.

Unfortunately for the wicked king, Abinadi promised that the king would eventually succumb to the same fate as that of the prophet, which the king does in a later story.

Alma

Some good did come from Abinadi's preaching, though. Alma, a priest of King Noah's, was listening to the prophet's words. And as he listened his heart told him that what he was hearing was the truth. After confronting his king, Alma was cast out of the royal house. Alma later wrote the words of Abinadi, eventually preaching the same principles to the same people.

Alma became the prophet and was the founder of God's church on the land. He preached to anyone who would listen and established churches all over the land.

Alma the Younger

Alma had a son called Alma the Younger. And when you follow his life—from his conversion until he is either taken by the Spirit or buried by the Lord—you get to read many conversion stories and sorrowful incidents and see why Latter-day Saints consider Alma the Younger one of the great missionaries in the Book of Mormon.

Mormon

Mormon was a Nephite prophet, military leader, and the man who consolidated the records that appear in the book that is named for him. Mormon lived during the middle of the fourth century A.D. His military life began when he was 15 years old, as told in the Book of Mormon. He soon became a general of great armies, and always fought against unrighteousness. Mormon was told by another Book of Mormon character, Ammon, that he would be the man who would gather and record the histories of the descendants of Nephi.

It was Mormon, seeing that the total destruction of his people was near, who began the consolidation of all the records from the descendants of Lehi, compiling them into a single volume, which he later turned over to his son.

> **" "   Words of Wisdom**
>
> A good book [according to Aristotle] must have structure and development which gives a unified impact from beginning to end. By this standard the Book of Mormon is not only a "good book"; it is a classic.
>
> —Apostle Jeffery R. Holland

Among the individual volumes of work contained in the Book of Mormon are two writings named for him, "Words of Mormon" and "Mormon." These books reveal experiences and sermons taught by Mormon, both as a prophet and military leader.

Moroni

There are two men called Moroni in the Book of Mormon. The first, known in the LDS community as Captain Moroni, was a great military commander around 100 B.C. A highlight of his life, and one of the most endearing stories in the Book of Mormon, is Captain Moroni's account of raising up a battlement that proclaimed the "Title of Liberty," a credo that his troops rallied around to defeat their enemies.

The second man called Moroni was the son of Mormon and the last living member of the Nephite civilization. It is this Moroni who appears atop the LDS temples as a symbol of the proclaiming of the Gospel of Christ into the world. Moroni's final task was to hide the records of the descendants of Lehi, which, as a resurrected spirit, were revealed to the young Joseph Smith in Palmyra, New York (see Chapter 11).

Two Thousand Momma's Boys

There are many accounts in the Book of Mormon of heroic battles and moments of greatness in the face of desperate situations. Like the "2,000 Stipling Warriors" who, at a young age and under the direction of another Book of Mormon prophet named Helaman, went to fight against the Lamanites in a terrible battle. Helaman called the warriors his sons, and although 200 of them were wounded, none of them died in the battle.

They were said to have the greatest courage among the Nephites. The Book of Mormon records that these 2,000 young men were taught not to doubt in God by their mothers.

And then there's Ammon, and Mosiah, and King Benjamin, and … well, the list goes on and on. The Book of Mormon works hand in hand with the Bible: Both testify to the coming of Christ, witness of his ministry, and forecast the state of today's world and the one to come.

One Book, One Translation

Like the Old Testament, the Book of Mormon is a volume of history of early civilizations. There are wars chronicled, and lots of faith-promoting stories—and even a few miracles. There are stories that touch a person's heart, and stories that may make the reader think, "Now why in the world would a person do *that*?"

Mormon Myths

Myth: The Book of Mormon replaces the Bible in the LDS Church. Although the Book of Mormon is central to the LDS culture, it is only part of LDS canon. Latter-day Saints consider the Book of Mormon to be another testament of Jesus Christ and a complementary work to the Bible, which was a record of the people from the Middle East.

One of the big differences between the Old Testament and the Book of Mormon, though, is that the Book of Mormon did *not* have several translators. In fact, only one person, Joseph Smith translated this book (see Chapter 12).

But long before Joseph discovered the book on the hill in upstate New York, this record was consolidated by one of the last ancient prophets in the Americas. His name was Mormon. The record of scripture had been given to him by a Nephite record keeper, to care for and keep safe.

Moroni's Challenge and Promise

Before Mormon's death, he gave the Book of Mormon to his son Moroni. Moroni eventually buried the record in a stone box. Before he did, Moroni wrote a challenge and promise in the last chapter of the Book of Mormon, regarding the validation of the work to which he was charged to protect.

Here's what he wrote:

> And I seal up these records, after I have spoken a few words by way of exhortation unto you. Behold, I would exhort you that when ye shall read these things, if it be wisdom in God that ye should read them, that ye would remember how merciful the Lord hath been unto the children of men, from the creation of Adam even down until the time that ye shall receive these things, and ponder it in your hearts.

> And when ye shall receive these things, I would exhort you that ye would ask God, the Eternal Father, in the name of Christ, if these things are not true; and if ye shall ask with a sincere heart, with real intent, having faith in Christ, he will manifest the truth of it unto you, by the power of the Holy Ghost. And by the power of the Holy Ghost ye may know the truth of all things.

Moroni's promise of knowing whether or not his words were God's words (through a personal acceptance by the reader), is critical to LDS philosophy. Every member of the Church of Jesus Christ of Latter-day Saints is counseled to read and remember this Book of Mormon verse, and decide whether the Book of Mormon is true, and its translator Joseph Smith was a man of inspiration or another nineteenth-century author of good fiction.

The Least You Need to Know

♦ Latter-day Saints consider the Book of Mormon the most important piece of scripture in their culture.

♦ Lehi was a righteous head of a Jewish house who escaped the destruction of Jerusalem. His relocation to the Americas meant the beginning of God's teachings to the New World.

♦ The Book of Mormon is full of epic stories and colorful characters who had both good and bad intentions.

♦ The Book of Mormon is meant to complement, not replace, the Bible.

♦ Moroni challenges anyone who reads the Book of Mormon to pray and consider its truth as God's truth.

Searching for Zion in the Midwest

In This Chapter

- ◆ The Church migrates to Ohio
- ◆ New surroundings, old problems
- ◆ The move to Missouri
- ◆ Our nation's only sanctioned extermination order
- ◆ The Haun's Mill massacre

Joseph Smith found great success in his early missionary efforts for the LDS Church. By 1830, 10 years from the time of his first encounter with divinity in the Palmyra forest, there were fewer than 100 members of the newfound Church. But by 1840, its numbers had swelled to 30,000.

However, before the Saints could enjoy peace as a community, and in their homes, they would endure years of persecution, violence, and economic hardship. Following Joseph's prompting to relocate from New York and Pennsylvania to Ohio, the Mormons would find temporary settlement on the shores of Lake Erie. But their tenure would not last, and after only seven years, the Saints would again be commanded to head south and west.

The Migration West: Ohio

Under the direction of Joseph Smith, the growing congregations of the LDS Church in the New York and Pennsylvania areas sold their properties and moved to the Ohio frontier, prompted by hostile neighbors and angry religious leaders. By late 1831, the LDS movement was reestablished in the northern cities of Hiram and Kirtland, Ohio.

But not everybody went along peaceably. Some of the new members who had established farms and businesses believed the Church leaders—especially Joseph—were more interested in their own personal success than that of their congregation. Even Emma, Joseph's beloved bride, was reluctant to move an eighth time in four years since marrying the Church leader.

But Joseph believed a move was not only commanded by God, but it would also be good for the Church to find a new home. It seemed the communities of northeast Pennsylvania couldn't live with one more religious uprising.

> **Words of Wisdom**
>
> They [Mormons] are good, honest people, who believe thoroughly in their religion.
> –Mark Twain, U.S. author and essayist

Strange Notions and False Spirits

But the problems Joseph and his followers faced in New York and Pennsylvania were nothing compared to their seven years in Ohio. Similar to what occurred in the Old World after the death of Christ, new religious factions began to form. People started to question the judgment of someone who would lead them away from their settlements into the frontier.

Everybody wanted to get into the act on dialog with God. As soon as the Saints had begun to settle in Kirtland, they began to interpret scripture and prayer by themselves (Joseph and his family came after most of them had already relocated). According to one account by a faithful member of the Church, some Church members "conducted themselves in strange manner, sometimes imitating Indians in their maneuvers, sometimes running out into the fields." Some of the more zealous converts would stand on tree stumps and preach to empty fields—actually thinking they were surrounded by congregations.

There was even a woman who claimed to be inspired by God to redirect the Saints to her own congregation. Joseph watched as many of the Church members were swayed by various outside influences, which he prayed about to get direction. He wanted confirmation that God had chosen him to lead the Church. His answer came in the form of the forty-third section of the Church's Doctrine and Covenants, which reads: "There is none other appointed unto you to receive commandments and revelations until [Joseph Smith] be taken, if he abide in me."

Trouble brewed from outside the Church, as well. As Joseph expanded the missionary effort, local preachers in communities surrounding Kirtland and extending hundreds of miles into other territories, became concerned over the alarming increase in conversions to Mormonism (which meant a decrease in their own congregations and the financial support on which they depended).

By the spring of 1831, communities were spreading word of the LDS movement. Unfortunately for the Mormons, the "word" being spread was anything but friendly.

What's Mine Is Yours, What's Yours Is God's

According to many outside the Church, Joseph and the Mormons had gone too far with a new divine revelation—the "law of consecration"—which taught that everyone should share their abundance and wealth with everyone else. This would be the first of several controversial directives that has labeled the LDS Church as "peculiar." In early February 1831, under the direction of the Lord, Joseph instructed the Saints to begin acquiring land in and around Kirtland, which would be contributed to the body of the Church for its use.

The Church was struggling to sustain its financial obligations, and many members were poor. Joseph believed that the law of consecration, which he was convinced was a revelation from God, would even the scales a bit. But the plan of all for one and one for all almost immediately fell into decay, which led to additional prayer by the Mormon leader.

The year of 1831 was not a banner year for the Smith family. Joseph's revelations concerning the law of consecration disturbed many people both inside and outside the Church. In one case, Joseph was dragged from his sleep, stripped naked, beaten, tarred, and feathered. Barely escaping castration and death, Joseph recovered from his wounds and the following Sunday, preached a sermon to a congregation that included his assailants, who attended more for the sake of mocking him. The mob had feared the Mormons would take their lands and steal their women.

Also, Joseph and Emma Smith lost to illness twin babies of their own and two other babies they had adopted. Compounding the frustration of Joseph and Emma's life, the couple were often separated from each other for long periods of time.

During their stay in Ohio, the Saints received many revelations from their leader. One such instruction was to build a temple, which would be used to perform sacred ordinances. The Kirtland Temple was the first temple built, and although it is no longer owned by the LDS Church, it set in motion the building of what are now more than 100 LDS temples worldwide.

The former Kirtland Temple, built in Kirtland, Ohio, was the first temple built by the Mormons. Although no longer owned by the LDS Church, the building still stands as a reminder of the early successes and challenges the Mormons faced on their journey to find a permanent home.

©Drew Williams (2002)

Mormonology

Latter-day Saints refer to **Zion** as "the place where the pure in heart dwell together." According to Joseph Smith, Zion would be established in Independence, Missouri, where Jesus himself would some day return to the earth and rule.

By midsummer 1831, Joseph had been instructed by God to create the land of *Zion* in central Missouri, in and around Jackson County, near the confluence of the Grand and Missouri Rivers. Once again, the Mormons uprooted their settlement and headed for strange lands 800 miles to the southwest.

One highlight of Joseph Smith's prophetic ministry came on Christmas Day in 1832. Joseph issued a prophetic statement that, more than 30 years later, would be fulfilled almost to the letter:

Thus saith the Lord concerning the wars that will shortly come to pass, beginning at the rebellion of South Carolina, which will eventually terminate in the death and misery of many souls; and the time will come that war will be poured out upon all nations, beginning at this place. ... And it shall come to pass, after many days, slaves shall rise up against their masters ....

The full account of Joseph's prophecy can be found in *History of the Church*, Volume 3.

More Misery in Missouri

The central United States in the mid-1800s didn't have highways or even decent trails, which made migrating a large body of people very difficult. In those days, with the exception of the skilled horsemen, the easiest way to get around was by boat on the river system.

The route of the migrating Saints started by steamboat down the Ohio River to what is now the southern tip of Illinois, where the Ohio and Mississippi rivers converge. Then, the Saints traveled upriver to St. Louis, where they transferred onto the Missouri River and up to Independence in Jackson County. The journey was a long and, for most of the farmers of New England, unpleasant trek into hostile and unsettled lands.

During their travels, many of the Church leaders—some of whom were also called to serve as missionaries—encountered other religious cultures, such as the Methodists, Quakers, and factions of nondenominational Christians simply referred to as "Free." The Church spread quickly, as whole congregations were baptized on occasion.

As the Church grew in size, so did its land holdings in central Missouri. In 1831, as the Saints first began their efforts to establish Zion, they could purchase tracts of land for as little as $1.25 per acre. The land would be later divided among the LDS families to live on and farm.

> **Mormon Myths**
>
> *Myth: The Shakers were a branch of the LDS Church.* Although several early LDS leaders were instructed to minister to the Shaker communities, there is no tie between the United Society of Believers in Christ's Second Coming (Shakers) and the LDS Church.

Missouri Finds No Favor

Life in Missouri didn't get any easier for Joseph Smith and his now several hundred followers. By the end of 1833, after their settlements had been destroyed by mobs, the Saints were once again learning that they had worn out their welcome. People from both inside and outside the Church were again questioning the integrity of Joseph Smith and his colleagues, debating whether he represented the voice of God or his own personal interest in ruling in a petty monarchy.

But those original residents of the Jackson County area decided that the surge in population that came with the migrating Mormons would ultimately result in serious political, cultural, and religious conflict.

The Protestant ministers of the region saw their congregations threatened by the "Mormon scourge." From a political perspective, it was clear that the growing number of Mormons in the area could threaten the economic landscape itself, which came to a peak when the Missouri River flooded in 1833 and destroyed the port at Independence. Commerce shifted north to Westport, leaving the town of Independence with a devastated economic situation.

The townspeople blamed the Mormons.

To compound the problem, Mormon missionaries had been courting Indian nations that were seen as a hostile people to the United States. Following the Black Hawk War, western Missouri pioneers feared the Mormons would enlist their Native American friends to overthrow the local communities.

Violence Begets Bloodshed on Both Sides

By summer, the townspeople had decided that enough was enough. Not only did they dislike the idea of Joseph and his Mormon confederates living in their town, they didn't much care for the newly established Mormon newspaper, or the new scriptures the Mormons had brought with them.

> **Words of Wisdom**
>
> I saw 190 women and children driven 30 miles across the prairie, with three decrepit men only in their company, in the month of November, the ground thinly crusted with sleet. I could easily follow their trail by the blood that flowed from their lacerated feet on the stubble of the burnt prairie.
>
> –Mormon pioneer Lyman Wight

In July, a mob, in cooperation with Missouri's Lieutenant Governor Liburn Boggs, stormed the Mormon-owned printing office in Independence, destroying it and everything in it. Its proprietor, W. W. Phelps, was dragged into the town square, where he was beaten, tarred, and feathered.

The mobs continued their pursuits, threatening that every Mormon man, woman, and child would be whipped unless they left Jackson County, Missouri. By spring of the following year, the Mormons had left Jackson County, but found no peace anywhere they tried to settle in Missouri.

On November 4, 1832, a bloody conflict ensued after members of a mob captured a Church-operated ferry traveling on the Big Blue River. Several people were killed from both sides, as word spread quickly to the Governor's office of a "Mormon uprising." Under the direction of Lt. Governor Boggs, Missouri militia were dispatched to banish the Mormons from the region.

Clouds of War Hang Over Missouri

By late 1833, the Mormons and the State of Missouri were at odds. Joseph Smith and his congregations were looking for political protection under the Constitution, while Governor Daniel Dunklin demanded civil obedience.

In the spring of 1834, the Mormons began assembling a "Zion's Camp," for the purpose of providing refuge to the Missouri Mormons. With the camp organized and armed, the tension between LDS leadership and the state militia heated to near-war levels.

Something terrible was about to happen, if somebody didn't back down.

Across four states, from northeastern Ohio (where Church headquarters remained until 1837), to the place that would later be called "Far West," Missouri, (north of Liberty, Missouri), Joseph Smith personally led a band of men to fortify the members of Zion's Camp. Eventually, with the exception of those families that were asked by their prophet to remain and settle in specific areas along the way, the Mormon population moved where Joseph directed them.

Fearing that a "Mormon invasion" to reclaim their lands in Independence was imminent, Governor Dunklin agreed to consider the Mormon leader's request to be restored to their lands.

After several town hall debates and legal negotiation, the Mormons disbanded Zion's Camp, with many of the men returning to Ohio, while the Missouri Mormons settled in Clay County just north of Jackson.

And It Came to Pass
Both the Oregon and Santa Fe Trails originated in Independence, Missouri.

Meanwhile, Back in Ohio

The Kirtland Saints enjoyed a respite of peace and modest expansion for about two years. Having constructed their temple in the spring of 1836, Latter-day Saints were introduced to many fundamental instructions that are still part of the Church's sacred proceedings. Revelations concerning substance abuse, the Priesthood of God, and temple ordinance were given through Joseph Smith to his people.

The LDS Doctrine and Covenants were approved by the body of the Church at a special conference and added to LDS canon.

The mission movement continued to expand as well, with new missionaries being called to preach and special witnesses of Christ, called "apostles," were ordained to a Council of Twelve.

But by the late summer of 1838, Joseph Smith was again fleeing for his life—this time taking all of his followers with him. The bad news got worse, however, as the Mormons fled Ohio to join with the rest of their flock in Clay County, Missouri. A familiar name was governing the "Show Me State" when the Mormons reunited—it was their nemesis, Liburn Boggs.

Governor Boggs's Death Warrant

Boggs already had dealings with the Mormons earlier in his career. A wealthy land owner from Independence, Boggs had participated firsthand in the overthrow of the first LDS movement in that region less than two years prior to his serving as governor. He was determined to have no Mormon settlement of any kind in his territory. On October 27, 1838, under official proclamation by the State of Missouri, Governor Boggs ordered his militia to destroy the Mormons. It would be the first time in the history of the Western World that a government-sanctioned order would be given to exterminate a group of people because of their religious affiliation. (Sadly, another such order would later be given in Central Europe by a rising government, which resulted in the death of millions of Jews.)

Words of Wisdom

Gentlemen, your cause is just, but I can do nothing for you.

–President Martin Van Buren, regarding Joseph Smith's plea for help in Missouri

Here's how Boggs worded the order to rid Missouri of what he called the "Mormon problem": "The Mormons must be treated as enemies and must be exterminated or driven from the state, if necessary, for the public good."

And the leaders of the Missouri militia, long-time opponents of the LDS movement, were determined to carry out that order.

Massacre at Haun's Mill

The tragic events following the Saints who attempted to remain at a place in Missouri called Haun's Mill have often been considered one of the most desperate times of their history.

After migrating from Green Bay, Wisconsin, Jacob Haun settled on property near Shoal Creek, in 1835. He had opened a mill, blacksmith shop and had built several small houses for his Mormon friends. Joseph Smith sent word out for all LDS families to move to Far West. Jacob Haun chose to ignore his prophet's counsel.

Three days after Governor Boggs's extermination order was given, a group of nine wagons carrying Church members from Ohio to Far West, stopped in Haun's Mill for a short rest. Their timing could not have been worse.

A mob of nearly 250 men hid in waiting, surrounding the mill, blacksmith shop, and several other buildings. While the men of the community were in the blacksmith shop, many of the women and children were going about their business of the day. The mob opened fire on anything that moved, eventually killing or wounding 30 people, mostly women and children. Perhaps the most despicable act of the marauding killers was when one of them put the barrel of his gun up to the head of 10-year-old Sardius Smith, and blew the top of his head off. The killer later said, "If he had lived he would have become a Mormon." Sardius's brother Alma, whose hip was blown away by a gunshot, witnessed his brother's and father's deaths, barely escaping with his own life.

And They Called Themselves "Christians"?

Once again, a people of Christian faith had been overrun out of contempt for their peculiar beliefs. However, in the case of the Missouri Mormons, it was by the hands of other Christians, which bore a sad testimony of the society of the Midwestern United States.

Still, the Mormons pressed on in perseverance, and as we will see in the next chapter, began to find harmony in their pursuits of refuge. But their sacrifice was yet to come— even that of their most favored leaders, the death of their prophet and patriarch.

The Least You Need to Know

- Persecution and violence followed the early Mormon settlers as they migrated first to Ohio and then to Missouri.

- The problems Joseph and his followers faced in New York and Pennsylvania only escalated as they moved farther west.

- In 1838, under official proclamation by the State of Missouri, Governor Boggs ordered his militia to destroy the Mormons.

- Some 30 Mormons were injured or killed during the massacre at Haun's Mill.

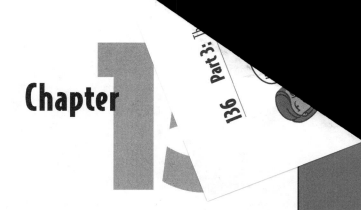

Chapter 14

Is *This* the Place?

In This Chapter

- ◆ On the move to Illinois
- ◆ A short refuge on the Mississippi
- ◆ From swampland to splendor: Nauvoo, the "city beautiful"
- ◆ The beginning of the end in Illinois
- ◆ Living and dying for the cause

By the close of 1840, the Mormons were considered pariahs in three states. Their leaders had been confined on charges ranging from trespassing to treason. With their financial situation in tatters and their lands illegally obtained by local mobs, all the Mormons had to live on was their faith.

However, it was their faith that prevailed in the many conflicts they experienced. No matter how difficult the confrontation, the early Mormons faced each situation with uncanny conviction that their leader was an inspired man of God, and that their cause was just.

Free to Escape

By the spring of 1839, Joseph Smith and several of his colleagues had been held prisoner for almost half a year. Their captivity began in late October

1838 in Independence. They were then moved to a small jail in Liberty, Missouri, where they endured cold winter months, confined in a space too short to fully stand. Joseph and his fellow captives were brought up on charges of murder, burglary, theft, larceny, and treason against the state of Missouri. But before the group could be brought to trial, their captors (whether out of sympathy or sensibility) allowed them to escape to Illinois, where the Saints were reassembling in and around the town of Quincy.

The following table highlights some of the various venues where the Mormons attempted to settle, and their circumstances for leaving.

Location	Approx. Dates	Est. LDS Population	Reason for Leaving
Palmyra, N.Y. Colesville, N.Y.	1818–27	<10	No work
Harmony, Pa.	1828–30	<60	Driven out
Kirtland, Oh.	1831–37	<10,000	Driven out
Independence, Mo.	1838	>12,000	Driven out
Nauvoo, Ill.	1839–45	15,000–20,000	Driven out

Refuge in Quincy

Once again, the Saints were forced west. But this time the Mormons were running from an entire state, not just moving to another town. In the mid-1800s in Midwest America, it appeared that people either hated the followers of this new religion or joined them.

And with their leaders spread out in jails in Liberty and Richmond, and others with Church members in St. Louis, the leadership of the Church fell upon a man whose name to this day, is linked with the pioneer legacy of Mormonism—Brigham Young.

Under the direction of Brigham, whom I'll talk about in depth in the next chapter, the Saints organized a migration out of Missouri, to the small Mississippi River town of Quincy, Illinois. There, the Saints found refuge with the townsfolk, and were even courted by the local politicians. Both the Whigs and Democrats thought that the large LDS vote would offer value as a political influence. Illinois' Governor Ford also hailed from the area and sympathized with the persecuted Saints on occasion.

Members of the state's upper political ranks were incensed by their Missouri counterparts and their actions toward the Mormons, and the governor's wife was said to have been moved to tears on hearing of the atrocities. In an article published in the Quincy newspaper, local leaders wrote: "We know of no language sufficiently for the expression of our shame and abhorrence of her [Missouri's] recent conduct."

 **Words of Wisdom**

Brethren, I have not apostatized yet, and don't feel like doing so.

—Joseph Smith, under pressure to deny his experiences as the founder of Mormonism

The huge population explosion from Quincy's own 1,200 to nearly 10,000 was too much for the small town. But the community bore the weight with little complaint. LDS leadership instructed some of the members to buy huge tracts of land on the western side of the Mississippi, in southern Iowa, where they anticipated making a fourth try at permanent settlement.

Nauvoo, the City Beautiful

Under Joseph's direction, the Saints continued to purchase land on both sides of the Mississippi, including most of the city of Commerce and its swampy surroundings. By midsummer, the city was renamed Nauvoo, which means "beautiful" in Hebrew.

But their mosquito-invested swampland was anything but beautiful. By the end of summer most of the residents along the river suffered from malaria, and some died from the disease. It was only through the onset of the mosquito-killing cold November days that the Saints eventually overcame the illness.

By 1840, Church membership was nearing 20,000, and the town of Nauvoo was becoming a major place for commerce—rivaling even St. Louis to the South. Elections were held, Apostles were assigned to leave for England to serve as special missionaries, and Joseph Smith was leading the faithful Saints. For a short time, the Mormons found a peaceful refuge of their own making.

During this time, Brigham Young and other Church leaders were serving missions to other parts of the country, with the Indians, and in Canada and the United Kingdom.

Joseph expanded the mission program of the Church to include efforts in central Europe and the Holy Land. He assigned his closest apostles to serve for several years in regions that included England, the Scandinavian countries, and Palestine. The result was a pouring in of thousands of new converts, who also settled in Nauvoo and became new citizens of the young nation.

Words of Wisdom

Verily I say unto you all: Arise and shine forth, that thy light may be a standard for the nations.

—Doctrine and Covenants 115:5

Their "city beautiful" was growing with the influx of European immigrants. Nauvoo had two sawmills, paved roads, a steam-powered flour mill, shops of various types, bakeries, blacksmiths, and tailors, and beautiful orchards. The Mormons had made a swamp bloom into a fertile, productive landscape of beauty. It would not be the first time they would enter a barren wasteland and bring forth a transformation.

Unfortunately, the following year again saw the spirit of contention from a crosstown uprising. And once again, the culprit was a Presbyterian minister from a nearby city. The Rev. B. F. Morris, a resident of Warsaw, Missouri, took the liberties of voicing his dislike for the Mormons in many of his sermons, much in the tone of his Missouri colleagues: "This diluted, fanatical and ignorant sect is about to be poured upon us by thousands … and thus like the locusts of Egypt consume every green thing in the land and wither away so far as they can every vestige of godliness."

The seeds of discontent were once again sewn, and this time would harvest fatal consequences for some of the Church's founding leaders.

Joseph Smith's final home in Nauvoo, Illinois. Nauvoo brought a brief respite of peace before the Mormons were forced to leave for unfamiliar territories to the West. Joseph and his family lived in this house from 1839 to 1843, and his son Joseph III later lived in the same home.

©Drew Williams (2002)

Ghosts of Missouri Haunt the Mormons

The beginning of the end for the Mormons in Illinois came partly with an endless pursuit by Missouri's Governor Boggs, to capture and extradite Joseph for his "crimes against the state." Boggs had been humiliated by Smith's visit to the White House where he asked for redress from President Van Buren against Boggs and the state of Missouri.

Adding to the trouble, Joseph's desire to create a strong local militia resulted in a well-disciplined, well-armed military strength that could rival virtually any other army in the region. Bundled with the perception that Mormons were troublemakers, the Nauvoo militia implied a reasonable threat to outsiders. And it didn't help any that the LDS battalion would put on demonstrations, military precision drills, and parades almost every week.

But the ultimate demise of the delicate fabric that was the Mormon settlement of Nauvoo came with the jealousy of the town's success, which overshadowed virtually every other settlement along the Mississippi.

In Warsaw, 17 miles to the south, and Carthage, also a few miles south, anti-Mormon political movements were growing. The population of the Mormon communities was growing rapidly, posing a force of both military and political strength. The reality that the outsiders didn't accept, however, was that Joseph Smith was building a religious-based community, not a political one.

Power in the Written Word

During the elections of 1842, Joseph's brother William ran for political office against anti-Mormon activists. Although the bully pulpit became both a podium for politics and a rostrum for religion, the real fight between Church and state took place in the many local newspapers. The power of the pen was not just mightier, but in the case of "*Mormonism* vs. *Everyone*," the pen was a precursor to the sword.

William Smith won the state House of Representatives race, and supported the publication of the *Nauvoo Neighbor*, which was mostly used to further the cause of Mormonism.

Meanwhile, back in Missouri, the now former Governor Boggs barely escaped an assassination attempt, allegedly by Joseph Smith's personal bodyguard, Orrin Porter Rockwell. Joseph was safe behind a writ of habeas corpus (which protected him from extradition to Missouri), while Rockwell fled to Pennsylvania under a false name. Although considered a lawman by some and renegade by most, Rockwell was often called the "Avenging Angel" by his Mormon friends.

And It Came to Pass

Orrin Porter Rockwell was one of the most colorful characters of early American history. Rockwell, whose name appears in LDS scripture, was the personal bodyguard of Joseph Smith. In a blessing given by Joseph, Rockwell was told that his life would always be preserved if he never cut his hair. Rockwell heeded his prophet's counsel and was never killed in a gun battle. Rockwell served as a U.S. Marshall, Indian fighter, and defender of many LDS leaders. At the time of his death of natural causes in June 1878, the longhaired Rockwell had "dispatched justice" by gun more than Wyatt Earp, Bat Masterson, and Doc Holiday combined.

Another election year rolled around in 1844. Joseph, still disenchanted with the way he was treated by President Van Buren, decided to launch his own political campaign for the office of President of the United States.

Joseph built a campaign that tried to appeal to the popular vote, despite the stigma that had followed the LDS faith. He pledged to remove the practice of confining indigents in "debtors prisons," he planned to annex Texas and Oregon, and he vowed to eliminate slavery by the end of the decade. "If I ever get into the presidential chair," he declared, "I will protect the people in their rights and liberties."

But Joseph's efforts were cut off prematurely with word that an internal plot had been created to not only remove him from Church leadership, but to kill him outright.

A Martyr's Death

General Napoleon Bonaparte of France once wrote, "It is the cause, not the death, that makes the martyr." Such was true of Joseph Smith. On June 27, 1844, Joseph and his brother Hyrum, who were both being held on trumped up charges in the nearby Carthage jail, were shot to death by a mob.

Prior to his death, Joseph had told his family goodbye, knowing it would be the last time he would see them. One last time, on his way back to Nauvoo, prior to leaving for Carthage, Joseph addressed some of his followers: "I am going like a lamb to the slaughter, but I am calm as a summer's morning. I have a conscience void of offense toward God and toward all men. If they take my life I shall die an innocent man, and my blood shall cry from the ground for vengeance, and it shall be said of me, 'He was murdered in cold blood.'"

In June 1844, while confined in the jail in Carthage, Illinois, Joseph Smith and his brother Hyrum were murdered by a mob.

©Drew Williams (2002)

Shortly after the death of their 38-year-old prophet and founder of the LDS movement, many Saints were grief-stricken rather than vengeful. Much to the surprise of both the Illinois governor and the surrounding communities, the Saints of Nauvoo never sought revenge for the murders of the Smith brothers.

Sadly, the death of Joseph and his brother most affected their mother Lucy Mack Smith. Within four years, Lucy had buried her husband and four of her sons.

The Least You Need to Know

- LDS leaders were allowed to escape and regroup, only to be captured again.
- Quincy, Illinois, provided refuge to thousands of homeless Latter-day Saints.
- The Latter-day Saints built a powerful city, Nauvoo, out of swampland; it served as a peaceful respite for a short time.
- Whether by vision or instinct, Joseph Smith knew his days were numbered.

Part 4

Pioneering a New World Religion

Before they found their refuge in the Wasatch Mountains of Utah, the Mormon pioneers had to endure nearly 2,000 miles of relatively uncharted wilderness, harsh climates, and personal hardships. Although the land to which they were banished was arid, unattractive, and difficult to farm at first, the transformation from desert wasteland to acres of productive farmland and orchards took only a few short seasons.

Through the pioneers of 1847 and those who followed, Joseph Smith's vision of "a mighty people in the midst of the Rocky Mountains" was finally realized. In the end, however, it was their incredible faith that led them to lay the foundation of the American West. Whether you've lived in Utah for generations or only a short time—LDS or not—the dominant presence of pioneer pride cannot go unnoticed throughout Utah's communities.

Chapter 16

New Leadership—and a Last Trek Westward

In This Chapter

◆ Church members decide on a new leader

◆ Disputes within the Church result in religious factions

◆ The challenge of leaving everything behind—again

◆ Faith once again fetches a high price during the last long trek westward

In 1844, the LDS Church saw the loss of its leader, Joseph Smith Jr., and his brother Hyrum. The Church had never known a time without Joseph at the helm. Nonetheless, under the careful leadership of those who were called to serve as "apostles, thousands of faithful Saints followed the direction of their 12 appointed leaders until a new "First Presidency" was appointed more than three years later.

To ease the matter of leadership, on August 8, 1844, after a day of debate over who should succeed Joseph as the new Church leader, the council of Twelve Apostles selected Brigham Young as their new voice. In that capacity, "Brother Brigham," as he was known, would see the Nauvoo Temple built, oversee the migration west and the settlement of the territory of Deseret (now the state of Utah). But he still had to wait until December 1847 before being sustained as president of the entire Church.

Brigham Young: The Great Settler

Brigham Young was born in Whitingham, Vermont, in 1801, the ninth of 11 children and a descendant of true American heritage. His father John was a devout Methodist and veteran of the American Revolutionary War, serving under George Washington.

The Young family was poor but hard working. Brigham's early years were spent in the fields and forests of Vermont, rather than in the classrooms. In his late twenties, he married his first wife Miriam. It was at this time that his brother Phineas brought home a copy of the Book of Mormon. Brigham spent the next two years reading and studying the book. He later wrote, "I weighed the matter studiously for nearly two years before I made up my mind to receive that book. I looked at it on all sides.... I wished time sufficient to prove all things for myself."

When Brigham was baptized in Mendon, New York, there were scarcely more than a few hundred Mor-mons throughout the region. But within the decade to follow, this close friend and companion of Joseph Smith would lead thousands across difficult lands, in desperate times, and would later serve more nearly four decades as the head of the LDS Church.

Known for his powerful stature and influence, Brigham later served as a mission president in Great Britain, where he and a companion observed or participated in thousands of baptisms in a single year.

Brigham Young was the president of the LDS Church longer than any other man, and saw more transition than any other Latter-day Saint of his time. At the time of his death in 1877, the Church had seen massive growth and included more than 150,000 members, had been banished from three states, and had settled one of the most wild and dangerous territories in Western America. Under Young's direction, the Church established three colleges (the first is now the University of Utah) and two newspapers, both of which are still the major news publications of the State of Utah. He was the first territorial governor of Utah, and his efforts as the first Utah settlement captain heralded the foundation of the now over 12-million-member Church of Jesus Christ of Latter-day Saints that calls Utah its home in the West.

Words of Wisdom

It is our duty to preach the Gospel, gather Israel, pay our tithing, and build temples. The worst fear I have about this people is that they will get rich in this country, forget God and his people, wax fat ... and go to hell.

—Prophet Brigham Young

Religious Factions Begin to Form

After the death of Joseph Smith, many of those who had served him in various leadership roles anticipated succeeding him as the Church's new leader. Many former apostles and friends of the prophet made vain attempts to carve up the Church's membership like a Sunday roast.

One convert, James Strang, left the Church to settle on an island in Lake Michigan, where he crowned himself king of "the Kingdom of Beaver Island." Strang claimed to be the authorized voice of God—right up until he was murdered by his own followers.

Then there was the Apostle Lyman Wight, who broke away from the Church after Joseph's death, leading a small body of the Church to the frontiers of Texas. Called "Colonia," the sect established a prophet, ministers, and priests, but was ultimately dissolved by 1852, due to debates over what was and wasn't acceptable canon.

There were other leaders, such as Sidney Rigdon—the one-time scribe of the Book of Mormon and former friend of the Church's founder. Rigdon, who had been shunned by Joseph Smith for his incessant efforts to stand alongside the prophet as "co-leader," attempted to sway the body of the Church to elect him as its guardian. To his displeasure, however, the Saints sustained their current Twelve Apostles as the body of leadership for the Church, with Brigham Young as the resident of the Quorum.

Sidney Rigdon led a small portion away with him to Pittsburgh, where he made an attempt at organizing his own version of a latter-day church. Rigdon and his church died in New York in obscurity in 1876.

Of all the factions that tried to make an impact on the early Church population, the most noted was the one founded in April 1860 by Emma Smith, Joseph's widow, and her son Joseph Smith III.

The 300-member "Reorganized Church of Jesus Christ of Latter-day Saints (RLDS)" was formed under the idea that any proph-etic leadership of the original church founded by Joseph Smith should be based on a bloodline from the LDS founder. The RLDS church established its headquarters in Independence, Missouri, where it remains today, renamed the "Community of Christ," which currently includes about 70,000 people.

> **Words of Wisdom**
>
> Pray as if everything depended upon God and work as if everything depended upon man.
> —Cardinal Francis Joseph Spellman, U.S. Roman Catholic clergyman

> **And It Came to Pass**
>
> Aside from sharing a common lineage to Joseph Smith, there is no formal tie or affiliation between any of the faction groups of so-called "Mormon spin-offs" and today's Utah-based LDS Church.

Leaving Behind the "City Beautiful"

By the end of 1845, the Mormons were forced to leave Nauvoo by mobs from the Illinois militia. They were forced to abandon their settlements, houses—even their personal possessions—and head west for the fourth time. The good news was, this would be their last move west. The bad news was, they made their migration during the worst season possible, across the most blustery terrain, in the most impoverished circumstances.

The winter of 1845 was exceptionally bitter, freezing the Mississippi River near Nauvoo. In February of 1846, the Mormons began their trek west. Some walked across the frozen Mississippi while it was frozen for a short period, but most traveled by ferry. Many of the Saints had no idea where they were going, following almost on blind faith in their 12 leaders—although Brigham Young and his advisors had already met with trappers and scouts who had been to the Great Salt Lake Valley. There was always a plan.

For many of the travelers, the trek would prove a last desperate effort in seeking permanent refuge from a life of persecution. Historically, the migration of the Latter-day Saints would bring the birth of the American West.

The Long Trek West

For the next seven months, the Mormon parade continued across the Iowa plains—the most difficult portion of their 2,000-mile journey. It took the pioneers nearly five months to cover the 300 miles across the plains, as opposed to the 13 weeks it took to make the final 1,000 miles over the Rockies, into Utah.

During their first few weeks, the travelers suffered through bitter cold and wet weather, as they attempted to make quarters in Sugar Creek, Iowa. But by mid-winter, the foot-deep muddy climate gave way to subzero temperatures, wreaking havoc on many of the unprepared settlers.

> **Latter-day Laughter**
>
> It was a much better day today on the trail. We only crossed through one mud puddle—but it was seven miles long!
>
> —Pioneer journal entry

Frostbite, hypothermia, and starvation visited the ill-fated campers, because many had left Nauvoo without heeding the advice of their leaders to prepare sufficient food and supplies for the long journey. Still, the Saints persevered at the Sugar Creek site until March, when they began their trek across Iowa.

During their trek westward, Mormons made settlements throughout the American beltline, from Pennsylvania, through the Ohio Valley, through northern Missouri, and across the American plains. Some of their makeshift lodgings can still be seen along what is now the nation's "Pioneer Trail."

©Drew Williams (2002)

Although concerned about where to cross the Missouri River once they reached it, Mormon leaders were more worried about how to get there, knowing that any journey back through Missouri would be risky to their weak and vulnerable caravans, primarily from anti-Mormon mobs and its former governor. The decision was made to cross diagonally from the southeastern corner of Iowa to a point on the southwest border, near Council Bluffs, and avoid Missouri altogether.

The Mormons would make their winter quarters across the Missouri River on a Nebraska hilltop. They may have avoided the Missouri rabble, but the trekkers were about to suffer the throes of the harsh prairie winds of winter.

And It Came to Pass

Not all of the Mormons were involved in the initial migration to the west. By the late summer of 1846, nearly 12,000 members of the Church were scattered throughout the Midwest. Nearly 4,000 Saints found temporary lodging on the Nebraska side of the Missouri River, with more than 2,500 camped in Indian territory on the east side of the river. More than 2,000 Saints were lodged throughout the new settlements of Mount Pisgah and Garden Grove, Iowa, and almost 2,000 Mormons lived in the St. Louis area. Although the most noted crossing was the initial Mormon trek that ended in Utah in July of 1847, the migration by the Saints continued for more than 10 years after

Winter Quarters Woes

Life on the trail west was hard. In Winter Quarters, just north of Omaha, Nebraska, many of the Saints, especially children, died from exhaustion and exposure to the cold.

Many of those who traveled along the seeming "forced march" across Iowa suffered from exposure, illness, and sheer exhaustion. To make matters worse, the traditional maladies that followed the rivers—malaria, tuberculosis, and pneumonia—affected many of the campers. By the spring of 1847, nearly 1,000 Saints perished at Winter Quarters. Survivors couldn't do much more than dig shallow graves for their dead, due to the frozen land. In many cases, no sooner were the dead buried than the coyotes were upon the corpses. Today, an LDS temple and visitor's center occupy a portion of the original campsite of the Saints.

To make the journey, the pioneers had to rely on their faith that God would eventually deliver them to a place foreseen by their beloved prophet, Joseph Smith.

Spring Brings New Hope

On April 16, 1847, the first *company* of wagons set out from Winter Quarters on their thousand-mile journey. Contrary to what many people think, the "Mormon Trail" actually runs somewhat parallel to the Oregon Trail, but to the north side of the Platte River.

Mormonology

A **company** refers to a group of organized travelers, sectioned off in even-balanced groups. In 1847, there were 13 migrating companies of pioneers, totaling more than 2,000 pioneers. Each company traveled separately, which included a company captain, who was the final decision maker for each group. Brigham Young led the first company of travelers, which included 148 people.

Company leaders thought they might not bring as much attention to themselves by avoiding the more frequented Oregon Trail, and were also certain of better food for their oxen. And although the ride across Nebraska was relatively smooth, there was always the fear of hostile Indians, outlaws, and wildlife.

Until the Oregon Trail turned north, the Mormons were able to follow with relative ease. However, after reaching what is now Laramie, Wyoming, the Rocky Mountains became a bit more difficult challenge. However, with the advice of some of the mountain men they met along the way (such as Jim Bridger and Miles Goodyear), Brigham and the other leaders were able to determine the best course to follow through the Rockies, en route to the Salt Lake Valley.

A Silver Lining

One product that came out of their journey was the invention of the odometer—the device used to count the distance a vehicle travels. During the long, often boring journey, Mormon leaders William Clayton and Orson Pratt devised a method for calculating the distance a wagon traveled, by the number of rotations made by the spokes on its wheel.

Dare I say it? Their clever invention was "revolutionary" in the way we calculate mileage.

Brigham Young's self-sustaining preparations were also realized with his introduction of "advance planting" of crops. Those companies that passed through an area in the spring would plant crops for the companies that came through during the harvest season. Brigham's foresight provided food and resources for those who followed—both man and beast. He and his company were well prepared for the journey; they would be the leaders of all the subsequent companies.

Interestingly, the Salt Lake Valley was not the first choice of the LDS leaders. During the months that followed the death of Joseph Smith, Brigham Young had asked permission from the governor of Arkansas to find permanent rest in his territory— but was refused.

Texas shared Arkansas' feelings for the Saints, and Young determined, after reviewing early maps, which were created by Catholic missionaries, and reports from the Lewis and Clark expeditions, that the Salt Lake Valley would be the place to make their final stand.

> **Mormon Myths**
>
> *Myth: Only white people were part of the Mormon trek west.* Although few in number, there were at least three black families that migrated west in the first parties that accompanied Brigham Young in 1847. The slaves of southern converts, these families eventually took up residence in Utah.

The Least You Need to Know

◆ Brigham Young's leadership withstood the entire history of Mormon persecution, leading to the settlement of the Salt Lake Valley.

◆ Leadership disputes within the LDS Church resulted in small religious factions, none of which are associated with today's LDS Church.

◆ Saints were required to flee their "City Beautiful" to avoid the growing mobs.

◆ Death and disease followed the Mormon pioneers on their long journey west, but their faith kept them going.

Chapter 17

This Is the Place ... Finally!

In This Chapter

◆ A long journey ends in a barren valley

◆ Building a city

◆ Brigham Young is elected leader

◆ After a rough start, the desert blooms

◆ Overcoming barriers to statehood

◆ Pursuing excellence in education

Is it possible the wandering religion of Mormonism could finally find a permanent place to dwell? It might be the second driest territory in the Union. It might include summer days of more than 110 degrees in many areas. It might be infested with scorpions, tarantulas, mountain lions, and rattlesnakes. Heck, it might also include its own salty version of the Dead Sea. But to the Latter-day Saints of the Salt Lake Valley, it was home at last.

The Mormons first rolled into the Valley in July 1847. However, it took them another 50 years to get their political, governmental, and legal matters in worthy enough condition for the Utah Territory to be considered a state. Brigham Young held onto the reins of both state (as governor) and Church leadership (as president and prophet) for many years. He was defeated as governor in an open election later in his life, but remained prophet of the Church until his death in 1877.

The State of Utah stands as a unique constitutional marriage between church and state. As it was with the early U.S. colonies in the East, the Salt Lake territory was founded on principles of religious freedom. Although, the principle of separating the two has been central to the Constitution itself, the strange alliance between the two fundamental liberties is still implied in many parts of Utah today.

Settling a Desert

On July 22, 1847, the advance party of Mormon settlers, led by one of Brigham Young's assistants, rode into the Salt Lake Valley. They were greeted with dry, parched soil as far as the eye could see. There were no trees, and the wildlife consisted mainly of rattlesnakes and rabbits.

The advance party's first order of business was to build a makeshift irrigation system, which they used to flood the land where crops would soon be planted, even though it would be a short season of growing.

> **Words of Wisdom**
>
> I would give you $1,000 for a bushel of corn raised in that basin.
>
> —Jim Bridger, early explorer of the West, referring to the challenge of farming the Salt Lake Basin

Brigham Young, who had taken ill from something called "mountain fever," was brought to the valley two days later by the man who would later become the third prophet and president of the Church, Wilford Woodruff. The arrival of Brigham and the leadership of the Church has since been commemorated, and a monument built, at a place now called Emigration Canyon.

Laying Out the City

The next order of business, after the irrigation project, was finding a place to build a city. Within four days of entering the Valley, Brigham and his associates selected a point between the forks of a creek, where the cornerstone of the new Mormon temple would be built. From that point, Brigham laid out in parallel, the streets of what would become Salt Lake City, with each street running parallel to the four sides of the temple site.

As part of the unique design of Salt Lake City's streets, with the exception of those four streets that provide the perimeter to the temple site, Brigham used numerical labels to identify each street. For example, if you were one block to the South of the temple site, which ran east and west, you would be at "100 South." Two blocks to the East would be "200 East."

And It Came to Pass

When Brigham Young and his colleagues were designing the streets of Salt Lake City, one of the unique features was in how wide the streets would run. Brigham took into consideration the space necessary to turn a fully hitched team of oxen around when deciding the width of each street. Being a man of vision, Brigham also designed the Salt Lake Temple to be built with large shafts running through, with openings on each floor. He anticipated that a device would some day be built to carry people up and down to each floor. Elevators were in fact added to the temple many years later.

For many people, the numerical labeling of Salt Lake City—and virtually every other city throughout Utah—might be confusing (especially when one city ends and another begins). But it's one more unique characteristic of the people who live on the western foothills of the Rocky Mountains.

With the city planned, the streets laid out, and the land flooded and planted, the arriving companies assisted in building a city out of nothing. They began by constructing a fort, which they would use as protection from hostile forces (Indians, outlaws—and any potential grudge holders from Missouri!).

By winter, the Saints were pouring into the Salt Lake Valley quite steadily. However, some were still camped back on the western edge of Iowa, across the river from Winter Quarters. In honor of Thomas Kane, who befriended the Mormons during their trek, the pioneers built a large settlement, which they named after him. Today, Kanesville is a thriving city across the river from Omaha, Nebraska.

Naming a New President

Although Brigham Young had served as the leader of the council of Twelve Apostles, following the death of their leader Joseph Smith, the body of the Church had no single leader.

On December 5, 1847, the council voted Brigham Young as the second president of the Church of Jesus Christ of Latter-day Saints. Announcement was made of his selection during the Christmas festivities taking place among the 1,000 members of the Kanesville settlement.

The Church had waited three years, but finally had its new leader and prophet.

Words of Wisdom

We have been kicked out of the frying pan into the fire, and out of the fire into the middle of the floor, and here we are and here we will stay.

—Prophet Brigham Young

A Tough Start for the Pioneers

The first winter in 1848 in the Salt Lake Valley was mild. Aside from the rodents and howling wolves, the Saints enjoyed a season of progress, as they worked to build their new homes and communities, and expanded their exploration into other areas surrounding the valley.

However, because the settlers had not yet had a chance to plant crops, good food was hard to come by. Everyone was on daily rations of eight ounces of flour. To supplement their food, the Saints ate wolves, crows, sego lily roots, and thistle tops. In some cases, where cattle had lain dead for who knows how long, people would cut away the exposed meat. Cattle, by the way, were a specific breed, also called oxen, and were used to pull wagons.

Then came the crickets. Due to a severe drought (something people who live in Utah still experience), the crops planted in the spring of 1848 were slight at best. But the horde of crickets that descended out of the foothills, combined with the drought, would spell winter starvation to the settlers. Millions of big, ugly crickets swarmed everything, devouring any green thing they could eat. The Mormons, it seemed, were once again outnumbered and outwitted by the "locals."

But a miracle occurred—one for which a monument now stands in Salt Lake City's Temple Square. While Charles Rich, one of Brigham Young's closest friends and advisors, was delivering a Sabbath day message, thousands of seagulls—which up to that point had never been seen in the Salt Lake Valley—descended on the fields and gorged on the crickets. According to the account of many witnesses, the birds would eat the crickets, and throw them up, just to eat new ones.

Within a few days, the airborne pest controllers had eradicated the area of the cricket infestation. Later, Utah would name the Western gull its state bird.

The Desert Blooms

By the early 1850s, the Territory of *Deseret* had been firmly established in a region known as the Great Basin. Its borders took in all of what is now Utah and Nevada, as well as the western region of New Mexico and Colorado, and most of Arizona.

Brigham Young had established the first of three colleges, the University of Deseret (now the University of Utah), a territorial currency, and all of the usual services offered by a small town. The Mormons were making good on their plans to make the desert "blossom as a rose."

Mormonology

Deseret, which means beehive, is a word used by the Jaredite people (from the Book of Mormon). The beehive is a familiar symbol of the State of Utah and of the LDS Church. When the pioneers crossed the plains and settled Utah, many of them brought small beehives, which they would use to pollinate their crops and orchards.

Communities including Fort Provo, Pleasant Grove, Springville, and Payson were formed to the South, while settlers moved into the Ogden and Bear Lake Valleys to the North. There was no turning back; the Mormons had finally found their permanent home. Nearly 100,000 Saints now lived throughout the region.

One of the earliest tasks assigned by LDS leaders was that of providing visual and written record of activity within the community of the Church. Although there have been many noted pioneer photographers, none are more recognized in the late nineteenth century for capturing the Mormon experience than George Anderson, seen here in his studio in Springville, Utah, with assistant Ralph Snelson. Ralph's grandson Mike operates Snelson's Photocolor Lab in Springville. A fourth-generation member of one of Utah county's first Mormon pioneer families, Mike personally processed all of the photos that appear in this book.

©Drew Williams (2002)

Music and the Spoken Word

One of the most notable icons of the LDS Church is its 360-member Mormon Tabernacle Choir. In 1867, in commemoration for the great tabernacle that was constructed to the West of the Salt Lake Temple site, choirs from the central Utah towns of Springville, Payson, and Spanish Fork assembled to provide the music for the Church conference held that October. They became known as the Tabernacle Choir, and have provided music at special events and all general conferences ever since.

In 1922, the LDS Church created a radio station with the call letters KZN (now KSL), which began airing broadcasts of a special program originally called *The Spoken Word*. The program, featuring words of inspiration and music by the Mormon Tabernacle Choir, is the longest concurrent broadcast program in existence.

Today, *Music and the Spoken Word* can be heard each Sunday morning on KSL, and is broadcast to radio stations throughout the world.

> **Latter-day Laughter**
>
> Colorful twentieth-century Apostle J. Golden Kimball recalled the story of a man who fell in love with a girl's beautiful singing voice and impulsively decided to marry her. The morning after their wedding the man looked at his new wife with curlers in her hair and no make-up. He looked once, then he looked again. On the third look he said, "Sing, for hell's sake!"

> **Mormon Myths**
>
> *Myth: J.C. Penney was a Mormon.* Although James Cash Penney was born in Missouri and eventually created the first headquarters for his growing department store practice in Salt Lake City, he was not a member of the LDS Church. His father was a part-time Baptist minister, his company's home office is in Texas, and today's headquarters for the J.C. Penney empire is in New York City.

The First Department Store

What do J.C. Penney, Sears, Saks Fifth Avenue, and other department stores have in common? They owe their department store origins to the early Mormons, and more specifically to Brigham Young. In 1868, he established Zion's Cooperative Mercantile Institution (ZCMI). The store's purpose was to bring a vast array of goods and products into Utah, to sell for the purpose of generating financial assets that would be distributed back to the community. Pricing would be uniform to reduce the risk of inconsistent profits and costs throughout the more than 100 stores that were created throughout Utah. The concept of a department store was born!

The Quest for Statehood

For nearly 50 years, after entering the Salt Lake Valley, the Mormons of the Utah Territory grew and developed Salt Lake City into a highly successful crossroads of the West.

However, the thrift and industry that Mormonism promoted also attracted others not of the LDS faith. In most cases, people who were not affiliated with the LDS Church, shared in the successes and challenges of their Mormon neighbors.

However, there was still one final, important event that needed to take place, which would solidify the LDS legacy of helping build the American West—statehood.

Unfortunately, despite all of the progress that had been made, the LDS Church still bore something of an unpopular stigma with the rest of the nation. The LDS practice of polygamy—the practice of having multiple wives at the same time—was, although considered by the leadership of the Church to be inspired of God, the single biggest roadblock to joining the Union.

Many of the territory's new residents did not agree with LDS philosophy, and due to limited voting rights by the Latter-day Saints (restricted because of their position on polygamy), the "Anti-Mormon Party" won various school and city elections in Utah by a landslide in 1890. Subsequently, they began transitioning the school systems from religious- to secular-based coursework. Moreover, even the property of the Church came into question, due to its position of violating Supreme Court rulings against plural marriages.

But in 1890, Church President Wilford Woodruff released a document called the "Manifesto," in which he spoke in the Church's behalf, renouncing the practice of plural marriage. Although it came as a tremendous strain to him and the 2 percent of the Latter-day Saints who were practicing polygamy, the Manifesto cleared the last barrier for Utah to be recognized as a star on the American flag.

We'll look more closely at polygamy in the next chapter.

The Glory of God Is Intelligence

One of the most passionate programs introduced by Brigham Young was that of institutes of higher learning. The University of Deseret was the territory's first college, and was later renamed the University of Utah. Today, the university is best known for its study in health care research (and an occasionally successful college football program).

In 1886, the Church leaders created the "Salt Lake Stake Academy," which later became the LDS Business College. Still owned by the Church, the school was created to offer "a spiritually grounded education founded on the divine doctrines and principles of the Church of Jesus Christ of Latter-day Saints."

Ten years earlier, Brigham Young had established an academy 50 miles south of Salt Lake City, in Provo. The school focused on providing higher education in areas of industry and business development. However, the school's main focus was to provide a spiritual foundation, deeply rooted in LDS principles of God, the arts, and strong family relationships.

In 1875, created from a bankrupt family-operated school in Provo, Utah, Brigham Young Academy was created. The old Academy building is now home to the Provo City Library.

©*Drew Williams (2002)*

Today, Brigham Young University is the largest privately owned university in the United States, with a student body of nearly 30,000. BYU has provided the seedbed for many breakthroughs in technology and business, and the school is also well-known for its highly competitive athletic programs, including (most seasons) a *really* successful football program.

And It Came to Pass

In 1918, a 14-year-old LDS boy had a vision. Philo T. Farnsworth of Beaver, Utah, figured out that electrons could transmit images through airwaves and into a console. He would call this idea a *television*. Farnsworth later attended Brigham Young University, where he studied breakthroughs in transmitting visual images. Farnsworth finally attained a patent for the television in 1927.

The Least You Need to Know

- ◆ The Mormon pioneers finally settled their own territory in Utah.
- ◆ City plans were defined by the ability to turn cattle around in the street.
- ◆ After four years, the LDS Church named a new leader, Brigham Young.
- ◆ After overcoming early hardships, the Mormon communities began to thrive.
- ◆ It took the early Mormons nearly 50 years to turn a territory into a state.
- ◆ Higher education was a priority for the early Saints.

Chapter 18

Meet the Wives and Kids

In This Chapter

- ◆ The practice of polygamy as a divine principle
- ◆ Plural marriage established in history
- ◆ Early laws against polygamy
- ◆ Prophet Wilford Woodruff's call for the end of polygamy
- ◆ The polygamy issue today: continued confusion with nonmember factions

Behind every good man is a better woman. Some of the Latter-day Saints expanded on this concept in the late nineteenth century by answering the divine call of polygamy—even Brigham Young had a wife for each week of the year. The idea of plural marriage has been around since the dawn of time. However, the Latter-day Saints were the first to embrace this practice in the Western World, in the late nineteenth century.

I remember when I was researching the LDS Church for myself, how odd I thought it was that a Western culture could justify such a bizarre and seemingly futile practice. I also couldn't understand how any woman would even want to *share* the same man. But after careful research, I realized that polygamy was a necessity to the Latter-day Saints during their early days, because it provided a safe haven for many women who had lost their husbands or had never been married. But more important, the early Saints believed the practice of plural marriage was divinely inspired but socially premature, and ultimately had to be abandoned.

Polygamy as a Divine Principle

It seems ironic that a religious culture whose own scriptures profess that "not any man among you have save it be one wife; and concubines he shall have none" (Jacob 2:27) would at one time have practiced *polygamy*.

Mormonology

Polygamy, or plural marriage, is the practice of taking more than one wife to one husband. Polygamy is an ancient tradition that was often practiced by the wealthy tribesmen of the Middle East. Throughout the Old Testament, polygamy is routine in the culture. Today, polygamy is still practiced throughout the world—but not by members of the LDS Church!

Words of Wisdom

The Mormons make the marriage ring, like the ring of Saturn, fluid, not solid, and keep it in its place by numerous satellites.

—Henry Wadsworth Longfellow, U.S. poet

But there was one catch: God commanded that his children "raise up a seed" unto him. And the primary purpose for living on the earth, according to LDS doctrine, is to multiply and replenish it, and to bring down God's spirit children (as you'll recall from Chapter 3).

From a social aspect, where the sexes are equal in population, everybody gets a relatively equal chance at finding that Mr. or Mrs. Right and settling down to building a family.

But for the Latter-day Saints of the mid- and late nineteenth century, the scales were tilted considerably in a higher ratio of women to men. Consequently, one of the very principle laws to which Latter-day Saints were required to live, could not be fully realized, unless something was done to balance the scale.

For one thing, Latter-day Saints have always been advised not to marry outside the Church. If you were LDS and your would-be spouse was not, you could not enter the temple, you could not be sealed for time and eternity, and you could not enjoy exaltation in the Celestial Kingdom (see Chapters 6, 24, and 26).

But those who were selected to practice plural marriage (by the prophet himself), were chosen because of their strong commitment to God, and the reasons for living a righteous life—to bring spirits into the world, as explained in Chapter 3. The women, at times, were also selected, but only after gaining permission from the "first wife."

Polygamy also offered women the opportunity to have the priesthood (held by a man), available to them. So in many cases, although the primary objective was to bring children into the world, there were cases plural marriage offered certain spiritual protection to women.

Raising one family on the frontier was difficult enough; raising multiple families was exponentially challenging. But those men and women who practiced polygamy, did so under strict obligation to God. There were no free-for-alls in the bedrooms.

The Roots of Polygamy

In the old days—the *really* old days—we know that men such as Abraham, Adam, and the other great voices of the Old Testament, took many wives, primarily for the purpose of increasing their posterity. Of course, the winner of prolific propagation was King Solomon, who had a mind-boggling 700 wives and 300 concubines. One might wonder how he could manage a kingdom, let alone an average of one woman for every eight hours, over an entire year. And just imagine all the in-laws he had to deal with!

The law of plural marriage was introduced to Joseph Smith by revelation in 1831, but not publicly acknowledged by the Church until 1852. Less than 2 percent of the people in the Church actually practiced plural marriage, and all had to be "called"—or spiritually selected—to be permitted to take more than one wife. In many cases older women who were unable to take financial care of themselves were brought into non-sexual roles in a plural marriage for the purpose of sustaining their own lives and receiving the blessings of having a priesthood holder to watch over them. Again, it's worth pointing out that this took place only under special circumstances as directed by the prophet, and only if the first wife agreed to the arrangement.

There are many people in the Church who have also noted that by introducing the law of plural marriage, the leaders of the Church staved off any potential problems associated with prostitution, due to the lopsided ratio of women to men. And certainly, there was no plan for women to have multiple husbands. This was a matter concerning priesthood availability and child propagation.

Whatever the reason, the notion that one man could be permitted to live and lay with more than one lawfully wedded companion enraged the traditional value system of the Christian world. With the introduction of polygamy, now outsiders saw the Latter-day Saints as stealing their land *and* their women.

And It Came to Pass

During the time when polygamy was sanctioned by Church leadership, those men selected to participate had to be interviewed and found worthy, both in spiritual character and moral fitness. Also, the man's first wife had to approve of his involvement in the program. When additional wives were brought into the family circle, they referred to each other as "sister wives." According to historical accounts, many of these arrangements produced righteous and strong children and were wonderful experiences for the Saints who participated. That's not to say occasional jealousy and bickering didn't occur among the multiwife homesteads. (I live with six girls and one wife, so I imagine it would have been quite an experience living with *six* wives!)

Government Mandates: One Man, One Wife

In response to what society had branded as an outrageous and hedonistic lifestyle by the Latter-day Saints, the Federal government introduced two pieces of law to address plural marriage.

Morrill Act (1862)

The Morrill Act, which was signed into law by President Lincoln, allowed the United States to cancel the citizenship of anyone who practiced plural marriage. Since the majority of members of the LDS Church were immigrants from other countries, they stood a great chance of not only losing citizenship, but also of being deported. Also, the Church was at risk of having its properties seized.

However, while the Latter-day Saints were in the West, settling the Salt Lake Valley, President Lincoln and the rest of the country had become preoccupied with a greater problem: the Civil War. Consequently, the Morrill Act was never heavily enforced, and a small number of Latter-day Saints continued to live with their divine belief that if one wife was good, many were divine.

Edmunds-Tucker Act (1882)

Twenty years after the Morrill Act, the LDS community found itself again under the scrutiny of the Federal government. The Utah Territory had come a long way since Brigham Young had led his people out of the wilderness and into the valley.

However, the nation had defined certain principles as being moral, and having more than one wife was definitely not part of the American charter. At least that's what everybody but the Latter-day Saints thought. Again, to the Saints, their Church leadership had reaffirmed polygamy as being both constitutional under the First Amendment, and a work of divine principle.

The Edmunds-Tucker Act prohibited "unlawful cohabitation" between one man and more than one woman. Whether married or not, the mere fact that more than one woman lived with the same man was enough to get everybody a free ride to jail, and their voting rights stripped.

Many polygamists went into hiding to avoid arrest. They still believed that their cause should be protected by the Constitution as an expression of their religious belief. But Congress, the United States Supreme Court, and most of the nation never agreed.

To the cynics, visiting with God in a forest was one thing, and maybe possible. Even discovering the record of an ancient people under a rock on a hill in New York was farfetched but still believable. But the idea that God had authorized a man to wed and bed more than one woman at a time? "No way!" said an angry nation.

The Manifesto

On April 7, 1889, Wilford Woodruff was selected as the third president and prophet of the Church. One of his first orders of business was to seek divine counsel to clear up the conflict that plural marriage had caused between God's children and the nation in which they lived. Woodruff soon ceased the practice of bringing the one-to-many marriage to the altar.

That following September, Woodruff issued a formal statement called the "Manifesto," which proclaimed an end—or rather, more of a *suspension*—to the practice of plural marriage. According to many historical accounts, there was a transition period in which additional marriages were practiced for a very short time that followed, and there were many hurt feelings and even personal family devastations over the matter. But the majority of obedient Saints heeded their prophet's counsel and stopped the practice. Some accounts say that after the Manifesto, husbands continued to offer financial and spiritual support to their extra wives and children, but remained intimate only with their first wives.

There are many Saints today who still believe polygamy is a divine principle, one that will be restored after the Lord's Second Coming, but which needed to be removed from the world out of necessity to live among the nonbelievers of this divine principle.

> **Words of Wisdom**
>
> I now publicly declare that my advice to the Latter-day Saints is to refrain from contracting any marriage forbidden by the law of the land.
>
> —Prophet Wilford Woodruff, from his Manifesto, 1889

Modern-Day Polygamists Are *Not* Latter-day Saints

So where do we stand today?

There are thousands of people throughout Canada, the western United States, Mexico, and in tribes in Africa and the Middle East, who still practice plural marriage. In fact, the State of Utah has mini-communities, who openly defy national bigamy laws. It's usually not until somebody tries to marry their own 14-year-old cousin, or someone is forced into a plural marriage, that state officials become publicly involved. But in this country, polygamy has been legally prohibited since the days of Abraham Lincoln. However, with the onset of the Civil War, polygamy wasn't actively enforced for several years. Pressure was put on the early Saints to abandon the practice as they moved closer to forming a state.

My wife and I were married in the Salt Lake Temple. Although polygamy hasn't been practiced in the LDS Church for more than 100 years, it remains a topic of interest to Church members and nonmembers alike.

©Drew Williams (2002)

For the most part, these multiwife one-husband households are ignored in Utah. But since this book offers a fundamental understanding of Mormonism, it's worth mentioning again: *None* of the people who are involved in plural marriages anywhere in the world are members of the LDS Church. Although these communities might read the Book of Mormon, practice LDS-based principles, and claim to have their own version of some type of priesthood, *they are not Latter-day Saints*. There are no such things as "Mormon factions." People are either members of the LDS Church or not.

But that's not to say that today's members of the LDS Church don't have strong opinions about the practice of plural marriage. Many Church members still believe it to be a divinely inspired practice and a principle of eternal living whose time is premature for current society. But whether they think so or not is irrelevant. Members of the LDS Church are obedient to God's laws, as defined by his leaders and by the civil laws of the communities in which they live. Although there have always been rumors of Latter-day Saints continuing to practice plural marriage, according to the statements made by LDS leaders, no plural marriage has been performed in the LDS Church since before Utah was made a state in 1896.

Marriage for Modern Times

As I'll discuss further in Chapters 24 and 26, marriage is the centerpiece of the LDS culture. Nothing can happen in God's plan without providing a vehicle by which his spirit children can come to the earth (as explained in Chapter 4).

For the LDS community, being lawfully wed, a Latter-day Saint man with a Latter-day Saint woman, God's eternal plan can be brought to fruition.

Generally, although the decision to have children is left to the couple and not the Church, Latter-day Saint families tend to be larger in numbers than the traditional 2.3 children households of America. You'll read more about the LDS principles behind families in Chapter 24.

Latter-day Laughter
Several years ago, my wife Carol and I were at a restaurant in Provo, Utah. A couple behind us was also waiting to be seated. Following a brief conversation, we invited them to join us. Almost immediately after the four of us sat down, the man told us that it was their first time in Utah. He looked around at the crowded restaurant and said in a low voice, "I wonder how many people in here are *Mormons*." Without letting on that my wife and I were LDS, I told him there were probably quite a few. He asked, "Do you think that if I moved here, they'd let me have more than one wife, too?" Apparently, not everybody knows Latter-day Saints stopped practicing polygamy more than 100 years ago!

Ever since the abandonment of polygamy in 1890, the shadow of that unique trait has hung over Mormonism. Many people inside the Church find it amazing that something, which was practiced by only a handful of Saints and ended more than a century ago, could leave such a strong social residue on a Church or its nearly 12 million members.

For Latter-day Saints, polygamy is just another peculiarity of popular discussion. But to the descendants of those plural marriages, it was a divine principle, albeit long before its time.

The Least You Need to Know

- Polygamy was originally a divine principle established to bring children of God to the earth.

- Only righteous LDS men and women were "called" to practice plural marriage.

- The Morrill Act of 1862 and the Edmunds-Tucker Act of 1882 were introduced to address plural marriage and quell public outrage over the practice.

- Polygamy among members of the LDS Church ended more than 100 years ago, with Prophet Wilford Woodruff calling for an end to the practice in his Manifesto.

- Some people still practice plural marriage today, but they're *not* Latter-day Saints.

Chapter 19

A Woman's Place

In This Chapter

- The many and varied roles of women in the Church
- The world's largest women's organization: the Relief Society
- The calling of "wife"
- Sustainers of the priesthood

Many people outside the LDS Church would offer a quick definition of the LDS woman's place: the home. And they wouldn't be all wrong. A recent proclamation to the world issued by LDS president Gordon B. Hinckley and the Quorum of Twelve Apostles asserts that an Latter-day Saint woman's prime responsibility is the nurturing of her children.

However, if a composite snapshot of women from the worldwide Church of Jesus Christ of Latter-day Saints were assembled, it would sparkle with variety: single women and widows, business owners and doctors, artists and athletes, and of course mothers and grandmothers.

The LDS Church embraces the leadership and wisdom of all women—single or married, mothers and the childless. Women of the Church are taught from their youth that man is not complete without woman, that women and men are equal in the eyes of God. Women, as well as men, are individual agents responsible for the lives they lead. Every person is accountable to God.

"O Woman, Great Is Thy Faith"

I love righteous women. I was raised by good women (my grandmother and mother). Even at my last duty station while in a so-called "Man's Navy," I worked mostly with women. I can't escape them. My exposure seems to have increased over time. Now, after 17 years of marriage, I live in a house with seven females, ranging in age from 5 to 43. Even our mailman is a woman!

It's a good thing, though, to be surrounded by so many daughters of God. One thing I have learned, however, is that if any man says he completely *understands* women, he's lying. No man can—we're not women, and our roles in life are much different.

When I was compiling the outline to this book, I realized that the best person to write a chapter about women in the Church would be a woman in the Church. With that in mind, I enlisted the help of my friend Erika. I think what you'll gain here is a firsthand understanding that women are not a lesser species than men, and that they share in all of God's gifts. In fact, man cannot obtain exalted glory without the enduring strength of the woman with whom he will stand throughout eternity.

> **Words of Wisdom**
>
> I know God will not give me anything I can't handle. I just wish that He didn't trust me so much.
> —Mother Theresa

The Roles of Women

LDS doctrine teaches that gender is determined long before mortal birth. The flashing, random connections of X and Y chromosomes are not what decide gender. Rather, it is taught that both men and women have an "eternal identity." Each spirit or soul is male or female—from the beginning to the end—eternally. This infinite gender carries with it a corresponding purpose. Women in the Church have responsibilities and expectations that are uniquely theirs.

The belief in an eternal gender lends importance to the LDS woman's role—the part she plays in the grand orchestra of life. Church leaders teach that it should not disturb either men or women that some responsibilities are bestowed upon one and not the other. Each woman born to earth has a divinely appointed purpose. First and foremost is the role of mother. A tremendous emphasis is placed on caring for children. Young women are taught from childhood to revere the position of matron in the home. They are taught that serving in one's own home is a higher spiritual calling than that of any other.

To some critics of the Church, this seemingly inordinate emphasis on the care of children is sometimes misconstrued as oppression—that LDS women are barefoot-and-pregnant slaves who bake cookies and change diapers all day. In modern times, however, this could not be further from the truth. The LDS Church indeed esteems motherhood as the ultimate contribution, but also values other accomplishments made by women. Women's roles, while focusing on home and family, expand to include a priority on college education, a charge to teach and support community affairs, and a call to serve as missionaries or teachers in the Church.

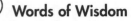 **Words of Wisdom**

A man is a great thing upon the earth and through eternity; but every jot of the greatness of man is unfolded out of woman.

—Walt Whitman, U.S. poet

And It Came to Pass

Minerva Teichert, one of 10 children, was born August 28, 1888, in Ogden, Utah, and was raised on an Idaho ranch. Minerva was taught to appreciate good art and music at an early age by her parents. At 14, she worked as a nanny for a wealthy San Francisco family, which exposed her to great works of art. She eventually graduated from the Art Institute of Chicago. After serving an LDS mission, Minerva settled with her husband in Idaho, and painted many historical accounts of the LDS culture. Today, Minerva's art can be seen in LDS temples, and fetch a high price at galleries throughout the country.

With the Church's worldwide membership, it would be impossible to broad-brush LDS women into one role. The female ranks of the Church include scientists, doctors, businesswomen, and educators. There are mothers, grandmothers, single women, and the childless. LDS women write books, create art that challenges souls for generations, and compose music. Others make just as significant an impact on humanity by their educated influence on their own sons and daughters within their homes.

Sisters in Action: The Relief Society

Picture a woman hauling a handcart across miles of desert nothingness. It's hard to imagine life for the women of the early LDS Church. But out of these hard times came what is now the world's largest women's organization: the Relief Society.

All adult women in the LDS Church are members of the Relief Society, which was founded in 1842. The minutes of those initial meetings are filled with accounts of how the sisters found work opportunities for the needy, took in the homeless, and made donations of food, shelter, and schooling.

The Relief Society was organized upon the initiative of the LDS women of Nauvoo, Illinois. These women of the early Church wanted to organize a society to strengthen the women of the Church, and to accomplish charitable works.

Today the Relief Society continues to accomplish charitable works, with its key purpose being the spiritual development of women. It also provides opportunities for leadership for adult women of the Church. Like all other Church positions, leadership is volunteer in the Relief Society; it comprises a president, two counselors, and a secretary. Working under the Relief Society president and her counselors are a number of volunteer committees that accomplish monthly meetings, organize visiting teaching, and provide Sunday lessons.

Here's just one example of their good works. My LDS friend went into early labor, completely unprepared for the new baby and the time spent away from her family. There was no one to care for their three-year-old son while her husband worked. He made one phone call to the Relief Society leader in their Church congregation. Within hours, members provided on-call service as babysitters. With apparitionlike grace and speed, women from the Relief Society set up the crib, washed and arranged baby clothes—then quietly disappeared. Meals were delivered for several weeks. Relief Society sisters cleaned my friend's house and mowed her lawn while her husband worked. With one phone call to the Relief Society, wheels of a great service machine were set in motion, blessing my friend in her time of need.

Most congregations also have one or two women who act as "compassionate service" leaders. These women give a whole new meaning to charitable service as they meticulously track Church members' major life events such as childbirth, hospitalizations, and deaths, to be prepared to coordinate assistance in times of need. Almost magically, the compassionate service leaders orchestrate a relief effort on behalf of sisters in need that could rival the Red Cross.

It is within the organization of the Relief Society that women in the LDS Church accomplish extensive service projects. The Relief Society is credited with producing mass quantities of items needed for worldwide disaster relief—goods ranging from food and clothing, to leper bandages and infant care kits.

> **Mormon Myths**
>
> *Myth: LDS women are not allowed to wear pants.* While LDS women are encouraged to dress modestly and wear skirts and dresses to Sabbath services and to the temples, there is no restriction about wearing pants in the house or anywhere else—they certainly do in mine!

> **Latter-day Laughter**
>
> A cheese-topped, hash-brown casserole affectionately called "funeral potatoes" is a staple at LDS funerals. It's traditional in many areas for the women's Relief Society to provide, cook, and serve for funerals in the congregation, and like the manna that fed the wandering Israelites of old, funeral potatoes always seem

These supplies are distributed through the LDS Church Welfare Program to people in need all over the world regardless of religion.

In addition to providing disaster relief, the women in Relief Society take on projects that are tailored to their specific community needs. In some areas, Relief Society sisters teach classes to combat adult illiteracy and teach English as a second language for immigrants. In other regions, sisters are instructed in subjects as varied as self-defense and automobile maintenance. (You'll learn more about the Relief Society in Chapter 22.)

Behind Every Good LDS Man ...

The LDS Church teaches that no man or woman is complete without the other. As the Apostle Paul taught in the Bible, "Neither is the man without the woman, neither the woman without the man, in the Lord." Thus a common goal of the men's priesthood quorums and the women's Relief Society is to bring people together in sacred marriage—and then to improve and enhance existing marriage relationships.

Why the emphasis on marriage? Mormonism teaches that the "new and everlasting covenant of marriage" (which is discussed further in Chapter 26), is the key to the highest level of exaltation after death. The covenant of marriage in the LDS temple opens the door to eternal life with God and Jesus Christ.

This should be especially interesting to those who stress equality between the genders, based on the following two points:

   ◆ Eternal life with God, the ultimate blessing of the priesthood, is not available to a worthy holder of the priesthood (a man) who stands alone in the world.

   ◆ A righteous LDS man must be sealed in eternal marriage to a woman who is as worthy as he is.

This significant doctrine demonstrates the interdependence and equality of men and women in the eyes of God. Neither individual can achieve exaltation without the other.

No "Shotgun Weddings" Allowed

Does this mean that LDS women are pressured into marriage to achieve some kind of reward in the next life? Moreover, are single women considered less worthy than those who are married? No.

The Church recognizes that God is a God of love and justice, and would not deny his children eternal reward for lack of opportunity. LDS women are encouraged to develop themselves spiritually, educationally, even professionally, and then to seek a righteous companion who has put the same effort into self-development. It is considered better to not marry at all than to marry a man who will not honor sacred covenants.

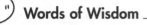

Words of Wisdom

There can be no heaven without righteous women.

—Prophet Spencer W. Kimball

Because of the emphasis on eternal families, half-member marriages—that is, marrying outside the LDS faith—are very difficult to manage in the LDS culture. Husbands cannot be sealed to wives, and children cannot be sealed to parents. The good news, though, is that if an LDS person does meet someone with whom they wish to share eternity, there's always those missionaries!

Barefoot and Pregnant? Not!

The LDS Church does not dictate a married couple's decisions on procreation. Church members are well-known for their large families, filling minivans and chapels with crews of Cheerio-toting youth. This tendency toward a generous-sized posterity, however, is more of a cultural phenomenon inside the LDS community rather than a doctrinal one. The LDS Church has made its position on families perfectly clear—the family is the most important unit in the Church, and it's up to the husband and wife to decide how many children comprise that family unit.

Prophet David O. McKay has said, "No success [in any field of endeavor] can compensate for failure [to lead righteously] in the home." That emphasis on the value of family life, along with the Church's teachings on women nurturing their children at home, contributes to large families.

Mormon Myths

Myth: LDS women are commanded to have as many children as possible. While Church leaders promote family and the rearing of children, there is no such thing as a "child quota." Those astounding families with a lot of children are the result of their desire for a large family, not church policy.

Ultimately, however, the weighty decisions surrounding child rearing—how many? how often? at what stage in life?—are decisions made between husband and wife, with inspiration from God.

The use of birth control is a woman's personal choice, not dictated by Church policy. However, husband and wife are encouraged not to postpone childbearing for reasons such a finances, schooling, or convenience. Rather, couples are encouraged to pray together for inspiration, adding God to their union. The Church teaches that women will be blessed as they sacrifice for their children. Through faith, growing LDS families find ways to sustain their lives.

Women and the Priesthood

In the Church, males hold the office of the priesthood while women are asked to sustain this priesthood. This is a grossly simplified description, but opens the door for discussion on what it means for women to sustain the priesthood in the LDS church.

Women have not, do not, and most likely will not hold the priesthood in the LDS Church. God gave the priesthood to the men and the baring of children to the women. That's doctrine, and it hasn't changed since the Jews wandered through the desert, Jesus walked the earth, and the Saints rolled into Utah. Lobbying for a change is not allowed.

Sometimes people in the LDS church casually refer to an entire group of men as "the priesthood," as if the *men* and *priesthood* mean the same thing—which they do not. For instance, a few select men occasionally attend a ward Relief Society meeting as part of their own assignments, perhaps to make an announcement pertinent to the sisters of the congregation. The sister conducting the meeting might say, "We welcome our priesthood guests here today."

This may be a kind gesture to recognize the men in attendance, but it doesn't mean the men stand in a position of authority in Relief Society meetings. "Sustaining the priesthood" does not mean that a woman or anyone in the Church is obligated to defer direction to men who are not their priesthood-appointed leaders. Rather, it means recognizing the men who have been established as having official responsibility or stewardship over a congregation, class, or organization. In the LDS Church, for example, women are called to be presidents and counselors in all Relief Societies, but are given spiritual advice and direction from a member of the Bishopric.

And It Came to Pass

One of my female friends was a missionary for the LDS Church in Quebec. Her experience in a mostly male-dominated arena gave her the chance to understand the LDS woman's relationship to the priesthood. At first, she resented reporting to 19-year-old male missionaries who were up to two years her junior. However, as her mission progressed, she saw the change that took place in the boys. She watched as these teenagers, challenged by their leadership responsibilities, evolved from immature boys to honorable, mature men (in most cases). Meanwhile, as an older sister missionary, she was free from some of the administrative duties of the priesthood, to do what she had come on a mission to do: Teach the people.

Some people incorrectly believe that LDS theology teaches that only men can receive divine revelation or hold positions of authority in the Church. On the contrary, a woman can be a priesthood-appointed leader, as in the case of a Relief Society or Young Women president. Women can also receive personal revelation and revelation for their families and church assignments. In fact, many members of the church say that women are more "naturally" in tune with the whispers of revelation than are men. However, when anybody is called to an office or job in the LDS Church, it is by direction of the Holy Ghost, and under the direction of the priesthood.

Duties of the priesthood are delegated to men and are patriarchal. *Blessings* from the priesthood are available to every righteous woman and man. Every member of the Church may receive the Holy Ghost, obtain personal revelation, and be endowed in the temple (see Chapter 24 for more about Patriarchal Blessings). The power of the priesthood heals, protects, and inoculates all of the righteous—women and men—against the powers of darkness. Most significantly, the highest priesthood ordinance—that of marriage in the LDS temple—can be received by only a man and woman together.

The Least You Need to Know

- Women play an important role in the LDS Church. There is a place for *every* sister in God's kingdom.

- The Relief Society sisters respond with flexibility and diversity to the needs within their local congregations and around the world.

- There is no greater calling for an LDS woman than that of wife and mother.

- While only men can hold the office of priesthood, women hold many positions of authority in the Church.

Chapter 20

Restoration of the Priesthood

In This Chapter

- ◆ The priesthood: the power to act in God's name
- ◆ The preparatory Aaronic Priesthood
- ◆ The Melchizedek Priesthood
- ◆ Apostles: special witnesses of Christ
- ◆ Open to all worthy LDS men

The holy priesthood has the power and authority to act in God's behalf in all things. For worthy Latter-day Saint men, the privilege of holding the priesthood (in other words, having some portion of priesthood office and authority), means being able to give blessings to family members, conduct the business of the Church, and participate in temple ordinances. LDS belief is that when the men of the Church act in the name of the Lord, they are actually doing the work of God himself.

Worthiness is based on an interview between the individual and the local Church authority. Matters including moral conduct, spiritual integrity, honesty, and Church attendance are considered when discussing worthiness.

In the LDS Church, the priesthood is broken into two divisions: the Aaronic Priesthood—or preparatory priesthood—and the Melchizedek Priesthood.

There are different offices within each priesthood body, which include deacons, teachers, priests, elders, and so on. In this chapter, we'll examine the various offices and functions of both priesthoods, and how they affect Latter-day Saint living.

A Priesthood to Lead God's Church

According to Latter-day revelation, from the days of Adam until the death of the last of Christ's apostles, the priesthood of God existed on the earth. Throughout each of the seven dispensations of man's history (discussed in Chapter 4), God's leaders became priests in order to conduct the affairs of God's kingdom.

> **Words of Wisdom**
>
> The rights of the priesthood are inseparably connected with the powers of heaven, and that the powers of heaven cannot be controlled nor handled only upon principles of righteousness.
> —Doctrine and Covenants 121:36

The duties and responsibilities included in the priesthood are designed to match specific aspects of Church law. For example, when a young man reaches the age of 12, and following a worthiness interview with his local leader. He will receive responsibilities for a portion of the Aaronic Priesthood, in which he will serve for approximately two years; after that, he will gain another portion of priesthood responsibility. He will continue to receive more responsibilities until he prepares for a mission and becomes an elder in the Melchizedek Priesthood—usually at the age of 19.

Sound complicated? Think of a man attaining various offices in the priesthood as if he were running for public office. Perhaps early in his political career, a young man who has a good understanding of the law, might run for a local position as a city council representative. In no way could he be prepared for the U.S. presidency, having served at such a local capacity. However, over time, the man decides to increase his sphere of influence, and runs for a seat in his state congressional district. Perhaps after a time of success in that capacity, he attains one of those coveted seats in the U.S. House of Representatives, or maybe the Senate. In doing so the man is gaining valuable experience, while increasing his responsibilities to the people for whom he serves.

> **And It Came to Pass**
>
> An "office" in the priesthood includes deacons, teachers, elders, and high priests. Worthy male members of the Church are ordained to these offices, based on worthiness and spiritual maturity. However, there are many positions within priesthood leadership pertaining to administering the business of the LDS Church. For example, a deacon may be called to serve as a counselor within his group—or quorum—of deacons, and an elder may be called to serve as a secretary within a bishopric—a level of local Church leadership.

In the LDS Church, the priesthood is bestowed upon all worthy male members who are at least 12 years old. Their responsibilities in various priesthood functions depend much on their level of spiritual maturity. Here, a deacon in the Aaronic Priesthood visits a Church member's home to collect donations for the needy, called "fast offerings."

©Drew Williams (2002)

There are many similarities between the political analogy and the priesthood. As the young man matures and continues to be worthy of Church responsibilities, he is given small levels of increased duties in the priesthood. He takes one small step, masters it, and moves up a notch.

Unlike the political analogy, however, a man is not elected to any office in the LDS Church, and he certainly doesn't (or shouldn't) aspire to any office. The priesthood of God is bestowed upon worthy LDS men who have demonstrated a capacity for understanding the priesthood, and are willing to perform their duties as prescribed by their respective priesthood office.

The sole requisite for holding any priesthood office is worthiness of the individual. Whether he is actually called to a position in the priesthood depends on inspiration from his Church leader.

The Aaronic Priesthood

The Aaronic Priesthood, which is also referred to as the lesser or Levitical Priesthood, is the preparatory priesthood. The priesthood was named after the Old Testament evangelist, Aaron, who served as Moses "spokesman." Holding the Aaronic Priesthood means that the man is preparing to administer the sacred blessings and duties of the Melchizedek Priesthood, which contains the fullness of God's priesthood. The fullness of the priesthood means that a man can officiate in all of the ordinances associated with spiritual government, direction and welfare of the body of the Church. For example, presiding over meetings, performing sacred temple work (like marriages), and serving missions, all require the Melchizedek Priesthood.

God established the Aaronic Priesthood during the time of Moses to preside over the law of "carnal commandments" (Mosaic Law). These laws, which were given to Moses on the Mount of Transfiguration, provided fundamental guidelines for God's children. According to the account in the Book of Numbers, just about every descendant of the House of Levi eventually received this priesthood. As such, Aaron and his sons were included in the list of those selected, and his name has since become synonymous with this priesthood.

For movie fans, the most visual reference of the priesthood of Aaron comes from the annual Easter showing of the Cecil B. DeMille classic *The Ten Commandments*. The powerful stature of Moses was portrayed by Charleton Heston, with his deep resonating voice. "Let my people go" never sounded so convincing! However, ancient scripture notes that Moses was actually a soft-spoken, somewhat introverted man, and it was his older brother, Aaron, who did most of the talking—although under the direction of Moses.

In the LDS Church, the Aaronic Priesthood includes the offices of deacon, teacher, priest, and bishop. The bishop also serves as the local president of the Aaronic Priesthood.

To discuss the various steps of the LDS priesthood holder, let's use my friend Ben as an example. We'll watch as he progresses through the ranks of both the Aaronic and Melchizedek priesthoods.

Deacons: Guardians of the Sacrament

I remember when I brought my Baptist parents to their first LDS church service. They were not quite sure what to think of the young deacons, who were between the ages of 12 and 14, walking down the aisles, passing plates from row to row. My dad was curious: How could these young boys be serving in a church in the capacity of deacon? I later explained that, aside from matters concerning actual priesthood authority, the LDS definition of a deacon and the Baptist definition are probably not as different as Dad might think. We just start ours out a little earlier in life.

As deacons, my friend Ben and the rest of the LDS boys his age are the youngest priesthood holders in the Church. Their most important role is performed during the Sunday service, when they line up in white shirts, stand as the sacrament prayers are read, and then proceed to pass the trays of bread and water through the congregation. Many LDS parents—including Ben's—take pleasure in seeing that for a few moments each week, the squirms and stirs of these emerging teenage boys can stay under control.

The Role of Teacher

As Ben gains experience and responsibility, he won't be excused from prior offices that he has held. For instance, when Ben turned 14, he was called to the office of a teacher, but was still invited to pass the sacrament along with the deacons. As a teacher, Ben was given the added responsibility of preparing the sacrament, which means he prepared the table on which the sacraments are placed, and filled the cups of water.

Ben also assisted his dad as a "home teacher" (discussed in Chapter 22), whose role it is to look after assigned families from within his congregation.

In the LDS Church, young men become involved in priesthood responsibilities beginning around the age of 12. From 12 to 14, a young man serves as a deacon (depending on his worthiness, as determined by his local Church authority). Likewise, he serves as a teacher from 14 to 16, and from 16 to 19, the young man serves as a priest.

Latter-day Laughter

While driving his dad's truck, 16-year-old Spencer received a speeding ticket. Knowing he was in trouble for getting the ticket—especially while driving Dad's car—Spencer reminded his dad about the day's Sunday school lesson: "Today, we talked about the fairness and patience of the Prophet Joseph Smith and we all agreed to live by his standards, setting an example for others." His father replied, "That's wonderful news, son, and to help you, you'll be walking to school for the next week, just like Joseph did when he was your age."

The Duties of the Priest

When Ben turned 16, he became eligible to be ordained to the office of priest, based on his personal worthiness. As a priest, Ben gained the authority to administer the sacrament prayers, and was also eligible to perform baptisms, as directed by his Church leaders. Ben also could assist the full-time missionaries in their work, in preparation for his own mission call, which will come when he turns 19. After his mission, Ben might go on to become a bishop, maybe even a Church Authority—depending on what the Lord decides for him. But Mormonism teaches that Ben will not (or should not) aspire to become anything in the Church other than a righteous husband, father, and neighbor.

Priests' responsibilities as senior members of the Aaronic Priesthood provide them with the experience necessary to prepare for the Melchizedek Priesthood.

The Bishops: Judges in Israel

In the LDS Church, the bishop is usually the local seat of authority on all matters pertaining to Church function. He leads a local congregation—called a ward—which is based on membership population in a designated area. There is no age requirement for a person to be called to the office of bishop. This calling, like the rest of the all-volunteer Church leadership, depends on divine inspiration. Also, no one in the LDS Church gets paid for a position that is held.

The bishop of the ward is part father figure, counselor, coach, sounding board, and judge. He is called by inspiration, at the direction of the general leadership of the Church in Salt Lake City, called the First Presidency (discussed later in this chapter), or someone directed by them. In this capacity, the bishop serves as the presiding high priest of the ward, and is president of the priest's quorum. The bishop has the responsibility of all spiritual matters concerning the hundreds of members of his ward. As with all of the local leadership callings, the bishop serves and receives no financial compensation of any kind for his time and effort.

> **Latter-day Laughter**
>
> How do you choose a bishop? Search for the most righteous, beloved, spiritual giant in the stake and call her husband.
>
> —Anonymous

The following list highlights only some of the responsibilities of the LDS bishops:

- Conduct and preside over all ward functions
- Supervise all local callings and appointments
- Make recommendations as to who is worthy to be called as full-time missionaries
- Perform priesthood blessings and counsel ward members

The bishop has certain abilities that come with his office, that entitle him to receive personal revelation in behalf of each member of his ward. The book of Titus, in the New Testament, describes the character of a man who would be considered for the role of bishop: "For a bishop must be blameless, as the steward of God; not self-willed, not soon angry, not given to wine, no striker, not given to filthy lucre."

Having the power of discernment, a bishop's job in the Church requires a great deal of time and personal sacrifice, not only from him, but also from his family. Bishops often spend most of their Sundays in Church meetings, and are frequently involved in other Church auxiliary programs, which take place throughout the week.

Perhaps one of the most important roles of the bishops of the LDS Church is that of steward over the Church's welfare program. In this capacity, bishops administer the *fast offerings* donated by local members to provide assistance to those members who are in need. Such assistance almost always includes food, but can also include other types of assistance, such as clothing and limited financial assistance.

> **Mormonology**
>
> **Fast offerings** are the financial contributions a family or individual makes, which represent the amount of money needed to provide two full meals. LDS members are asked to fast at least one day per month—usually the first Sunday—and offer to the Church the funds they would have spent on two consecutive meals.

Bishops are also responsible for the activities that take place within the buildings owned by the LDS Church. All local meetings must be approved by the bishop, and must be part of the Church's sanctioned programs.

Bishops also have the opportunity to meet at least annually with each member of his congregation, to discuss the paying of tithes. During the meeting, called "Tithing Settlement," each individual gives an accounting of his or her status as a full tithe payer. A full tithe represents 10 percent of an individual's financial or personal income over the year. To help with the individual's accounting, the bishop retains a year-to-date report of all contributions made by each person under his stewardship, which he shares with the person during the interview. (I discuss tithing in detail in Chapter 21.)

Whether or not an LDS bishop is successful in his role as steward over a congregation depends not only on his willingness to remain close to the Spirit, but also on the members of the congregation and their willingness to accept him as the Lord's representative. Nobody knows in advance who the next bishop will be. There's no campaign, no lobbying, nothing other than inspiration from God.

> **Mormon Myths**
>
> *Myth: Women are not allowed to lead in the LDS Church.* Women have the right to the same honors and privileges afforded by priesthood blessings as men do, but they may not hold the priesthood. Women do serve in valuable leadership roles throughout the LDS Church, including as members of the various general boards of the Church's auxiliary programs, the women's organization known as the Relief Society, the Young Women's programs, and as leaders in the children's program.

The Melchizedek Priesthood

Let's get back to my friend Ben. The seven years Ben spent in the various offices of the Aaronic Priesthood allowed him to prepare for his role as an elder of the Church, and to get him ready for his calling as a missionary, and future husband and father.

After an interview with his bishop to determine worthiness, 19-year-old Ben received responsibilities of the Melchizedek Priesthood and was ordained to the office of elder. He needed the experience and knowledge of this priesthood before being called on a full-time mission, and prior to entering the temple.

The Melchizedek Priesthood, otherwise known by its formal name of "the Holy Priesthood after the Order of the Son of God," was named for the high priest and king of Salem, Melchizedek, of Abraham's time. Melchizedek lived so obediently to the Lord's commandments that the Apostle Paul noted his deeds in his epistle to the Hebrews. Melchizedek was "made like the Son of God; abideth a priest continually." (Heb. 7:3) The Melchizedek Priesthood is the higher priesthood in the LDS Church. It is the priesthood by which all other authorities and duties are directed.

Although not always, men who are not born into the LDS Church—meaning they are converted to Mormonism at some later time in their lives—often receive the Melchizedek Priesthood after serving as priests in the Aaronic Priesthood for a period of time. This gives them an opportunity to better understand what the priesthood is about, and how it functions in the Church and in LDS families before receiving it for themselves.

The Melchizedek Priesthood includes several important offices. As in the Aaronic Priesthood, men ordained to the various offices in the higher priesthood do not lose their former priesthood functions. For example, when directed by his local leader, an elder in the Church may use his authority as a holder of the Aaronic Priesthood to baptize or to administer the sacrament.

Elders Carry the Word of God

As a 19-year-old man, Ben came a long way since the days of being a squirmy, 12-year-old deacon. Ben became a full-time missionary for the Church of Jesus Christ of Latter-day Saints, and served at his own expense for the 24 months. (I discuss missionaries in Chapter 25.)

As an elder, Ben was authorized to take on these responsibilities:

♦ Preach the Gospel

♦ Pronounce blessings of healing and comfort where needed

♦ Participate in the sacred ordinances of the LDS temples

♦ Serve as a home teacher

♦ Serve in various adult leadership capacities within the Church

High Priests: The Power to Preside

After returning from a successful mission, Ben married, had children, and became a high priest in his local congregation. The role of the high priest in the Melchizedek Priesthood is to serve in presiding responsibilities over the Church. Bishops, for example, although functioning through the Aaronic Priesthood, are high priests.

Once a man is ordained to the office of high priest, he may be called to serve in a variety of leadership capacities, many times throughout his life. A stake president, for example, is responsible for a larger area of Church boundary than what a "ward" congregation includes. Stake presidents preside over 10 to 12 wards, with each ward having a bishop. In the LDS Church, a "ward" represents a local congregation, and where a family or individual lives determines which ward they belong to—you don't get to choose. Check out Chapter 22 for more information on Sabbath Day activities and congregational structure.

I know a man who has served as bishop on two separate occasions, mission president on three occasions, temple president and stake president. And in spite of all his callings in the Church, he *still* managed to help his wife raise their 14 children!

Sound confusing? Let's use a football metaphor. There are two "camps" in God's "NFL": the Aaronic Priesthood, which includes the offices of deacon, teacher, priest, and bishop; and the Melchizedek Priesthood, which includes elders, high priests, patriarchs, and apostles. Each office has its own special responsibilities in the LDS Church. The bishop must hold the higher priesthood (Melchizedek), to preside over the congregation. However, under God's game plan, his *office* (bishop) serves as the presiding high priest in the Aaronic Priesthood.

Patriarchs Provide the Visions of Our Lives

The patriarchs of the Church are high priests who have been selected to provide local congregations with important insight into their lives as Latter-day Saints. The men who serve as patriarchs normally do so for the rest of their lives, or unless they become incapable of serving.

Ben is now the patriarch of his area, which includes several wards. For the rest of his life, Ben's role will be to provide members of the Church with individual Patriarchal Blessings. These special, one-time blessings identify for the receiver his or her lineage in the House of Israel, and highlights his or her personal traits on which he or she may focus throughout life. In Chapter 24, we discuss Patriarchal Blessings in greater detail.

Priesthood blessings, as directed by the Holy Spirit, allow Latter-day Saints to administer to the spiritual welfare of individuals. Anyone can request a blessing. Church membership is not required.

©Drew Williams (2002)

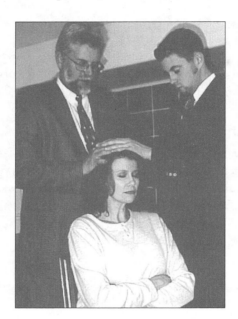

Apostles of the Lord

While Jesus was on the earth, he ordained men to the office of apostle as part of his organizing his Church. Apostleship was passed from man to man, based on authority from Christ himself. Members who had served with Christ, and those who came after, including Paul and Timothy, were called to be the leaders of the Lord's ministry.

The organization of the Church of Jesus Christ of Latter-day Saints is managed and directed by the inspiration of the president of the Church, who is also the prophet of the Church, and with the assistance of his two counselors and the Quorum of the Twelve Apostles. Together, these 15 men—all ordained as apostles—serve not only as the governing body of the Church, but as "Special Witnesses of Christ."

Apostles are members of the Melchizedek Priesthood, who have been selected to serve for the duration of their lives as prophets, seers, and revelators. Although all of the apostles hold the keys of leadership over the entire Church, only the senior ranking apostle holds the authority associated with the position of president and prophet.

There have been 15 presidents of the LDS Church since its organization in 1830. I discuss their lives in Chapters 27 and 28, as well as the life of Church founder Joseph Smith in Chapter 11, and his successor, Brigham Young, in Chapter 16.

> **Mormonology**
>
> **General Authority** is the term used for members of the Quorum of the Twelve Apostles and other selected Church leaders (including members of the Quorum of Seventies and area presidents). Some temple presidents are also considered General Authorities.

All Worthy Male Members May Participate

Although the priesthood at one time excluded men of color, any worthy male member of the Church may now hold the priesthood. This modification to LDS ideology took place in 1978, after the prophet and president of the Church, Spencer W. Kimball, met with other General Authorities in the Salt Lake Temple. This issue stands out as one of the two most debated topics in the LDS Church (the other being polygamy, which is discussed in Chapter 18).

Among Church members, there are many opinions regarding the origins of the ruling that restricted men of color from holding the priesthood. Two scriptural passages are often used in reference to the matter, including Genesis 4:15 (Cain receives a mark to distinguish him and his progeny from the rest of Adam's children), and the Latter-day scripture in 2 Nephi 21. In this second reference, a tribe of people were unwilling to listen to God's commandments, resulting in "the Lord God [causing] a skin of blackness to come upon them."

> **Words of Wisdom**
>
> We have pleaded long and earnestly in behalf of these, our faithful brethren ... supplicating the Lord for divine guidance. ... The long-promised day has come when every faithful, worthy man in the Church may receive the holy priesthood.
>
> —Official Declaration given by LDS Church President Spencer W. Kimball, September 30, 1978

The matter concerning men of color and the priesthood was debated for many years in the LDS Church. In the early 1960s, during the time of change on racial equality throughout the southern states, the LDS Church released a statement in support of equality for all races, without reference to the Church's own position on men of color being forbidden from the priesthood.

The issue is still a difficult topic to discuss, especially for some of those men who were personally affected by it. But for faithful Latter-day Saints—regardless of race—the matter was resolved with President Kimball's revelation in 1978, in which the priesthood was extended to all worthy men of the Church. The Church has since encouraged all of its members to look forward and experience the progress and success of the Church, rather than waste time on matters that no longer warrant attention.

The Least You Need to Know

- The priesthood gives worthy LDS men the power to act in God's name.

- The Aaronic Priesthood, or preparatory priesthood, includes the levels of deacon, teacher, priest, and bishop.

- The Melchizedek priesthood provides the binding power of God's government and leadership.

- Apostles are called to be witnesses of Christ.

- The priesthood is available to all worthy LDS men.

Part 5

Modern-Day Revelation

In this part we examine how, through more than 170 years of struggle, setbacks, and finally settlement, Mormonism has affected our modern-day society. Today, nobody is pushing handcarts along dusty trails or through snowy plains of middle America. No one is roasting buffalo droppings to stay warm. For Latter-day Saints, the hard journey of establishing and raising a righteous culture before the Lord has grown into a highly successful, rapidly growing, worldwide religion.

This part will look at how Latter-day Saints still are very much involved with such ancient commandments as paying tributes to the Lord, honoring the Sabbath Day, walking in faith, raising righteous families, and sharing the Gospel.

Tithing and the Word of Wisdom

In This Chapter

◆ How sacrificing a little brings greater returns

◆ Healthy living doesn't mean shutting out the world

◆ Morality issues: from clothes to sexuality

◆ The abortion question

◆ Striving for spiritual excellence

Latter-day Saints believe in living lives that are rich in good health and success. They don't believe God wants people to wander the world in misery. But to walk in faith that all will be well with them and their families means more than just reading scripture and going to church. Tithing, an ancient commandment from the days of Moses, and the Word of Wisdom, a modern-day revelation on how we should treat our mortal bodies, are significant laws. As long as LDS people live by these commandments, they believe they will be blessed with longevity and personal success.

For almost 180 years, the Latter-day Saints have enjoyed the companionship of what they believe to be God's only true messengers and mouthpieces on the earth—his prophets. Through these great men, they have been counseled to share their material success. As well, LDS people consider the human body to be a temple of the Lord. In these matters, Latter-day Saints believe that what they have is God's anyway—they're just borrowing from him for awhile.

Tithing: Paying "Fire Insurance"

A so-called humorist once wrote that if Latter-day Saints wanted to give themselves a raise, they should just stop paying their *tithing*. This man, I thought, must have never experienced the blessings associated with giving back a tenth of what was already the Lord's in the first place.

Mormonology

Tithing equals 10 percent of anything considered a material "increase" to an individual. For example, if a person makes an annual income of $50,000, then his or her tithing would be $5,000, which is paid to the Church. If he or she wins a car, tithing would equal 10 percent of the value of that car. LDS scripture found in the Doctrine and Covenants, section 64, verse 23, says that those who pay their tithes "will not be burned" at the day of the Lord's return. In a lighthearted sort of way, Latter-day Saints sometimes refer to tithing as paying "fire insurance."

God does not need money. He doesn't need riches of any kind. In fact, I can't think of anything our Heavenly Father needs at all. However, one thing that Latter-day Saints all around the world know that God expects, is obedience to all of his commandments. Latter-day Saints, don't look at obedience to divine law as a hobby. Church members listen to what God says with great attention and reverence. Paying tithing is one of those commandments that is not negotiable.

Paying tithing is so important in the Church that LDS people cannot enter the temple without doing so. But here's the catch—there's no bill generated by the Church. Nobody stands at your door from Church headquarters and force you to pay up. Paying tithing, although a commandment, is still left to the individual.

Tithing constitutes 10 percent of gross earnings, measured on an annual basis. That means 1 out of every 10 dollars goes back to the Lord. For LDS farmers in many countries, 1 out of every 10 chickens, pigs, bushels of grain, or the revenues they produce go to God's work.

Since the days of Moses, the Lord has commanded his people to pay tithes and offerings to him. Such activity has a twofold purpose in the Church. First and foremost, paying tithing affords Latter-day Saints a powerful tool of faith. I could reference scores of experiences in the lives of the LDS people and other Christians throughout history and around the world, whose lives were blessed beyond belief, because they followed this small act of obedience. Second, tithes and offerings are used to fortify the work of the Lord throughout the world. Here are some ways the Church uses these tithes:

♦ To build new chapels and temples

♦ To build the efforts of the missionary program (although missionaries are not paid)

♦ To provide Church education programs

♦ To help with genealogical research

♦ To offer humanitarian service to those in need, as directed by Church leaders

In LDS Church services, there are no plates passed through the congregations to collect tithes and offerings. All tithing is paid privately to local Church leadership, or directly to Salt Lake City. At the close of each Sunday Service, Church leaders make an accounting on a name-by-name basis of the tithes and other offerings made. The entire amount is sent to Church headquarters. Funds are disbursed to local congregations on an as-needed basis.

At the end of every year, each member of the congregation—even the children—have the opportunity to meet with the bishop or branch president, to make an accounting to the Lord. This may sound very "business-like" and in a way it is. Each member of the LDS Church has an obligation to do all he or she can to help others.

> **" " Words of Wisdom**
>
> The time has now come for every Latter-day Saint, who calculates to be prepared for the future and to hold his feet strong upon a proper foundation, to do the will of the Lord and to pay his tithing in full. A part of tithing is no tithing at all.
>
> —Prophet Lorenzo Snow

Just Say No to Drugs (and Coffee, and Tea, and ...)

As I travel throughout the world on business, many of my meetings take place over food. Almost every time, the issue of why I don't order coffee at breakfast, or wine with a meal, or drinks after dinner, becomes a topic of conversation.

The idea that Latter-day Saints don't drink alcohol, smoke or chew tobacco, or take illicit drugs is not difficult for people outside the Church to understand. In fact, many health-conscious people and cultures practice similar habits. Our "peculiarity," however, is often raised when we throw coffee and tea into the list of no-no's.

The LDS dietary guidelines, which is called the Word of Wisdom, are part of Latter-day scripture. This is found in Section 89 of the Doctrine and Covenants. Like tithing, living the Word of Wisdom is a commandment that is taken very seriously. LDS people cannot enter the temple if they do not live the Word of Wisdom.

> ### Latter-day Laughter
>
> There are people who deprive themselves of each and every eatable, drinkable and smokable, which has in any way acquired a shady reputation. They pay this price for health and health is all they get.
>
> —Mark Twain, U.S. writer and humorist

Although the guidelines taught in the Word of Wisdom make good general sense regarding health practices, living by this decree has as much to do with obedience as it does with good health. There are millions of people who smoke, drink, and do whatever, who live to ripe old ages. My great grandfather, in fact, lived to be 99 years old, and he couldn't work a single day without his liquid "buddies," Jack Daniels and Jim Beam.

The Apostle Paul said in Romans, "The kingdom of God is not meat and drink; but righteousness." Latter-day Saints believe that their bodies are "temples of God," as quoted throughout the scriptures. A temple is to be kept clean, pure, and undefiled both inside and out, and so are their bodies. However, living the Word of Wisdom does not give Latter-day Saints a guarantee that something won't go wrong with their health, but it won't hurt them, either.

> ### And It Came to Pass
>
> During the time when towns had wooden sidewalks and shootouts at high noon, the main social establishment was the saloon. One unspoken rule was that saloons were only for men and the occasional "working woman." Saloons were seen as an improper establishment for wives and children. In the late nineteenth century, chemists mixed mild chemicals with carbonated water to create nonalcoholic alternatives to water and milk. Serving these "soft" drinks, the pharmacy's soda fountain became a popular place to socialize for the rest of the family while the menfolk kicked things up at the saloon.

But there is a spirit of the law and a letter of the law, and often, this is where things get fuzzy. The letter of the law states that no hot drinks, such as coffee or tea, should be consumed. However, LDS Church leader Prophet Gordon B. Hinckley was asked by Mike Wallace on a *60 Minutes* broadcast whether he drank soft drinks with caffeine. "No sir, nothing," was his reply. The *spirit* of the Word of Wisdom encompasses consuming anything that might pose the potential for addiction.

Latter-day Saints have been given clear directives on such things as alcohol, coffee, tea, and drugs. The rest is up to the individual and his or her spiritual consideration of what would constitute living the Word of Wisdom. For example, decaffeinated coffee is still coffee.

People outside the Church often assume that our restriction from coffee and tea is due to the caffeine, so chocolate must be taboo as well. Although there may be obvious reasons for not drinking hot drinks like coffee—possibly due to potential health risks—Latter-day Saints take the Word of Wisdom at face value and apply it in faith. But we still bring plenty of heart-shaped boxes home to our favorite ladies on Valentine's Day, and our kids still get sick on Cadbury eggs at Easter.

The Word of Wisdom offers guidelines on other food choices, too. For example, we are to eat meats sparingly. We are to ensure a high content of grains and vegetables are part of our diets.

For many people outside the Church, Latter-day Saints who pay tithing and live the Word of Wisdom do so under great restriction from life's potential choices and social opportunities. For temple-worthy Latter-day Saints, however, there is nothing missed and everything to gain by keeping God's commandments regarding a higher quality of life. I guess it's the Lord's way of saying, "Eat right, live right. Your soul depends on it."

Good Old-Fashioned Morality

Okay, now comes the part where I tell everyone how all Latter-day Saints are short-haired and clean-cut, with white shirts, suits, long flowing dresses, and shiny name tags. Of course, I'm kidding. Actually, this perception is a common stereotype, but not always the case.

We have been counseled by our prophets not to watch R-rated movies. We've been told that earrings (one pair), are for ladies only. We've been advised not to follow the trendy fashions of society, or to succumb, in general, to worldly influences.

So let's look at some of these things Latter-day Saints consider important, which the world may think is *extreme* in self-discipline.

Clothing Fit to Wear

Nobody has ever been criticized for having good taste in attire. But before everybody starts thinking I live in a home that Ward and June Cleaver built, let me assure you, there is a place for tie-dyed clothes, sweatpants, and mascara in LDS homes. (Especially if there are seven women in the house!)

When it comes to morality, the so-called "window dressing" of fashion is considered the first line of defense in maintaining good composure and protecting virtue. Although the matter of what Latter-day Saints wear is highly subjective in LDS households, they again depend on common sense and sound advice from their leaders. One consistent message regarding fashion is "conservative dress." Wearing short shorts, for example, or shirts that expose shoulders and midsections are unacceptable attire.

Simply, Latter-day Saints believe that being well-groomed and modestly dressed invites a spirit of dignity and respect for one's body. (And who really wants to wear skin-tight vinyl pants anyway?)

> **Words of Wisdom**
>
> Never lower your dress standards for any occasion. Doing so sends the message that you are using your body to get attention and approval.
>
> —*For the Strength of Youth* pamphlet (produced by the LDS Church)

Body Piercings and Tattoos

If we're lucky to be born with all of our parts intact, we don't have any extra holes where there shouldn't be, or marks that weren't there in the first place. That pretty much sums up the LDS position on body piercings and tattoos. The exception, according to Church leaders, is that *women* who choose to may wear one pair of earrings—and everyone should leave the permanent brandings to the range cattle. But for people who were converted to Mormonism, tattoos and all, nobody will advise them to see a plastic surgeon to have it (or them) removed. Just don't get any more.

Viewer Discretion Is Advised

Did you know that once we look at something—anything—it stays imprinted in our memories forever? In ancient Greek mythology, Medusa was an evil creature with the head of a woman and hair made of serpents. Legend was that anyone who looked at her ugliness was killed and turned to stone.

One position that the LDS Church has consistently taken is that of intolerance for pornography and immorality and excessive violence in visual entertainment. As with Medusa of old, viewing such things kills the spirit and hardens the heart over time.

LDS people believe there is plenty of alternative entertainment available to the world that doesn't pander to its audiences.

While the media continues to justify the production of so-called "adult entertainment," Mormonism preaches total avoidance of materials deemed even questionable by conservative standards. But based on the rising popularity of morality advocates in our society, and the seeming shift on family focus, one might think that "Mainstream America" is awakening to a new standard.

It's not just the Latter-day Saints who try to live prudently, either. In an Associated Press poll in the early 1990s, 80 percent of those Americans interviewed found the amount of profanity in film to be unacceptable. More than 70 percent of those polled found the current trend in focusing on sexual content to be objectionable. During his leadership as the fourteenth prophet of the Church, President Ezra Taft Benson stressed that Latter-day Saints should not watch R-rated movies due to the excessive profanity, violence, and immoral behavior often shown. And if you think about it, do you know of *any* R-rated movie that doesn't include strong language or depict some level of immoral or graphically violent behavior?

Not the Same Old Song and Dance

One of the most emotional sources of influence comes from the type of music Latter-day Saints listen to. Again, Mormonism takes a highly interpretive position on the matter of what should be deemed "good" and "bad" music.

LDS households aren't just enjoying the Tabernacle Choir and Donny and Marie on eight-tracks in our family rooms. Like fashion, film, and the other issues I've already mentioned, the type of music Latter-day Saints listen to can bring the spirit into their lives, or it can chase it away.

LDS people also believe in "bustin' a move," "cutting a rug," "shakin' it," or whatever the term for dance is these days. Dancing is often a part of LDS courtship. Some have even found their spouses at Church-sponsored dances. Dancing is a popular activity in the Church, however everyone is encouraged to show respect for his or her dance partner, avoid full-body contact, and not engage in suggestive or sexually enticing moves.

What constitutes "good music" can mean anything from a Moody Blues reunion tour to a concert by the National Symphony. Mormonism cautions listening to music containing messages that would discourage strong, moral character in the listener.

But showing care in the choice of music they listen to doesn't mean Latter-day Saints don't rock the house once in awhile either. Heck, although there's not a very strong field of rock veterans, there have been a few LDS musicians in the mainstream, including Randy Bachman (of Bachman Turner Overdrive and The Guess Who), The Jets, and Gladys Knight. Okay, there's the Osmonds, too.

Many people in the LDS Church like to debate who is and isn't a member of the Church in the entertainment industry. In fact, there are whole websites dedicated to this topic! Rocker Alice Cooper, actor Steve Martin, and the cast of the television show *Touched By an Angel* are often part of the "yes-they-are" lists. Alice Cooper (aka Vincent Furnier), the original "Mr. Nice Guy," although a strong family man, was never a member of the Church. Although he might be a "wild and crazy guy," Steve Martin isn't LDS either. And although CBS has filmed every season of *Touched By an Angel* in Utah, none of the cast are "Saints."

The Power of "F" Words

Here are three Latter-day maxims of truth: The word "flip" in conversation is not a verb to describe rotating something in midair, "fetch" is not a retrieval command given to a dog, and "freak" is not a noun used to describe a scary, crazed individual. These are words commonly used as substitutive expletives for the more acidic, infamous "F" word.

Like the rest of the world, Latter-day Saints get angry, too. And, by heck, when they do, they can really throw out the swears! But LDS vernacular is replete with a host of substitutes for the stronger curse words more widely used. They may be poor substitutes for the evil expletive, but they're better than dropping "F-bombs" all over the place.

> **Mormonology** _____
>
> **Choose the Right** is a common phrase among the LDS culture. The term connotes always striving to make good decisions, which result in good consequences. As a reminder of this, many Latter-day Saints throughout the world wear rings with "CTR" (or the language equivalent) engraved on them.

"Yippie-Skippie" is a personal favorite that I got from a dyed-in-the-wool-Baptist-editor friend. This wonderful expletive drips with just enough spice to make it the perfect term to describe anticlimactic moments!

How we speak reflects a great deal about us. People often judge us by the words we choose and how we use them. A strong vocabulary and the ability to communicate in any language are signs of intelligent, well-disciplined people. Mormonism promotes strong character of speech and a command of our language as part of a wholesome, God-loving lifestyle. And although, as I sit here and write this, feeling like such a hypocrite—counting how many times I let those cusswords slip out while on the golf course (all my golf buddies are choking on these words, I'm sure)—I'm trying my dang best to reflect what *good* LDS practices include, by golly!

And It Came to Pass
The thirteenth prophet of the Church, President Spencer W. Kimball, was being wheeled in for throat surgery in a Salt Lake City hospital. The intern pushing his bed became frustrated en route to the operating room, taking the Lord's name in vain. To this the old prophet, half-conscious, lifted himself up and said, "Please don't say that. I love him

Sexuality

Okay, we won't be delving into anything too deep here. Simply, Latter-day Saints believe in the basic standard of *one* girl per boy, no boys-to-boys and no girls-to-girls. It doesn't work with fire hoses, and it doesn't work with people, either. And no, it's got nothing to do with homophobia, and everything to do with God's design. It wasn't Adam and "Dave" in the Garden of Eden. Man was not meant to be alone, so God "made him a woman, and brought her unto the man." (Genesis 2:22)

LDS youth, such as these girls at camp, learn about virtue and morality well before the dating age. They are encouraged to wait to date until about age 16, and are commanded to avoid all sexual activity until after marriage, and then only with their spouse.

©Drew Williams (2002)

Physical intimacy between a husband and his lawfully wedded wife (not "wives"), is ordained by God as a sacred experience, between the two of them (not one, not three—just the husband and wife). It is, in fact, the means by which they bring God's children into the world. Sexual activity of any kind is forbidden outside of marriage; even intimate kissing is discouraged until after the vows. (With that said, refer to Chapter 18 for the discussion on plural marriage—something that hasn't been endorsed by the LDS Church in more than 100 years!)

Abortion and the Right to Live

Throughout the world more than 46 million unborn children are killed each year. Ninety-five percent of all abortions performed, according to Illinois Right to Life, are done so as a means of birth control. Such statistics are staggering to a culture that promotes the very sanctity of life. Such numbers are often devastating to the thousands of families who are not able to conceive or bare children of their own.

> **Words of Wisdom**
>
> I stand in admiration of women today who resist the fashion of abortion, by refusing to make the sacred womb a tomb!
>
> —Apostle Neal A. Maxwell

For Latter-day Saints, unless rape results in a pregnancy or there are life-threatening circumstances to the mother (both are relatively rare), participating in abortion is akin to participating in murder.

Living by God's Rules

LDS ethics for life may seem stringent by other standards. However, members of the Church of Jesus Christ of Latter-day Saints make no apologies for striving to follow all of God's commandments—even if they seem out of step with worldly trends and peer influences.

Latter-day Saints are very much a part of the human family. God sets up the rules, and they try to live by them. But LDS people often fall short of their goals because, essentially, they're imperfect. Latter-day Saints believe that without the atoning sacrifice of Jesus Christ, no one—LDS or otherwise—would have the chance of returning to God. That's why the process of repentance is so important in the Church.

Don't be shocked if you occasionally see LDS males—especially young adults—walking around with a pair of posts or loops in their earlobes. You might hear an LDS guy order a cup of joe, you might even see a Latter-day Saint coming from one of those cinematic no-nos. Remember that we all sin "and fall short of the Glory of God."

In this day and age, some people are still compelled to follow worldly trends. It's not right, but for the most part, Latter-day Saints strive to pursue spiritual excellence in keeping all of God's rules—even on the golf course.

The Least You Need to Know

- Tithing is a 10-percent investment that yields eternal profits.

- Latter-day Saints feel that their bodies are temples and should be respected; addictive substances such as cigarettes and coffee are to be avoided.

- Conservative lifestyles offer Latter-day Saints a broad base of good, wholesome choices in life.

- Unless there are extenuating circumstances such as rape, Latter-day Saints consider abortion akin to participating in murder.

- Latter-day Saints generally shun worldly trends and strive for spiritual excellence in keeping all of God's commandments.

22

Remembering the Sabbath Day

In This Chapter

- ◆ The significance of the Lord's day
- ◆ Sacrament: partaking of the symbols of Christ's atonement
- ◆ Sunday school, quorums, and other functions of the Church
- ◆ The joy of working with the youth
- ◆ The typical stages in an LDS person's church-going life
- ◆ The "ideal" Sunday: what to do (and not do) on the Sabbath

All Christian faiths practice some level of reverence for the Sabbath. It is the day when congregations meet and share spiritual thoughts, read scriptures, and sing hymns to God. Latter-day Saints look at the Sabbath as a time to gain strength to face each new week. For those local Church members who have been assigned various leadership, teaching, and administrative duties, the Sabbath is a busy day, but is still looked upon as a labor of love. Their responsibilities require an earlier start to Sunday activities, by conducting the business of the Church, as well as preparing lessons for the day's three-hour worship service.

For the general congregation, the Sabbath often brings a spiritual retreat as LDS people prepare their families for the day. Because many LDS Sabbath services begin Sunday morning, getting ready for meetings and making sure they have the right lesson plans, the cookies for the nursery, and all of the kids in the minivan on time can be a challenge. But no matter what their involvement in the Church might be, for Latter-day Saints, the Sabbath is the time to renew personal covenants made with God when they were baptized. With that weekly renewal comes a reassurance that they will find the strength to survive another one of those busy work weeks.

Celebrating the Lord's Day

Because Latter-day Saints recognize the Sabbath as being the Lord's day, it's not only an obligation but also a great privilege to enjoy the right to turn away from the world, even if only for a single day. But the Sabbath day and the activities in which Latter-day Saints participate on Sundays share one common theme: remembering the atoning sacrifice of the Savior Jesus Christ, and acknowledging that humanity cannot progress spiritually without recognizing the grace of God in all things.

Sabbath day activities often include formal family gatherings, where each member participates in discussion, song, prayer, or family business matters.

©Drew Williams (2002)

Latter-day Saints believe God is a God of order and runs his kingdom in an organized manner. Similarly, perhaps one of the best examples of order in the Church is demonstrated each Sunday. No matter where you go, Sabbath meetings in the LDS Church all operate the same way and include four core components: Sacrament, adult Sunday school, youth meetings, and Priesthood/Relief Society. These meetings are conducted the same way around the world.

And It Came to Pass

I often travel to other countries with my work, and recall one September when I had the chance to attend Sunday services in Tasmania, Sydney, Utah, London, and Northern Ireland—in that order. I was amazed that in all five cases, the meetings were consistent, even down to the same songs and similar lessons. This consistency is key in maintaining the strong fiber between Church members worldwide. A stranger can enter a chapel 6,000 miles away from home and feel as if he or she is visiting extended family for the first time.

The LDS Church is an unpaid, all-volunteer church—meaning that all of its members are responsible for the spiritual growth, education, and business activities of the Church. With the responsibilities that come with an all-volunteer organization, Latter-day Saints can find Sabbath day activity an invigorating part of life. Participation in Sunday functions is always based on divine inspiration, and includes specific instructions from Church leaders both locally and from Salt Lake City.

The Lord made his plans clear to Moses, as recounted in the Book of Exodus: Remembering the Sabbath day and keeping it holy was not a suggestion. In Genesis, God sanctified the seventh day (at the beginning of his earthly ministry, Jesus changed the Sabbath to the first day of the new week). For Latter-day Saints, the biggest part of sanctifying the Sabbath is during the three-hour worship service. During this time, Latter-day Saints share spiritual instruction, songs of praise, and prayer—all provided by members within the congregation.

Participating in Sabbath services could mean assisting with a special musical number, helping children provide a spiritual thought during a youth meeting, or even providing a portion of the Sunday sermon.

Sacrament

Christian Sunday meetings often include music, prayer, collecting tithes and offerings, and copious amounts of preaching. The *Sacrament* meeting is the single most important event of an LDS Sabbath day observance. This 70-minute period is a time when covenants of baptism are renewed by partaking of the symbols of Christ's atonement, which Latter-day Saints do as part of each week's services.

For those in attendance—both LDS people and members of other faiths—the Sacrament provides the opportunity to remember the atoning sacrifice of Jesus Christ. Although not obligated to do so, all worthy Church members participate by eating a piece of bread and drinking a small cup of water. In the days of the pioneers, Sacrament participants would break the loaves of bread and often pass a single cup from person to person. (What a true test of faith, to drink from the same cup after scores of others!) The bread and water symbolize Christ's body and blood, which all Christian faiths believe were sacrificed for the redemption of man in the Garden of Gethsemane.

Mormonology

The **Sacrament** is a sacred ordinance performed each Sunday, in which Latter-day Saints eat and drink the symbols of Christ's atonement. At the Last Supper, Christ used bread to signify his body, and wine to represent his blood, and talked about how both would be sacrificed for mankind. Latter-day Saints substitute water for wine.

Mormon Myths

Myth: Only Latter-day Saints may take the Sacrament. All attendees of Sacrament services may partake of the symbols of the Lord's atonement (except for members who have been instructed not to). Visitors not of the LDS faith are invited to participate, and often find comfort and a time for spiritual reflection when doing so.

Following brief remarks by a member of the bishopric and after a song and a formal prayer, young men of the Aaronic Priesthood, who have been considered worthy (morally clean, honest, pay their tithing, and so on), pray over the bread and water and pass them to the congregation.

The atmosphere during a Sacrament meeting is solemn and reverent, not loud or full of yelling over the pulpit. The type of reverence demonstrated in Sacrament meetings is more of a time to renew faith in God, meditate on simple messages of faith and obedience, and consider the influence of Christ in the lives of Latter-day Saints.

In some circumstances, members of the LDS Church are not permitted to take the Sacrament due to some form of Church disciplinary action. Such circumstances that might prohibit a Church member from participating would include moral transgression, violating the Word of Wisdom, or some other personal issue that is not in accordance with LDS teachings. In these cases, after a time of repentance, which is decided by Church leadership, the Church member is permitted to again take the Sacrament.

After the prayers and passing of the Sacrament, members of the congregation spend the remainder of the meeting listening to music, presentations on doctrinal principles, and the testimonies of their fellow members. Families sit together and often the feeling of congregational solidarity abounds. This association tends to build close ties among Latter-day Saints, and is fortified through their Sacrament worship.

> ### Words of Wisdom
>
> O God, the Eternal Father, we ask thee in the name of thy Son, Jesus Christ, to bless and sanctify this bread to the souls of all those who partake of it, that they may eat in remembrance of the body of thy Son, and witness unto thee, O God, the Eternal Father, that they are willing to take upon them the name of thy Son, and always remember him and keep his commandments which he has given them; that they may always have his Spirit to be with them. Amen.
>
> —Sacrament prayer for bread

Sunday School: Not Just for Kids

Church buildings buzz with even more activity during Sunday school. Meetings include member participation in a variety of ways, ranging from round-table discussions about marriage and raising families, to acting out stories from Church history for the children. Regardless of the activity, however, Sunday school meetings always follow a plan, which is usually based on a monthly message or year-long teaching schedule.

What makes LDS buildings particularly unique is that they are often shared by two and three different congregations with overlapping meetings. For example, in my church building, another congregation begins its sacrament service at 9:00 A.M., followed by Sunday school at 10:00 A.M., and Priesthood/Relief Society meetings at 11:00 A.M. My congregation conducts meetings along this same cycle, but they begin at 11:00 A.M., and another congregation begins its cycle of meetings at 1:00 P.M. So for several hours, there are always two congregations split up and wandering around in the building at one time. But everyone knows when and where to go, so no one gets lost.

As part of the three-hour weekly service, the Sunday school organization comprises the largest auxiliary within the LDS Church. Families separate into their respective age groups for classes. For young children, Sunday school activities represent the balance of the Sabbath's services (after Sacrament). Older children and adults spend about a third of their time involved in these activities; the other two thirds are spent in Sacrament worship and meetings (which I'll explain in a moment).

Depending on the size of the congregation and availability of resources, adults may be offered a variety of Sunday school classes. Subjects include family preparedness, marriage enrichment, temple attendance preparation, and Gospel doctrine. The Gospel doctrine class is the main attraction for Sunday school participants. It follows a four-year cycle, which includes in-depth study of the Old and New Testaments, Book of Mormon, and Church doctrine and history. Here, the main body of the local congregation that does not have other Sunday school responsibilities, meet together to share testimony and learn the Word of God.

Strong family ties are especially important in the LDS Church like this father and daughter on a picture-taking outing.

©Drew Williams (2002)

Priesthood Quorums

Priesthood *quorums* are essential to all LDS families, and perform some of the most critical functions in the Church. All men in the LDS Church hold some level of priesthood—depending on their worthiness, maturity, and needs of the individual and the Church.

Following a brief opening exercise of song and prayer, members of the priesthood usually separate into their respective groups or quorums, which are defined by their office (elders with elders, high priests together, and so on). If the congregation is not big enough to warrant break-out sessions, the adult men will meet in two groups—elders and high priests—while the younger men get together in a separate meeting.

Quorum meetings follow strict organizational outlines, as provided by Church headquarters. Meetings include instruction on matters concerning leading the family, studying the lives of Church officials, and performing priesthood ordinances—holy functions performed by a person who has been ordained as a worthy priesthood holder in the Church. Such ordinances include offering the Sacrament prayers, administering to the sick, baptizing, and officiating in the blessing of children.

Mormonology

A **quorum** is an organized assembly of men who share the same priesthood (for example, "elders," "high priests," and "deacons"). Quorums comprise the leadership body throughout the Church, with the most senior quorum—the "First Presidency" and "Quorum of Twelve Apostles"—being the governing body of the Church.

The LDS Church is a service-oriented organization. All work pertaining to the spiritual and personal welfare of its members come through the priesthood quorums. During winter months, for example, members of the Aaronic Priesthood will provide coordinated schedules to shovel walkways for the elderly and on Church property. Priesthood meetings often include in-depth discussion about important principles of morality, spiritual success in the workplace or in school, and often invite a spirit of emotion.

And It Came to Pass

Jesus pointed out that watching over each other is a commandment given to all people. He said that by loving and serving our neighbors and friends, we draw closer to him. Such service can come in many different ways. One rainy Sunday morning, my friend found that one of his cattle—a big bull—had escaped his property and was tearing up a neighbor's fence line. With the help of some Church members, and following several soggy hours of slushing through pasture, my friend recaptured the bull. A few weeks later, he hosted a huge barbecue for all of his friends who had helped. The bull was invited as well, to provide the main course.

Quorums typically include a president and counselors; however, the priests' quorum includes a president and two "assistants" who help him. This is because the priests' quorum is always headed by the bishop of the local congregation, who is also the president of the Aaronic Priesthood (see Chapter 20).

Presidencies of all quorums are responsible for activities performed in and by their respective quorums. The idea is that as Latter-day Saints spend time learning about what God expects of them, they will in turn serve him by loving to serve others.

Latter-day Saints truly try to be their brothers' keepers. This example is best demonstrated by the Church's policy on visiting other families within congregational boundaries. The Church's Home Teaching program serves as a vehicle to look after its members. In this program, two members of the priesthood are assigned to a handful of families as home teachers to look after the families' well-being on a monthly basis. When the home teachers arrive, they provide a short message from the First Presidency of the Church, offer prayers, give blessings, or offer other services pertaining to spiritual or temporal needs of the assigned families. The home teachers then make a monthly accounting of these families to their priesthood leaders.

Relief Society

For the women of the Church, the Sabbath day brings the chance to gather part of the time for *Relief Society* services. The oldest women's auxiliary organization in the United States, the Relief Society was organized by LDS Church founder, Prophet Joseph Smith, in 1842.

Designed to offer "relief of the poor, destitute, the widow and orphan," according to Smith's charter, the Relief Society is clearly the cornerstone of the LDS Church's welfare system. Like all of the organizations within the Church, the Relief Society is organized at the congregational level (wards, branches), and includes a president, two counselors, teachers, and other positions as needed. All positions are managed by the sisters within the congregation, but fall under the direction of the local Church leadership.

There have been books written about the many acts of service the Relief Society Sisters have performed. These ladies are often considered as the glue that holds a congregation together during difficult times.

You'll learn more about the Relief Society in Chapter 19, but here's a sample of what Relief Society sisters do:

- Prepare meals for families in crisis
- Gather clothing and supplies for the poor

Mormonology

The principle auxiliary organization within the LDS Church, the **Relief Society** is designed to support, sustain, and extend service by and to the sisters of the LDS community and the welfare of their families—and any others who might require compassionate assistance.

Latter-day Laughter

Q: How many Relief Society sisters does it take to change a light bulb?

A: Four. One to fix refreshments, one to bring the tablecloth, one to design the centerpiece, and one to call the bishop to suggest that a change is necessary.

- Visit the sick, homebound, and less fortunate

- Enrich the lives of the women in their communities

- Organize and administer to members' temporal needs

- Stand as witnesses of God's unconditional love

Because the LDS Church considers the wife to be equal to her husband, both Relief Society and priesthood share the same lesson topics during Sunday meetings; but for the sisters, messages are targeted toward the spiritual and temporal welfare and general "health" within the family. The Relief Society teaches the sisters of the congregation how to support the principles in each lesson, whereas the priesthood brethren learn how to apply those principles in their performance of priesthood responsibilities (discussed in greater detail in Chapter 20).

Many people both inside and out of the LDS community often mention that Latter-day Saints take care of their own. This is true. For example, should an LDS family find itself in times of financial hardship, the Relief Society president—under the direction of Church leadership—will visit the family and assist in itemizing what their personal needs might include, by way of food and clothing. As a follow-up, members may be invited to receive limited temporal assistance from the Church.

The Relief Society is also well connected to community needs. Often, when a crisis such as an earthquake, hurricane, or other catastrophe strikes a region of the world, the Relief Society mobilizes throughout the Church to lend assistance where they can.

During the many conflicts and hardships people faced during the Bosnian conflicts throughout the 1990s, for example, members of the LDS Church were asked to contribute whatever they could to the families and children who were barely surviving in those hostile circumstances. Among the many efforts by the Relief Society's General Board, was the call to all congregations to donate clothing, blankets—even toys—to be supplied to these regions. Within a few weeks, the sisters had to ask that LDS Church members stop contributing, because they couldn't fit anything else on the cargo planes.

Whether collecting blankets or clothing, preparing meals, visiting the sick or elderly, or just picking up the spirits of a neighbor, the Relief Society sisters are always prepared to offer any type of compassionate service they can.

Primary and Youth Meetings

Here's a fun recipe: Take one ordinary LDS chapel. Add a congregation comprised of dozens of children, ranging from age three to twelve, and a handful of adults armed only with Cheerios, chalk, cookies, and course manuals. Next, throw in a couple of people in front of the group, holding big posters—usually depicting Jesus, a temple, and LDS leaders—then stir lightly with itchy church clothes, and let bake for two hours. The result? A typical Sunday Primary meeting.

Actually, many members who have served in the various capacities within the Church seem to agree—the most fun of all the Church's organizations comes from working in the Primary. This is the group in which the young children of the Church separate from their parents and learn the foundations of Church principles.

> **Words of Wisdom**
>
> Whosoever shall receiveth one of such children in my name receiveth me: and whosoever shall receive me, receiveth not me, but him who sent me.
>
> —Jesus (Mark 9:37)

These meetings can be very animated times of discovery for both teacher and student, as children are completely involved, including offering opening and closing prayers, providing spiritual thoughts, reading scriptures aloud, and even preparing talks for the congregation.

For young LDS children, Primary offers the chance to begin developing their public speaking skills, as they step to the podium—often with a parent nearby—to offer a short message about God, Jesus, Church, or family. For parents, it is a magical time, especially on the annual Sunday when the Primary presents the Sacrament program. During this event, the stand in front of the chapel comes alive with wiggles and giggles, as the entire program is offered by the children.

Church Meetings in Singles' Congregations

Aside from Jesus Christ, the center of any Latter-day Saint's life is the family (a topic I'll discuss in detail in Chapter 24). But there comes a time when all young adults have to leave the nest and start their own families. To ensure that these new families start off properly, as they prepare to leave home, older youth and young adults are encouraged to leave their family congregations and attend a local "singles ward." This voluntary separation encourages proper courtship and peer-socializing among Latter-day Saints, all under the watchful eye of a loving bishopric or branch presidency.

For the singles congregations, all of the same Sunday meetings take place with the exception of the young children's meetings, known as Primary.

Where there are larger concentrations of Latter-day Saints, church attendance is also based on peer-to-peer relationships. For example, families meet in family wards, singles meet with singles, and even cultures are often given the option of combining—such as Navajo or Vietnamese branches—or even all-deaf congregations. Although this is not a mandate, these types of congregational arrangements are established for convenience of Church members who share common interests and issues.

Here's one example of the four "typical" stages in an LDS person's church-going life (depending on the choices he or she makes):

◆ LDS children are born into families that usually participate in a local congregation. As the child grows, he or she will attend the various youth functions, and will take the Sacrament with the rest of the family.

◆ After leaving high school, the child might choose to attend college or military service. In the case of college, the child might elect to live at home while attending school, if the family happens to live near the college or trade school the child wants to attend.

◆ The third stage in this scenario might go two different ways: In the case of college, almost everywhere in the United States, and in other locations in the world where the Church is popular, a student or singles congregation exists. During military service, the member's records transfer to each new duty station. If the young adult chooses to serve a mission, his or her membership and records are transferred to the mission where the member will remain for the duration of the mission call.

> **And It Came to Pass**
>
> When Latter-day Saints move to another location—no matter where—their Church records are transferred with them (as individuals, not necessarily as a family unit) to the new local congregation. Once the records arrive, the LDS member can participate in meetings, receive callings, and record tithes.

◆ Somewhere along this path, the young LDS person might meet and marry his or her spouse. Now, instead of attending a singles ward or branch, the newlyweds will transfer their records to a local "young married" congregation (where available), where they will remain, usually, until after graduation from college, they move out of student housing, or win the lottery and buy a house.

Okay, I can already see the mail piling up from LDS people all over, telling me that they never went to college or met their spouses there, or they skipped past the second stage and went right to stage four. I said it was one "common look" at life. And I was just kidding about winning the lottery!

The "Ideal" Sunday

Let's take a look at how our society has evolved over its perception of Sabbath day observance. Going back a couple of millennia, the pre-Christ church of God (aka the Jews), focused more attentively on this important day.

Here are some Sabbath activities that were sanctioned for the day:

◆ Enjoying a simple meal (prepared the previous day)

◆ Spending time in prayer and song

◆ Attending religious services

◆ Reciting verses from the holy scriptures

Here are some of the activities that were frowned upon (and which are still taboo in LDS circles):

◆ Hunting and fishing

◆ Water sports

◆ Shopping

◆ Housework

◆ Golf (and all other sporting activities)

In the ancient days, the consequence for the Israelites not observing the Sabbath: *death*.

Now, it's probably a good thing that we no longer get rocks thrown at us for watching the final round of the Masters or soaping up the minivan on those sunny Sunday afternoons. However, Latter-day Saints, along with the rest of the Christian world, consider the Sabbath to be a day when everyone focuses on something or someone other than themselves. Latter-day Saints try to affirm on a weekly basis that they are not the center of their universe, and without Christ, those rocks have a better chance of making it to Heaven.

I asked my wife what she thought the ideal Sabbath was to her. She didn't hesitate, offering several suggestions that included breakfast served in bed, making sure our girls were properly dressed and prepared for church before she got up, starting dinner ahead of time, and something about foot massages.

Not that I mind serving up the occasional meal-on-a-mattress, my wife's ideal day correctly pointed to one of three key elements of the Sabbath; along with worshipping God and resting from our worldly labors, serving others is perhaps the most valuable and enriching component of the day. I guess the foot massage *could* apply.

Ultimately, though, the final word on the Sabbath is remembering God, and his Son, Jesus Christ, who gave Latter-day Saints all of those other wonderful aspects of their lives, even the work they generally perform on the other six days of the week. For Latter-day Saints, it's "TGIS" (Thank God It's Sunday!).

The Least You Need to Know

- Honoring the Sabbath day is a commandment of God.
- The Sabbath allows us to renew covenants.
- Church work involves everyone—even the children.
- Latter-day Saints love to provide service to others.
- You can find "rest" in serving the Lord on his day.

Chapter 23

Thirteen Articles of Faith

In This Chapter

◆ A look at the 13 basic principles that sustain LDS faith

◆ No one creed comprises a complete LDS ideology

◆ Freedom to believe what you wish

◆ Living to serve God

Most religions include a core set of fundamental beliefs. Such tenets include matters pertaining to God, prayer, eternal life, and issues regarding the temporal operation of that religion. Generally, Christianity shares a common creed of a belief in Christ, acceptance of the Bible as being God's word, and the assurance of a heavenly life beyond mortality if one accepts Christ as one's personal savior and redeemer. Like the rest of the Christian community, Latter-day Saints believe in these common threads.

Since its organization in 1830, Mormonism has often been perceived as an oddity in the Christian world, due to its peculiarities in such matters as living prophets, new scripture, and unconventional lifestyle choices. In his efforts to address general questions pertaining to the Church's basic beliefs, Prophet Joseph Smith provided 13 points of reference. The Church soon adopted these as its "Articles of Faith." Although these principles offer a fundamental understanding of Mormonism, they are not a comprehensive view of all of the Church's beliefs and doctrine.

God Is Not a Three-for-One Special

Article 1: "We believe in God, the Eternal Father, and in His Son, Jesus Christ, and in the Holy Ghost."

As you learned in Chapter 2, one of the most distinct elements of LDS theology is the belief that God, his Son, Jesus Christ, and the Holy Ghost, are three individual beings who act under a common basis of understanding and purpose. Given any circumstance, each member of the Trinity would take the same course of action, since they are all guided by the same perfectly balanced set of moral principles and character.

According to LDS teaching, this is how the eternal triad works:

◆ We pray to God, through his Son, Jesus Christ.

◆ Jesus serves as our mediator between our Heavenly Father and us.

◆ All things that God wants us to know, he reveals to us through the Holy Ghost.

We Pay the Price for Our Own Bad Choices

Article 2: "We believe that men will be punished for their own sins, and not for Adam's transgression."

Latter-day Saints believe the purpose for existence is to gain an understanding of what God expects them to know and do so they may some day return into his presence, and receive all that he has.

Think of eternal life with God as graduation from the school of mortality, with God the Father being the Dean of Everything, and Jesus Christ as the Professor of Everything. Once we have passed through the challenges of what life's courses teach us, we graduate (that is, we die), and are given accolades based on which of life's courses we passed. We are not responsible for anything Adam did, nor is he responsible for anything we might do.

Words of Wisdom

Adam fell that men might be, men are that they might have joy.
—2 Nephi 2:25

For Latter-day Saints to gain the knowledge of what they will need to pass into God's presence (which includes how they live their lives and what sacred covenants they must accept), they have been given perhaps the most important *and* most controversial gift—free agency. That is, they are free agents—each of them is responsible for their own actions and no one else's.

Mormonism teaches that the only original sin is that of disobeying God's commandments. We're all guilty of that at one time or another based on the choices *we* make today, not because of something someone else decided. Although Adam willfully volunteered as the spiritual fall guy for the human race, we are still ultimately responsible for what we do in life.

Everyone Has a Chance at Salvation

Article 3: "We believe that through the Atonement of Christ, all mankind may be saved, by obedience to the laws and ordinances of the Gospel."

I remember the first time I was ever yelled at in church. It was when I attended a sermon as a young boy in Missouri. It was a Protestant church—not very big, but full of nice people. I just couldn't understand what was getting the reverend so riled. It was a discussion about salvation.

After about 20 minutes of hollering, the pastor calmed to a whisper. The organ music rose in the background, while he turned into a gentle, almost pleading man. I was amazed at this transformation, when he stepped to the side of his pulpit, moved forward on the platform, and leaned as if he were about to tell us all a little secret.

Then the good reverend sprung it on us. All we had to do to become saved—to live with God again—was to walk up to where he was standing, recite a short prayer, and acknowledge that Jesus had come into our lives. That was it. No other strings attached.

But I liked it right where I was. I didn't know why, but something told me it just wasn't necessary to get up out of my seat and walk to the front of the building to be noticed by the Lord. Did that mean I was damned for all time?

I remained mired in confusion over this matter for more than 10 years. I always wondered why Jesus couldn't just come up the aisle and save me right where I was sitting. What was so special, I thought, about the front of the church? And who gave this guy the right to mete out salvation like food rations to the homeless?

What does this have to do with the Third Article of Faith? Simply, LDS people believe that Christ atoned for our sins whether we acknowledge that he did or not. Christ paid the price for our mistakes and transgressions while in the Garden of Gethsemane, and nobody can change that. It was a gift—something rendered to the world so that we would have the opportunity of being resurrected after death. But there was a price. All he asked us to do in return for his gift was to keep his commandments and follow his *Gospel.*

Mormonology

Gospel refers to the plan of salvation as defined by the ministry of Jesus Christ. As it is literally defined, it is the "Story of God." For LDS people, the Gospel encompasses God's eternal plan for his children to follow, in order to return to his presence. Latter-day Saints refer to the first four books of the New Testament as the "Four Gospels."

That's where Mormonism and the rest of Christianity begin to part ways. Traditional Christianity insists that an individual must profess acceptance of Christ as his or her personal Savior, in order to be counted among the chosen of heaven, and to escape what they often call the fiery pits of Hell. LDS people believe salvation—the gift of resurrection after death—is guaranteed to everyone. But here's the catch: To achieve exaltation (to live in the presence of God forever), we have to change the way we live our lives, follow God's council, the Gospel of Christ, and endure to the end.

Everybody gets saved—but not just anybody can live in God's presence for eternity. Worthiness through our actions makes all the difference.

A Four-Step Process to Prepare for God's Kingdom

Article 4: "We believe that the first principles and ordinances of the Gospel are: first, Faith in the Lord Jesus Christ; second, Repentance; third, Baptism by immersion for the remission of sins; fourth, Laying on of hands for the gift of the Holy Ghost."

Latter-day Saints believe these are the fundamental guidelines everyone must meet to return to God's presence after our mortal lives come to an end. As such, the first principle—having faith that Jesus Christ is the savior of the world—combines conviction with action.

For LDS people, "faith" is a verb. Something has to happen for faith to work. The Apostle Paul called faith the "substance of things hoped for." It's one thing to believe something is true or real without actually ever experiencing it. It's far more difficult to commit to it without having the knowledge that it's true or actually exists.

Words of Wisdom

Is not faith in a living God a beautiful thing? It is the highest attainment of the mind of man.

—Prophet Lorenzo Snow

Having faith in Jesus as being Lord over all things requires us to believe not only *in* what he says, but also to actually *believe* what he says, and then to apply what he says to our lives. We have to do as the Lord commands us, relying on the reassurance that the consequences will bring blessings.

And It Came to Pass

Many might remember, as children, watching older friends ride their bikes. The idea that people could balance themselves on a two-wheeled, manually powered mechanical device might have seemed complicated to our young minds. We all wished we knew what our friends had mastered. But when our first bikes arrived, our wish turned quickly into faith that we could hop on and ride along with everyone else. Our faith was tested. We fell, but we kept getting better. We knew we would eventually master the skill of bike riding. Our choices were clear: We could either continue to learn and progress, or give up. We had yet to experience the actual success, we just knew it was possible. That's faith.

That's where the other three components of this principle come into play: repentance, baptism, and receiving the Holy Ghost. According to LDS teaching these three elements depend completely on having the faith that what Jesus taught was true, and that through faith, we—as individuals—receive a personal witness that his Gospel has been restored to the earth.

From any Christian's point of view, it's probably safe to say that faith in the Lord is a fundamental principle of salvation. It's probably also reasonable to conclude that we, being sinners, must repent, to actually show a contrite spirit unto the Lord.

But then comes another leap of faith—that of baptism. Baptism by whom? By what authority? Is it a baptism by sprinkling or by immersion?

Baptism is the initial step into the LDS Church, and is also a key difference with many other Christian churches. Baptism by total immersion, by one who holds the appropriate priesthood authorization, is a powerful and sacred rite. We know that Christ—although a perfect man—was baptized to "fulfill all righteousness." He was obeying the commandments of his Father.

Following the Great Apostasy (the time when the power and authority to act in God's name was removed from the earth, as discussed in Chapter 9), the concept of baptism was altered and interpreted by men in different ways. The notion even evolved to claim that babies—those who, according to LDS teaching, do not stand in judgment before God—required baptism. It is popular among some Christian sects today.

Words of Wisdom

Faith is not to have a perfect knowledge of things; therefore if ye have faith ye hope for things which are not seen, which are true.

—Alma 32:21

LDS children, based on scriptural guidelines, are baptized at the age of eight. That's the age Latter-day Saints believe the Lord has revealed that a child begins to be capable of accepting responsibility for his or her actions. Receiving the gift of the Holy Ghost follows the ordinance of Baptism and empowers the receiver with the right to have the Holy Ghost as a constant companion, so long as that individual remains worthy.

Leadership in God's Church Does Not Require a Degree

Article 5: "We believe that a man must be called of God, by prophecy, and by the laying on of hands by those who are in authority, to preach the Gospel and administer in the ordinances thereof."

Have you ever noticed the number of people throughout the ages, who claimed they had the right to spiritual leadership and authority—but were never actually called by God, endorsed by Christ, or validated by the Holy Ghost? Formal education in religious theology has never been a prerequisite for God's chosen mouthpieces.

Take the patriarchs of old, for example:

◆ Noah, "who found grace" in God's eyes, according to the account in Genesis

◆ Abraham, who was blessed with a righteous posterity

◆ Moses, who was called to the ministry via a burning bush

All three of these men had important common characteristics. They were simple men, not educated by the world in the studies of theology. They weren't rich men either—and in Moses' case, not even eloquent in speech.

Why did they catch God's eye?

In the Book of Abraham (which is part of the LDS "Pearl of Great Price"; see Chapter 10), such men are described as "many of the noble and great ones." They were part of God's leadership during our pre-earth life, ordained before the world was.

Words of Wisdom

Before I formed thee in the belly, I knew thee.
—Jeremiah 1:5

There are many called to the service of God, but few are chosen for the task of leadership. LDS people know these leaders as men who have been tested through life's trials, and have consistently chosen to follow God. It is an education plan designed by God, administered by God, and those who graduate are selected by God.

Give Me That Old-Time Religion

Article 6: "We believe in the same organization that existed in the Primitive Church, namely, apostles, prophets, pastors, teachers, evangelists, and so forth."

When Latter-day Saints talk about the primitive church, they're not referring to cave paintings and stone knives. The primitive church is the church that existed from the time of Adam, in which all of God's revealed truths and principles were taught, under divine authority, as defined by God, through Jesus Christ.

And It Came to Pass

During the period called the "meridian of time," (when we switched from B.C. to A.D.), Jesus established his Father's government upon the earth, fulfilling what was, up until that time, the Law of Moses. The Savior appointed not only the Twelve Apostles who served under his guidance, but also key people to serve in various capacities, including ministers, pastors, and evangelists. In all cases, based on an unbroken line of authority, these various leaders were directly ordained and set apart by either Jesus or one of his delegates by laying his hands upon each of their heads and ordaining them to their respective offices. LDS people believe that the same remains true today since the Restoration of the Gospel in 1830 (that is, the founding of the LDS Church).

God Still Talks to His Children

Article 7: "We believe in the gift of tongues, prophecy, revelation, visions, healing, interpretation of tongues, and so forth."

A wise man once said that it's easy to believe in the dead prophets of history, but difficult to believe in the living prophets who walk among us today. On the contrary, Latter-day Saints believe that, beyond the words found in the Bible, and beyond the lives of the prophets of old, our Heavenly Father is still alive and is very much involved with the dealings of mankind. It is through the power of the holy priesthood, which we believe was restored to Prophet Joseph Smith, that man is still able to hear the words of a living God.

The Bible Is God's Word, But Wait, There's More ...

Article 8: "We believe the Bible to be the word of God as far as it is translated correctly; we also believe the Book of Mormon to be the word of God."

The Bible contains many wonderful and sacred passages. It offers Latter-day Saints a look into the Laws of Moses, and the life of Jesus Christ as he fulfilled those laws.

This may come as a real shock to many Christians: Every version of the Bible was assembled by committees!

From the time of the early Masoretic writings of the Old Testament accounts, which were assembled nearly a century after the birth of Christ, the contents of the Holy Bible have been a source of debate. Even today, people continue to rewrite the Bible, attempting to interpret and simplify God's word, often weakening its messages in the process.

> ### Words of Wisdom
>
> The Book of Mormon is the most correct book of any book on earth. ... A man would get nearer to God by abiding by its precepts than by any other book.
> —Prophet Joseph Smith

LDS people use the King James Version of the traditional scriptures, which were assembled in England in 1611. They believe this version to be the most accurately translated of the Bibles that have been compiled, and are part of the Church's Standard Works (see Chapter 10). Latter-day Saints believe that the Book of Mormon, another testament of the Savior Jesus Christ, is also holy writ. It contains the record of a people here in America, with whom Christ visited after his resurrection, of whom he mentions in John:10.

Stay Tuned; God *Still* Has Some Things to Say

Article 9: "We believe all that God has revealed, all that he does now reveal, and we believe that he will yet reveal many great and important things pertaining to the Kingdom of God."

The idea of receiving revelation is another one of those divine principles that has led to much confusion and sadness in the world. "False prophets," it seems, come in abundance.

LDS leaders, especially the men who have been called as "Prophets, Seers, and Revelators," cannot lead LDS people astray from God's will. This concept is easy for them to understand, since they believe those who have been called and ordained as God's messengers were called to such roles through the power of the Holy Ghost, by the will of the Father, and in the name of Christ. It has nothing to do with education, status or income. And it *certainly* has nothing to do with politics.

> ### Latter-day Laughter
>
> Blessed is he who expects nothing, for he shall never be disappointed.
> —Alexander Pope, English poet

The House of Israel Is Reunited at Last

Article 10: "We believe in the literal gathering of Israel and in the restoration of the Ten Tribes; that Zion (the New Jerusalem) will be built upon the American continent; that Christ will reign personally upon the earth; and, that the earth will be renewed and receive its paradisiacal glory."

The collapse and utter destruction of the nation of Israel was foreseen by the prophets of old and the Savior, himself, and remains a high point of contention even today. About 700 years before Christ, Israel was separated and disbursed by the Assyrians and Babylonians. Ten of the 12 tribes of Israel were taken captive and assimilated into Assyrian culture, while the tribes under the House of Judah were enslaved by Nebuchad-nezzar. Thus, the "remnant" of the House of Israel represented the entire nation.

Today, there are many who speculate the location of the lost 10 tribes. But as the tenth Article of Faith suggests, at the time of his return, Christ will have restored those lost bloodlines to their proper places, and the nation of Israel will recognize Jesus as their king and Savior.

Also, LDS people believe that the Kingdom of God will be established on American soil. This belief is not out of any patriotic leaning, but because they believe that the Founding Fathers were inspired by God to create a nation where the practice of open and free philosophies—for the most part—could go unrestricted, allowing for God's word to be restored to the world.

Everyone Has a Right to Believe What They Wish

Article 11: "We claim the privilege of worshiping Almighty God according to the dictates of our own conscience, and allow all men the same privilege, let them worship how, where, or what they may."

Although assertive in their callings as missionaries to the world, LDS people do not practice what I call "guerilla religion." They do not aggressively seek out to tell others that what they believe is wrong or inappropriate. This couldn't be better illustrated than when Salt Lake City hosted the world for two weeks in February 2002. During the nineteenth Olympic Winter Games, LDS people were instructed by Church leaders to be kind, hospitable, and gracious hosts, and not to proselyte Mormonism to the mass of visitors. Even the missionaries in the area were asked to offer answers to Church-related questions, and that if someone were to inquire of the Church and its philosophies, the matters be addressed delicately and in a way not to be intrusive.

LDS people believe everyone has a right to his or her beliefs. They might not always agree with what somebody believes, but it remains the other person's choice as long as those beliefs do not infringe on the rights of others.

And It Came to Pass

Every six months, when the LDS Church assembles for "General Conference," which takes place at Temple Square in Salt Lake City, a few people gather outside the Church's assembly hall. They pass out leaflets and yell derogatory remarks to passersby, making every effort to sway people from attending the conference. Inside the assembly the Church's General Authorities are gathered (the prophet, apostles, and other high priests of the Church). On one occasion several years ago, one of the Twelve Apostles, Elder Ashton, noted the hecklers in his remarks and asked, "Whatever happened to giving somebody the benefit of the doubt?" Those people were allowed to remain and continue their right to free speech, mostly ignored, while Church members tried to pay as little attention to them as possible.

Government Is Not a Bad Thing

Article 12: "We believe in being subject to kings, presidents, rulers, and magistrates, in obeying, honoring, and sustaining the law."

Mormonism is a worldwide religion, with more than 11 million members in countries spanning the globe. Latter-day Saints have temples in more than 100 locations around the world, and schools of higher learning in places where they are not even allowed to proselyte. Members of the Church are subjects of kings and citizens of democracies. Latter-day Saints embrace the idea of actively participating in secular government.

During its early years, prior to becoming a state, there was virtually no line between politics and religion in the Utah territory. The president of the Church, Brigham Young, was also governor of the territory. It's one of few times when religious leaders governed a land by the same principles as the popular religion. In many cases, there still exists an *unspoken* overlap between LDS tradition and Utah government.

Mormon Myths

Myth: All LDS people in the United States are Republicans. LDS people may have begun leaning toward the Republican Party because of Abraham Lincoln's soft position on their plea for religious freedom. But the notion that all Latter-day Saints are Republicans is totally untrue. There are many LDS Democrats. I even met one once, I think.

Basic Beliefs on Being a Decent Human Being

Article 13: "We believe in being honest, true, chaste, benevolent, virtuous, and in doing good to all men; indeed, we may say that we follow the admonition of Paul—we believe all things, we hope all things, we have endured many things, and hope to be able to endure all things. If there is anything virtuous, lovely, or of good report or praiseworthy, we seek after these things."

This article encompasses much that is virtuous about LDS life. Honesty and integrity are powerful traits of anyone, and in the LDS philosophy, they are characteristics of righteousness.

Whenever a person investigates a religion, much will be dependent on what is taught or believed or defined as religious dogma. Perhaps what's more important, though, is in how its people live their lives on Monday through Saturday.

The Thirteenth Article of Faith does an excellent job of summing up *how* LDS people would like to be seen. It still remains with them as to how well they live up to this description.

The Least You Need to Know

◆ The Thirteen Articles of Faith provide the template for how LDS people live their lives.

◆ Although the 13 Articles offer a fundamental understanding of Mormonism, they are not a comprehensive view of all of the Church's beliefs and doctrine.

◆ Religious freedoms should be afforded all people.

◆ LDS people aspire to live in a way that is righteous and faithful to God.

Chapter 24

Families Are Forever

In This Chapter

- ◆ The family as an eternal unit

- ◆ An LDS institution: Family Home Evenings

- ◆ Knowing their heritage teaches LDS people who they are

- ◆ The gift and responsibility of bringing children into the world

- ◆ The Patriarchal Blessing: a spiritual roadmap that provides direction to LDS lives

For Latter-day Saints, the family is the fundamental unit of the Church. Everything comes down to the welfare of their families. This is perhaps one of the most distinct characteristics of LDS culture. They believe their families are part of an eternal round, which was set up by the Heavenly Father long before the world began.

A key responsibility for Latter-day Saints is in bringing God's spirit children into the world. Accordingly, an LDS family is often much larger than other families. Having children is regarded as not only a privilege, but a divine commandment. While in the Garden of Eden, Adam and Eve were commanded to "be fruitful and multiply and replenish the earth." LDS people believe that through the Heavenly Father's eternal plan, they may enjoy their posterity throughout eternity, and as such, live with their families forever. For Latter-day Saints, bringing God's children into the world is a distinct honor God allows them to enjoy, and a right that they believe should only occur lawfully and legally in binding marriage between a man and a woman.

The All-Important Family

In 1997, the First Presidency of the Church of Jesus Christ of Latter-day Saints prepared a formal statement. The "Proclamation on the Family" is for every family around the world. It emphasizes the fundamental institution of marriage between a man and a woman—an institution that is not only ordained by God, but an eternal expectation.

The Proclamation further states that the sacred powers associated with procreation are only to be used between a man and a woman who have been lawfully married as husband and wife. Husbands and wives, according to the leaders of the LDS Church, are responsible for loving and caring for each other and for their children. It's a sacred duty; one that will not be taken lightly by God should spouses/parents fail to do their jobs. The Proclamation points out that these responsibilities include physical and spiritual needs of the family. Fidelity is also stressed as a commandment, with dire consequences at the day of judgment should spouses not remain faithful in their moral obligations to each other.

If you ever visit an LDS home, you will most likely see a copy of this Proclamation displayed on a wall. It's very important to members of the LDS Church.

> **Words of Wisdom**
>
> There is nothing any of us can do that will have greater long-term benefit—particularly for our children—than to rekindle wherever possible the spirit of a happy home and to once again provide a stable family environment where children can develop under the watchful, loving eye of virtuous parents.
>
> —Prophet Gordon B. Hinckley

The Eternal Bond

If you look at the world today, many aspects of risk posed to society are targeted at the family unit. According to a recent Carnegie Corporation study on young children in America, of the 12 million youth under the age of three, 25 percent live in poverty and in single-parent homes. One out of every three will have suffered some form of physical abuse by the age of one. In 1996, there were nearly 8 million families in the United States without fathers, and more than 30 percent of all births occurred out of wedlock.

Okay, so that was just the tip of the bad-news iceberg. There is another side to the picture, one that Latter-day Saints hold as the center of family focus:

♦ All of us are children of heavenly parents.

♦ We are created in the image of God.

♦ Parents can help society by raising strong, righteous families.

♦ Everyone can live with their families forever, by following God's council.

And It Came to Pass

If you look at the research, sociologists have shown that the benefits of a stable marriage, one in which both the mother and father are actively involved in the lives of the family members, include the following perks:

♦ Married people are physically healthier, live longer and take fewer risks that could compromise their lives.

♦ Married people are happier, suffering less from depression and fewer clinically diagnosed mental psychiatric maladies.

♦ Married people tend to conserve their financial resources, and provide a healthier economic lifestyle for their children.

The knowledge that families can be eternal provides LDS people with a spiritual connection to each other and to their personal values. LDS leaders have taught that when children are equally involved in family life and are respected as human beings all family members enjoy a much happier family life.

Sparing the Rod?

Whether to use force when correcting a child is often the cause for debate among families everywhere. LDS leaders, citing the most current research on disciplinary actions with children, believe that homes in which children are disciplined with unprovoked, nonabusive consequences (without being physically hurt), raise less aggressive, more sociable youth. In these homes, children maintain a stronger spirit of attachment to and within the home.

The notion that we should physically punish children was born out of the early Judeo-Christian philosophy that we were all born in original sin, as part of the fallen species of man. Such ideas were further ratified by early Calvinistic philosophies that children required heavy punishment and light sprinklings of love.

For LDS couples, it is a solemn responsibility to raise their children with love and careful attention. The term "discipline," in fact, can mean almost opposing things. On the one hand, the term is often used to connote punishment, and on the other, it means to teach (as in "disciple," or being a student of something or someone). In the case of "discipline," most LDS people prefer the latter definition.

There are several key verses in the Old Testament that, to the untrained reader, might seem as encouragement to strike our children. Here are a few from the book of Proverbs:

- "He that spareth his rod, hateth his son. ..."—(13:24)

- "Withhold not correction from a child: For if thou beatest him with a rod, he shall not die. Thou shalt beat him with the rod, and shalt deliver his soul from hell."—(23:13–14)

- "Foolishness is bound in the heart of a child; but the rod of correction shall drive it far from him."—(22:15)

Words of Wisdom

I have never accepted the principle of "spare the rod and spoil the child. ..." Children don't need beating. They need love and encouragement.

—Prophet Gordon B. Hinckley

Mormonology

The Hebrew translation of the **rod** from the Old Testament denotes the "Word of God," as written in the holy scriptures, or spoken by Church leaders. Often, the term is misunderstood to mean a stick with which to fight or strike.

Sounds pretty ominous for how we should treat those wayward children—except for one small detail. The Hebrew translation for *rod* is "Word of God." That changes the meaning just a bit. "Thy rod and thy staff," for example—part of the Lord's Prayer (Psalms 23)—refers to God's comforting words, with reference to the staff of a shepherd, which is used to gently direct his flock. Now let's revisit the quotes with the appropriate translations:

- "He that spareth the Word of God [meaning the scriptures, Church leaders, Gospel principles, etc.], hateth his son: He who loveth his son corrects ["teaches?"] him early on [during his youth]."

- "Withhold correction from a child: For if you teach him using the Word of God, you will deliver his soul from hell."

- "Foolishness is bound in the heart of a child; but the Word of God will drive it away from him."

Family Home Evening

In 1915, the Church initiated a program to encourage weekly family interaction, calling this activity "Family Home Evening." The practice of gathering at least once per week as a family has since become an LDS institution.

The Church has formally set Monday night aside for this purpose, although families are free to decide whatever time and day is best for them. The necessity of the program is more to ensure consistent family time, and the opportunity for family members to cultivate their talents (but Mondays are the encouraged nights).

Many families make sure there's a weekly gathering for spiritual meetings, and one for family-focused activities. Whether gathering together to watch *Monday Night Football*, taking a walk, or playing games at the kitchen table, the notion that those who play and pray together, stay together, is very real for LDS people.

Setting aside Monday evening for unrestricted family time is so important to the Church that its leaders, including Prophet Gordon B. Hinckley, formally requested to community leaders around the world to consider Monday evenings as a time for family functions "without conflicting loyalties" outside the home.

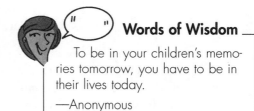

Words of Wisdom

To be in your children's memories tomorrow, you have to be in their lives today.

—Anonymous

And It Came to Pass

Before joining the Church I visited a large LDS family in northern California. Each Sunday following Church services they would meet to discuss the day's events, read scriptures, and sing songs. I was amazed when listening to the youngest boy, little more than five years old, read difficult passages of scripture. This family had established early in their marriage that Sunday would be set aside for conversation, planning, and other matters. Now, more than 20 years later, my own family of nine follows the same pattern. We use Sunday as our day because of my frequent travel schedules. Our Family Home Evenings also allow our girls to share the day's events and discuss important matters in their lives. But when they can, my girls do share Monday evenings with Mom, involved in some type of fun activity.

The Importance of Family Histories

We're all related (whether we like it or not). Everyone is a descendant of Adam and Eve, and a spirit child of God. Searching out ancestors is often the subject of a great deal of time and effort for LDS families. Latter-day Saints believe they have an obligation to help those family members who have passed, who were not given the opportunity to accept the Gospel of Christ. One of their responsibilities is to redeem their dead ancestors, and link generation to generation. In line with this objective, the LDS Church has become the single largest family research organization in the world, offering its historical records to anyone with a desire to look up their ancestry.

> **Words of Wisdom**
>
> Only the Mormons are extending the blessings of the atonement of Jesus Christ to those beyond the grave.
> —The late Bishop Dr. Krister Stendahl, Stockholm Lutheran Church

If you want to know more about your mother's cousin's uncle's father's great, great, great grandmother, the Family History Library in Salt Lake City will probably have the information. This extensive resource for family historians throughout the world contains more than two billion names from current civilizations and from those long since past. Although many of the records are original, some of the documents on file include copies of royal pedigrees that date back to the Nordic kings of the fourth century!

Each weekday, the Family History Library receives more than 2,000 visitors and eager researchers. A few people even claim to have traced their lines back to Adam himself, although this is virtually impossible (without inventing connections along the way), due to the lack of information and limited records kept during the Dark Ages. Some families, however, have successfully traced their heritage as far back as the fifteenth century, and if they're lucky, will connect into some line of royal heritage that goes back even further.

These records are accessible to the outside world. Anyone can have access to the histories and names. You can learn more about the Family History Library at www. familysearch.org.

Everyone in the Church is encouraged to get involved with family research. This interest is based on modern-day revelation that all people who have ever lived will have the opportunity to learn of the Gospel of Christ and its saving principles. For this purpose, seeking out family lines is not a hobby—it's a spiritual obligation.

Once Latter-day Saints know who their ancestors are, they can perform sacred ordinances that will allow those ancestors to enter into God's presence. That's where the temples come into play, as I'll discuss in Chapter 26.

Researching LDS family histories include three basic elements:

◆ Identifying deceased family members

◆ Identifying those family members who were not members of the Church, who require God's ordinances to enter into his presence

♦ Ensuring that those ordinances are performed in the temple on behalf of those who are deceased

LDS people are also encouraged to set up and participate in family organizations. Finding members of a particular lineage and gathering together under one common ancestry provides families with an extended look back to their respective heritage. Family organizations also provide people with a common bond, and get more people involved in the search for their roots.

And you never know, maybe you'll find that lost rich uncle after all!

Size Doesn't Matter, But ...

There's a popular LDS joke that goes: Why do Mormon women stop having babies at 35? Because 36 are just too many. All kidding aside, LDS families do tend to run larger than the national average of 2.3 children. For Latter-day Saints, bringing children into the world is not only an obligation to God, it is a great joy to be surrounded by children.

Children are a source of great joy to LDS families.

©Drew Williams (2002)

As such, LDS families often live up to the commandment of being fruitful and multiplying. Historically, many LDS people come from large families, have large families, and love being a part of large families. The love of family and children runs deep in the LDS culture. Prophet Ezra Taft Benson once said, "The family is the cornerstone of civilization and no nation will rise above the caliber of its homes." In many cases, parents who are able to have only one or two children—or none at all—choose to adopt.

Mormon Myths

Myth: LDS people don't practice birth control. The decisions on when to have children, how often, and how many are highly personal and sacred matters with LDS couples. LDS people are left to their personal choices on family size. The Church itself, however, takes no official position of endorsement or restriction on regulating birth control, except in the case of its firm condemnation of elective abortion.

My friends, the Terrys, have taken God's commandment of "multiplying" to considerable proportions. Mike and Trish, who have been married for 27 years, have managed to raise a family of five girls and nine boys (all single births). Mike, a self-employed cement mason, and Trish, a former ski instructor, still hike Utah's Rocky Mountains, rock-climb, ski, and camp together as a family. Each child in the Terry home is loved, nurtured, and watched over by older siblings, with Mom and Dad always nearby. There is no lack of love in this family of 16 individual personalities.

Bringing children into the world is a divine gift and responsibility for LDS families. For Mike and Trish Terry, the more the better. Here they are with their 14 children.

©*Drew Williams (2002)*

According to LDS revelation, LDS people are to live honorably and bear and raise righteous children before God. Each new child to the family unit brings a unique personality, new challenges, and great joy into the lives of everyone. LDS families are encouraged to counsel with the Lord on all matters concerning family size and organization.

Patriarchal Blessings

There are many offices within the Church of Jesus Christ of Latter-day Saints. As I mentioned in Chapter 20, patriarchs are ordained high priests, with the special calling of revealing individual characteristics and personal lineage of Church members. Each stake within the Church—an extended boundary that includes 10 to 12 congregations (wards and branches)—has a designated high priest who serves as the patriarch for that region.

Based on worthiness and the ability to understand these personal revelations, every LDS person is entitled to one *Patriarchal Blessing* in his or her lifetime. This blessing is given by the patriarch, recorded, and later a written copy is given to the receiver. There is no age requirement other than what is advised by the recommendation of the person's local Church leader. In these blessings, Latter-day Saints learn more about who they are, what their talents might include, and the courses they will take as they create their own families. They are discouraged from sharing the contents of these blessings with others outside their immediate families.

The Patriarchal Blessing has been called "a paragraph from the book of our life's possibilities." These special blessings afford a look into the recipient's individual traits, and provide a very personal review of the Lord's expectations of each person on a case-by-case basis. Patriarchal Blessings can be used as a roadmap for personal growth in the Church and throughout life.

Mormonology

The **Patriarchal Blessing** is given once in the life of every worthy Latter-day Saint. Its contents reveal sacred principles and unique traits about the receiver. This blessing also includes a declaration of lineage for the individual, indicating to what bloodline, either literal or adoptive, the person belongs.

And It Came to Pass

In one particular region of South America, in the small communities within the Amazon rainforest, Latter-day Saints are scattered across long distances. Often, the Church members are in isolated areas, and have to use the great Amazon River itself as a primary means of transportation. In one case, an LDS family living in a remote village outside of the city of Manaus was anxious to receive the Lord's personal message for them. They traveled several days over river and through the jungle to receive their Patriarchal Blessings. They later said of their trip that it was a worthwhile journey to receive the personal direction of the Lord.

Patriarchal Blessings also share a bit of personal lineage concerning which of the 12 tribes of Israel the Church member descended from. This blessing also includes, for example, information about special gifts such as the receiver will counsel children or become a strong leader in the Church. There might also be mention of specific artistic or musical abilities not yet realized.

Latter-day Saints consider these blessings very sacred and personal, and seldom share the contents of the blessings with others outside their families. These blessings are the only blessings formally recorded verbatim in the records of Church members. A person gets only one Patriarchal Blessing in his or her life, but it will take that person a lifetime to gain a good understanding of what's contained in it.

The Least You Need to Know

- Families are the foundation of civilization itself.

- Family Home Evenings are an important part of LDS family life.

- Tracing family heritage is a way to link generation to generation and to redeem the deceased.

- LDS families view bringing children into the world as not only an obligation to God, but a great joy.

- Every worthy Latter-day Saint receives the Patriarchal Blessing once in his or her life.

"Every Nation, Kindred, Tongue, and People"

In This Chapter

- ◆ Every Church member is obligated to be a missionary—every day of his or her life

- ◆ What's involved in missionary work?

- ◆ One God, one world: tolerance for all religions

- ◆ How Mormonism differs from Catholicism and Protestantism

The Church of Jesus Christ of Latter-day Saints is the fastest growing Christian religion in the United States. A key factor supporting the growth is found in the 60,000-person-strong missionary program of the Church. Seeing two young men in dark suits, often with bicycles, has become an icon in the LDS Church worldwide. Often overlooked, however, are the thousands of young women and older couples who also volunteer for full-time missions. Those who are called to missions serve for a specific length of time, and live in the communities where they are assigned. Missionaries do not choose where they serve or what language they might be required to learn. They submit their request through their local leaders, and the rest is up to Church leadership in council with the Lord.

The concept of missionary work is not specific to Mormonism. Many Christian faiths share a love of service to God. In fact, there are many aspects of "mainstream Christianity" that Mormonism shares, which we'll examine in this chapter. Latter-day Saints believe that, since there is only one God, he has only one program, which they believe to be owned, operated, and directed by the Lord Jesus Christ. As such, God's plan for his children doesn't apply to a particular culture, country, government, or language. Rather, the world is God's handiwork, and LDS people see it as their responsibility to share his good news with the people who inhabit it.

Bicycles Built for Two: Missionary Work

The missionary program of the Church began almost immediately after the Church was founded in 1830 as word of mouth spread the Gospel from family to family in the upper Finger Lakes region of New York, and in northeastern Pennsylvania. Martin Harris and Oliver Cowdery were among the first missionaries called to the service. Over time, through a consistent Church government and ongoing desire for more Latter-day Saints to share their new faith with others, the Church missionary program grew as new pairs of *elders* were called to missions.

One of the symbols of the LDS culture, missionaries volunteer for two years of full-time service to the Church at their own expense. They are frequently required to learn a new language before leaving on their mission, with a short time for preparation.

©Drew Williams (2002)

Boys born into active LDS families are taught to prepare for a mission from an early age. While still in the junior youth programs, called "Primary," (see Chapter 22), LDS boys and girls between the ages of three and 12 are instructed on spiritual matters concerning Church culture, the atonement of Christ, and the relationship between Heavenly Father and his children. The boys begin preparing for missions during this time, working to live worthily for such a calling, and putting aside the necessary finances they will need to pay for their mission expenses.

Although they serve the ultimate role as wife and mother, LDS women can choose to serve a mission, but they are not categorically encouraged to do so. A woman's mission does not have the same amount of focus and often emphasis as that placed on the mission of a young LDS man.

The bottom line is, the LDS Church does not send out people to serve missions because those people need to gain some sort of special understanding or personal spiritual experience. Rather, those who are called to serve do so with the objective to teach the Gospel of Jesus Christ, or in the formal statement of the LDS Church, "to bring souls unto Christ."

As they progress through the Aaronic Priesthood programs of the Church, as Deacons, Teachers, and Priests (see Chapter 20), young LDS men begin taking on greater Church duties. These 14- to 18-year-old boys offer assistance in teaching Sunday school, visiting families, and seeing to various leadership roles among their peers (all in preparation to serve full-time missions). Young women also gain similar experience in the various leadership opportunities they become involved with.

Mormonology

Elder is the title used by men who serve missions for the LDS Church. The term is also used for a specific office in the Melchizedek Priesthood, and is also used to identify high-ranking Church leaders.

Mormon Myths

Myth: *All LDS boys are required to serve missions.* Many LDS young men do serve full-time missions. However, when issues relating to a young man's personal, physical, mental, or emotional fitness are not up to Church guidelines, young men are often honorably excused from serving.

The Missionary Lifecycle

Beginning at age 19, the young men who are called to serve do so for a 24-month period. Sister missionaries, which include single women over the age of 21, serve for 18 months. For married couples with older children, or no children at all, the time of service varies from 6 to 36 months, again, depending on the type of mission.

Everybody's missions begin when they arrive at the Missionary Training Center (MTC), where they spend four to eight weeks. The MTC in Provo, Utah, is the largest of its kind, with more than 23,000 missionaries trained in 50 different languages each year. Other Church-owned missionary training centers are located throughout the world, including London, Tokyo, Buenos Aires, Manila, and Mexico City. These smaller centers provide training to missionaries originating from those regions.

While at the MTC, missionaries learn how to teach the Gospel of Jesus Christ, and often do so in a new language. Many of the missionaries who leave the MTC learn foreign languages with reasonable fluency within a few short weeks. Former LDS missionaries are often recruited for State Department positions and internships because of their multilingual abilities, cultural experience, and high standards of living.

Once missionaries complete their training, they move into the mission area. These areas can comprise a whole country, or a single city, depending on the location and population of the Church. Other than via mail (electronic or "snail"), missionaries are permitted to contact their homes only in cases of emergency and on special holidays. They are instructed to focus their attention on the spiritual welfare of the people who live within their mission boundaries.

Latter-day Laughter

Two elders were traveling through the African bush when they came across a large lion. One of the elders dropped his scriptures and began to run. The other elder, trying to keep up, questioned his companion's decision to flee. "We'll never be able to run faster than that lion," he exclaimed. "You're absolutely right," replied the other elder, "I just have to run faster than you."

—Anonymous

While on their missions, elders may not date or engage in any excessive physical recreation. They do not watch television or go to movies without permission, and they do not listen to popular music. They are never alone (Church policy), and must follow a strict daily routine of prayer and teaching. The regimen might sound peculiar, but the Church believes the calling to be a missionary is a sacred opportunity, requiring the strictest focus and self-discipline.

If called to remote venues where the Church is not well-established, the elders might serve in leadership positions. But wherever they serve, for most of the Church's missionaries, those two years "in the field" provide the greatest spiritual influence they will ever experience.

After two years of living out of suitcases, often wearing the same meager selection of five white shirts, three suits, and two pairs of shoes, elders return to their home wards (wherever their immediate family lives), where they are released from the calling of full-time missionary. The sister missionaries have already been back six months. Single women who wish to serve missions attend the same training programs as the elders, and they follow the same code of conduct. Sister missionaries are involved in all aspects of missionary work with the exception of performing the priesthood functions of baptism and confirmation. As for their choices of fashion, it's long dresses or skirts, conservative blouses or sweaters, and good walking shoes.

The next step on the LDS agenda of life for returned missionaries: Marriage!

Missionary Callings Vary

There are many types of Church-sponsored missions. Some are considered "teaching" missions in classrooms, some are research oriented, and some are proselytizing missions. For example, in Nauvoo, Illinois, the place from which Latter-day Saints were banished in 1845, the Church has reclaimed much of the old part of the city where married couples serve as tour hosts, dressing in period clothing. Missionaries also serve on Church-owned farms throughout the world, and in remote locations, providing medical and educational assistance. At the Family History Library in Salt Lake City, couples serve as researchers and name extraction specialists. Responsibilities include researching family lines and assisting the more than 2,000 visitors each day. Regardless of where they serve, those who participate in the missionary experience do so at will and with no financial compensation.

During the 2002 Winter Olympics in Utah, this 25-story photo poster of an Olympic figure skater was attached to the Church office building as part of the city's backdrop for the two weeks of sporting events.

©Drew Williams (2002)

One God, One World, One Religion

I find it amazing that, as I travel throughout the world, many religious people find it easier to denounce Mormonism as the conjurings of a nineteenth-century crackpot, while they understand even less of their own religion's origins or doctrine. LDS people feel strongly about their religious beliefs. All Latter-day-Saints must pray for confirmation to truly stand as individual witnesses of the restoration of Christ's Church. However, they do not actively participate in discounting other religions, or spend time and resources attempting to disprove other faiths.

LDS missionaries, while they believe Mormonism to be the only completely endorsed religion of deity, face many different religious cultures in the world. One thing LDS missionaries are counseled to always remember is tolerance for other faiths. People have the right to believe what they want. Latter-day Saints encourage everyone to seek out God, to understand the atoning sacrifice of Jesus Christ, and to study the *logic* of what is being taught.

With more than 11 million members of the Church of Jesus Christ of Latter-day Saints spanning more than 150 countries, the influence of Mormonism is worldwide. The LDS culture extends into government leadership roles, the television and movie industries, music groups, and professional athletes. There are LDS schoolteachers, authors, heads of public universities, and Fortune 1000 companies—even royal families.

And It Came to Pass

Early in their marriage, Alice and Willard Marriott wanted to create a business so that they could support their family. They opened a chain of fast-food root beer stands. The Marriott family eventually expanded their business into the hospitality industry. Today, standing as a testament to what two people can accomplish, Alice and Willard Marriott's hotel chain is part of a multibillion-dollar business empire. Amazing that all of those wonderful hotels were built on the strength and reputation of hot dogs and root beer! (By the way, it's a myth that the Marriotts owned A&W Root Beer, supposedly named for "Alice & Willard.")

Although started in the upper regions of nineteenth-century New England, the LDS experience transcends a nation or single culture. In fact, since 1996, more Church members live outside the United States than within.

With the dramatic increase in the growth of the LDS Church, even the tradition of keeping our highest leaders—the quorum of the Twelve Apostles—based in Salt Lake City, is changing to meet the demands of Church membership. Currently, several of the Twelve Apostles have relocated their families to broader regions of the Church, to attend to member needs and to show a stronger Church presence throughout the world.

The LDS contribution to world needs is often seen during times of struggle and tragedy. On many occasions, following natural disasters, for example, Church leadership mobilizes local congregations to participate in contributing extra finances, resources, and materials to those who suffer. Church affiliation does not matter when suffering or hardship is involved. Latter-day Saints believe that there is no greater calling than that of service to their neighbors—even if those neighbors happen to live thousands of miles away.

Modern Tenets of Christianity vs. Mormonism

When LDS missionaries prepare for their assignments, they are cautioned to always present the Gospel using the Spirit as their guidance. Missionaries are discouraged from entering debates on the merits of Mormonism vs. other Christian faiths. The missionary's purpose is to preach the Gospel, answer questions about Mormonism, and provide priesthood assistance where needed.

So what are the distinct differences between Mormonism and the other two camps (Catholicism and Protestantism)? Often, many people assume the LDS Church is a spin-off of some puritanical Protestant cult, but that's not the case. The primary difference is in the LDS belief that God still reveals truth to his children, and that they may inherit everything God has—if they live righteous lives. Let's take a look at some of the common differences between Mormonism and other Christian faiths that LDS missionaries are frequently asked to explain:

> **Words of Wisdom**
>
> Wherefore the Lord said, forasmuch as this people draw near me with their mouth, and with their lips do honor me, but have removed their heart far from me, and their fear toward me is taught by the precept of men.
>
> —Isaiah 29:13

◆ **Catholicism.** The Catholics believe their church is based on the scripture found in the New Testament that says Jesus gave Peter the keys to the church (which he did). Peter's followers later built a holy shrine on a hill outside Rome, where he was allegedly crucified (about A.D. 65). The Christians were persecuted for almost 250 more years, until the death of the Roman emperor Diocletian in 313. Constantine was the first Roman emperor to publicly adopt Christianity, which he did in battle against Diocletian's military. Upon his succession to emperor, the Holy Roman Empire was born, also giving way for the organization of the Catholic Church. But according to LDS doctrine, with the last of Jesus' apostles being gone for more than two centuries, by now the true Church of Christ and the subsequent keys of authority to manage it were no longer upon the earth.

♦ **Protestantism.** The Protestants were a group of ex-Catholic reformers whose ideologies were founded on the notion that Catholicism was corrupted and had fallen away from Christ's true teachings. In various Protestant charters, God's church includes independent and autonomous religious groups, organized through a democratic process, which attempt to follow the teachings of Christ as explained in varying interpretations of the King James Version of the Bible. Latter-day doctrine supports the notion that many Protestant faiths possess portions of God's true church, but lack divine authority and the day-to-day details of holy government.

♦ **Mormonism.** Members of the Church of Jesus Christ of Latter-day Saints believe that the keys to God's kingdom, as defined and organized by Jesus Christ, must be conferred on a man directly by another who holds the same keys, and who was also ordained. These keys were lost with the death of the last apostle, about 100 years after Christ was born. When the keys to God's kingdom were lost, the world fell into the Dark Ages and did not enjoy the blessings of having the true Church of Christ on the earth, until its restoration through Joseph Smith in 1820.

Now, before everyone runs to mail the publisher religious nastygrams, remember that this book introduces the fundamentals of Mormonism, and how those fundamentals compare and contrast with mainstream Christianity. I make no attempt to debate the validity of other religions, and merely make reference to them here, based on historical information and their accepted doctrines, and to further explore some of the issues LDS missionaries face on a daily basis.

And It Came to Pass

Orson F. Whitney, an early twentieth century LDS Church apostle, once wrote of an experience he had with a member of the Roman Catholic Church. "The issue is between Catholicism and Mormons," the man said to Whitney. "If we are right, you are wrong. The Protestants haven't a leg to stand on. For if we are wrong, they are wrong with us, since they were a part of us and went out from us; while if we are right, they are apostates whom we cut off long ago. ... If we have the apostolic succession from St. Peter, as we claim, there is no need for Joseph Smith and Mormonism; but if we have not that succession, then such a man as Joseph Smith was necessary."

Scriptural Doctrine

As I pointed out in earlier chapters, the notion that God's messengers recorded his teachings shouldn't come as a complete shock to anyone. The question, however, as to what should serve as canon vs. conjecture, has been the stuff of spiritual debate throughout the ages.

Every Christian religion considers some form of the Bible to be the Word of God. In their 1963 charter, the Southern Baptist Convention, for example, states that the Bible was "written by men divinely inspired." The Protestants believe that the 66 books that comprise the Holy Bible are the all-encompassing works of God. However, the contents of both the Old and New Testaments were debated by Christian sects for hundreds of years. Also, the New Testament, in general terms, was first mandated by Emperor Constantine more than 300 years after the life and ministry of Christ and his apostles, and the general landscape of the Holy Bible as we know it today came from another king—England's James I—some 1,300 years later.

The Catholics also use the post-King James Version (KJV) Bible as canon, along with *apocryphal writings*, which were included in the KJV until about 1630. Mormonism is the only Christian religion that does not take the Bible to be the definitive volume of God's word. This does not detract *in any way* from the importance of the Bible.

In Chapter 23, I discuss the Church's 13 Articles of Faith, which includes the LDS position on the Bible being holy writ, as well as the Book of Mormon being another testament of Jesus Christ.

Latter-day Saints, as stated in the Eighth Article of Faith, believe the Bible to be the Word of God, and that the Book of Mormon, another Testament of Jesus Christ, is also the Word of God (see Chapter 23). Missionaries are often asked if the Book of Mormon is the "Mormon Bible." Indeed, it is *not*. The Holy Bible is part of LDS standard works, as I discussed in Chapters 7 and 8.

However, because the Bible has been translated, retranslated, and retranslated yet again, much of its spiritual content has been altered. The King James Version, Latter-day-Saints believe, contains the most accurate accounts from the original records of those particular books found in the Bible. LDS missionaries

Mormonology

The **apocryphal writings** comprise the Apocrypha, a group of books that have been considered dubious and unproven "holy" writings from the Old Testament collection. Religious scholars have debated their authenticity throughout the many iterations of the Holy Bible. Modern-day revelation given to Joseph Smith indicates that these books once contained valid doctrine, but have lost many of their truths due to misinterpretations.

often quote biblical scripture that show direct ties that tell of the other record that will come forth out of the ground (which Latter-day Saints believe to be the Book of Mormon).

The Separation of Three Distinct Beings

We've already examined the notion of the Holy Trinity (see Chapter 10), as it was originated in the Nicene Creed of A.D. 325. (Again, under the "solemn" direction of a king—this time, Constantine the Great—to exhort "his will that religious peace should be established.")

For the Catholics, God is the Supreme Being, Jesus "sitteth at the right hand of the Father," according to the revised creed of A.D. 381, and the Holy Ghost who, along with the Father and the Son, are to be worshipped as part of the Holy Trinity.

Heck, even many Baptists with whom I used to affiliate don't *really* believe Jesus, Heavenly Father, and the Holy Ghost were the same person, based on what the Southern Baptist Church calls its "Faith and Message" adoption of 1963. God, according to the statement, retains "distinct personal attributes," while Jesus Christ is "the eternal Son of God ... now exalted at the right hand of God," and the Holy Ghost is the "Spirit of God. ... He exalts Christ" and "cultivates Christian Character." Simply, how can any one person be two or more people, based on this or any other intelligible doctrine?

As shown in the discussion of the Articles of Faith in Chapter 23, and the Holy Trinity in Chapter 10, LDS Church members are taught that three distinct beings comprise the Godhead. According to LDS thinking, it doesn't make sense to believe that God the Father, who "made man in his own image," should look any different than we do. Nor would his Only Begotten Son, Jesus Christ, be the same person.

> **Words of Wisdom**
>
> Don't waste your time worshipping sports heroes, rock stars, movie idols, or CEOs. Please, just worship God, your Heavenly Father.
>
> —Steve Young, former football quarterback and member of the LDS Church

Living Revelation

Mainstream Christianity, it seems, believes God is alive but no longer communicates with his children. The general masses of Christianity rely on holy writings from prophets who have been dead for thousands of years. For many people, the concept of God still communicating seems at first to be outlandish. However, according to many of the missionaries I've spoken with, this notion frequently leads people to wonder, "Why wouldn't he?"

LDS people believe God is alive and well, and still talks to the world. Through his Only Begotten Son, Jesus Christ, our Heavenly Father continues to lead his children. We believe that every individual is worthy of direct inspiration for his or her life, so long as it is in harmony with the Gospel of Christ, as revealed through his appointed prophets.

In this section I've reviewed some of the unique characteristics of Mormonism, and what LDS missionaries often discuss with the inquiring minds of the world. Obviously, there are many facets of the Church that can't be covered in an introductory book like this one. If you're interested in a more in-depth look at the LDS Church, see the books in Appendix B, or go to the official website of the LDS Church, www.lds.org, for more information about LDS doctrine. Oh, and if you ever meet somebody who tells you they know all about the LDS Church, be skeptical. According to the leaders of the Church—even *they* are still trying to learn the doctrine.

> **Words of Wisdom**
>
> The vice of our Theology is seen in the claim that the Bible is a closed book and that the Age of Inspiration is past.
>
> —Ralph Waldo Emerson, U.S. essayist and poet

But the bottom line is this: If you're seriously interested in a deeper understanding of Mormonism, there is no better source than Salt Lake City (or a local LDS Church leader in your area).

I have a lot of respect for anyone who is willing to dedicate a portion of their lives to any worthy, spiritually uplifting cause—LDS or otherwise. On behalf of the missionaries, the next time you see them, honk or wave. Although we all might not be on the same page in the same hymnbook, most Christians are still after the same thing: a place in God's kingdom, where we will be happy and safe.

Besides, no matter what religion they might be, you have to give credit to people—especially young men and young women—who feel so strongly about serving the human race that they would postpone college, marriage, and careers to dedicate themselves to assisting with the spiritual needs of others for any length of time.

The Least You Need to Know

- The missionary program of the LDS Church has been active since the founding of Mormonism.

- The core of Mormonism is that there is only one God, and thus, only one true order of Godliness.

- Many Christians focus their attention on criticizing the LDS way of thinking, leading many to ask, "What would Jesus do?"

- The Bible is part of the collection of LDS sacred works, but it isn't everything.

Part 6

Latter-day Landscape and Leadership

Let's wrap things up with an examination of two distinct and highly visible icons of Mormonism—its temples and its prophets. More than 100 temples dot the earth, and 15 men have held the position of God's Prophets since the restoration of his church. This part provides you with a basic understanding of how temples fit into the LDS equation, and how each of the Church's Prophets lived their lives in a unique fashion to be called to such a sacred office.

We'll also examine the unique practice of temple work, and how temples are different from Sunday houses of worship. By the way, if you happen to live in an area where an LDS temple is being built, you can take a complete tour inside the building before it is dedicated as a House of the Lord. Be sure to check with local Church leaders if you'd like free tickets during the open-house events. Once the doors close and the dedication takes place, only the most worthy Latter-day Saints may enter these sacred buildings.

Chapter 26

Houses of the Lord

In This Chapter

- ◆ Temples: sacred places of worship for the worthy
- ◆ A look at ancient and modern-day temples
- ◆ Sacred temple ordinances that are required to return to heaven
- ◆ The holy ordinance of marriage
- ◆ The LDS belief in the eternal family

God has commanded his people to construct temples since the days of Adam and Eve. Only the most sacred ordinances (ceremonies), those that pertain to exaltation and eternal life, take place in the Houses of the Lord. Just as Solomon's temple once stood to serve God's highest orders of worship, Latter-day Saints enjoy the benefit of temple work as part of the Church's mission to redeem the dead. They do not attend church services in temples, nor are temples open for any work on Sundays. They attend temple sessions, first, on their own behalf, and then on behalf of others who have died.

As the membership of the LDS Church grows, so does the need for more temples. Apostle James E. Talmage has said of temples: "A temple is more than a chapel or church, more than a synagogue or cathedral; it is a structure erected as the house of the Lord, sacred to the closest communion between the Lord himself and the holy priesthood."

Perhaps the crowning testament to LDS activity is in members retaining a level of worthiness that allows them to participate in temple ordinances. There are more than 100 LDS temples throughout the world. Church members participate in an interview every two years, to review their worthiness to keep company in God's Holy House. Latter-day Saints who attend the temple often find more richly blessed lives. They have been promised that they will experience greater love in their homes, and their children will feel just a bit safer from worldly influences. Even their jobs seem a little less hectic when they get a good "spiritual workout" in the Lord's House.

Temples in Ancient Times

The idea of dedicating certain buildings to high ordinances of Holy origin is not a new concept. In ancient history, the children of Israel held church services in synagogues, as they do today. However, their high and sacred ordinances took place in, first, the Holy of Holies, found inside their tabernacles, which was a mobile structure—good for long-term desert wanderings.

Sacred worship soon moved from the tents to the *temples*. Temple activity was performed by the high priests of the ancient church. All offerings made on the altars of the temple were designed to address specific needs of God's children. There were unique offerings for health, for harvests, but most especially, for instruction from God on matters concerning the disposition of his government.

Mormonology

A **temple** is a high and holy sanctuary of worship to God. Only the most sacred ordinances—such as the endowment, sealing families together, and vicarious work for those who have died—take place in LDS temples, and only the worthiest members of the LDS Church are allowed to attend.

The earliest, most notable temple, Solomon's Temple, was built around the year 1000 B.C. Ancient legend says that Moses himself was present when the Ark of the Covenant was placed in this new temple.

Solomon's Temple was destroyed in 600 B.C., then rebuilt a century later, only to be destroyed again in 37 B.C. About 17 years before the birth of Jesus, under the direction of Herod, the temple was rebuilt in a political effort to pander Jewish favor. Its ultimate demise lay with Emperor Titus' Roman soldiers, during the conquest of Jerusalem in A.D. 70. The temple was destroyed for the last time, and replaced with a shrine to the Roman god Jupiter.

Modern-Day Temples

God's children have come a long way from the ancient times. Although there was considerable "wandering through the wilderness," as described throughout Chapters

14 through 17, Latter-day Saints did finally find their destination in the West. As did the community of God from ancient times, the LDS community began building temples at the direction of Prophet Joseph in 1832, while the Saints were somewhat settled in Kirtland, Ohio. The purpose of the temple was to provide a sacred sanctuary for divine revelation and a place to perform the sacred ordinances of the Gospel in behalf of those who had not had the opportunity to do so while alive.

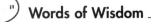

Words of Wisdom

Establish a house, even a house of prayer, a house of fasting, a house of faith, a house of learning, a house of glory, a house of order, a house of God.

—Doctrine and Covenants 88:119

Today, the Kirtland Temple (pictured in Chapter 14) is owned and operated as a tourist facility by the Community of Christ—a small splinter group from the LDS Church.

The Washington, D.C., Temple is the largest LDS temple in the world. This temple, which is actually located in Maryland, is one of just more than 100 buildings worldwide in which worthy LDS marriages are performed, families are sealed together forever, and other sacred ordinances are performed on behalf of those who have died.

©*Drew Williams (2002)*

The next temple of modern times was built when the Saints fled to Nauvoo, Illinois, in 1841. The temple in Nauvoo was still under construction when the saints began their trek west, after being evicted from Nauvoo by an Illinois militia. However, as in the days of Solomon, this modern-day House of the Lord was eventually ravaged by an arsonist's flames in 1848, and further destroyed by a tornado in the spring of 1850. The temple lay in ruin for the next 156 years.

Even before the Latter-day Saint community migrated to Nauvoo, LDS Prophet Joseph Smith had planned to build additional temples in Missouri, to replace the temple that had to be abandoned in Ohio. The Church was not able to begin any of the buildings. In fact, the temple in Nauvoo was completed and dedicated two years *after* the death of Joseph in 1844, *and* after the Saints began their migration west.

In June of 2002, on the anniversary of the death of Joseph and Hyrum Smith, at the time of their martyrdoms, the Prophet Gordon B. Hinckley dedicated the new Nauvoo Temple, which was rebuilt on exactly the same spot as the original.

Why the Fuss Over These Fancy Buildings?

For members of the Church of Jesus Christ of Latter-day Saints, one of the highest privileges in the Church is to bring their spouses to the altars of the temple. There, they are married not just for the period of their mortal lives, but for all eternity. Latter-day revelation explains that this privilege is required for exaltation in the next life.

And It Came to Pass

In 1980, my ship, the USS *Coral Sea*, returned to California from extended deployment in the Pacific and Middle East. My parents came to take me back to our home in Michigan and stopped in Salt Lake City at the suggestion of an LDS shipmate. On Temple Square, alongside the brass-domed Tabernacle, stood the Salt Lake Temple. It was our first formal encounter with "Mormons." Mom was surprised we weren't allowed to tour the temple. "It's not about secrecy," said a sister missionary. "It's because of the sacred nature of what takes place inside." I was fascinated. What could be so sacred to keep it hidden from public view? My curiosity about Mormonism increased, which led to my own baptism—coincidentally—in a building adjacent to the temple in Oakland, California, in 1982.

Temple work focuses on the family. Paraphrasing the words of Tevye, from the epic film *Fiddler On the Roof*, participating in temple ordinances helps LDS people find out about who they are and what God expects of them.

The Guy with the Horn

Many people who see an LDS temple are familiar with the golden statue that stands atop the highest spire. Most who are not familiar with LDS doctrine, would say that the statue was a reference to the angel Gabriel, from the Book of Revelation. They would be partially correct. There is a reference to an angel flying through the skies in Revelation 14:6, which reads, "I saw another angel fly in the midst of heaven, having the everlasting gospel to preach unto them that dwell on the earth, and to every nation, and kindred, and tongue, and people."

This angel was the angel Moroni, a character discussed in the Book of Mormon (see Chapter 13). Moroni restored the plates that contained the record of his people—a Meso-American culture long extinct, which Joseph Smith translated.

Moroni is the symbol of the message of the Restoration of the Church of God going out to the entire world, and stands on almost every temple built by the Church.

Sacred Ordinances (Not Secret Rites)

The ordinances of the temple can be grouped into three categories:

◆ Endowment for the individual

◆ "Sealing" covenants (which include but are not exclusive to marriage)

◆ Vicarious work on behalf of the dead

Following a series of questions that are asked by local Church leaders, which validate a Church member's worthiness, the individual attending the temple for the first time does so for his or her own benefit. This process is called the *endowment*.

During the temple experience, the individual learns important matters concerning the requirements for returning into the presence of God. A person goes through the temple endowment for his or her benefit only once.

> **Mormonology**
>
> **Endowments** are highly sacred blessings given to worthy Latter-day Saints, which deal with covenants made inside the temples of the Church. The endowment includes a spiritual cleansing of the participant, which is preparatory to returning to God's presence.

The New and Everlasting Covenant of Marriage

The covenant of marriage is one of the most sacred of all Latter-day Saint functions. Let's use real life to explain the Latter-day principle of eternal marriage. Imagine that you have fallen in love with the most wonderful person you have ever met. Imagine that you can think of no better place than to be with this person for the rest of your life, and you marry this person.

Now let's roll forward several years *after* the honeymoon period wears off—when things are starting to droop more than they used to, and the sound of marital bliss is frequently drowned out by the sounds of children crying, "She pulled my hair!" "He looked out my window!" "She touched my chair!" You still look into your spouse's eyes and find yourself just as happily married, or even more so than when you first wed.

Mormon Myths

Myth: LDS temple marriages do not include divorce. The "New and Everlasting Covenant" of marriage is an essential part of God's Plan. However, some marriages don't work out. Although still an infrequent occurrence, should mates choose to go in different directions, the choice is theirs.

Perhaps many of you are lucky enough to have known someone like that, or be in such a relationship yourself. Have you ever thought or hoped from time to time, that it would be nice to share the experience of your spouse's company forever? In the words of Prophet Gordon B. Hinckley: "Was there ever a man who truly loved a woman, or a woman who truly loved a man, who did not pray that their relationship might continue beyond the grave?"

And even though they might have to listen to all of those "hair-pulling" and "window-looking" stories from their kids, most parents wouldn't trade their children for *any* price.

"Forever" is a possibility that Latter-day Saints take seriously. When LDS couples kneel across the altar of the temple, they are pronounced husband and wife forever. The sacred covenants that LDS couples make in the temples offer families the assurance that they will be together throughout the eternities.

There are also LDS couples whose marriages were not performed in the temples. These couples may later choose to go to the temple and be sealed to each other, and to any children that have been born, based on their worthiness and desire to do so. Temple ordinances for couples already married are the same as if the couple was attending the temple on their wedding day.

By the way, there are no caulk guns or tubes of glue involved when families are "sealed" together. The term refers to an ordinance in which a man who holds certain priesthood authority *spiritually* binds the couple or family together in a special prayer, conducted with the participants kneeling over an altar in the temple. The participants are required to dress in all-white clothing, symbolizing the purity of the ordinance taking place. For Latter-day Saints, being sealed is an awesome spiritual experience.

This experience is especially common with the conversions of whole families—and is very special for those in attendance. For Latter-day Saints, being sealed together as an eternal family unit gives us a peace of mind that is unmatched in worldly experiences or ceremonies.

In 1996, I met a new LDS convert in northern Australia. He was preparing to attend the temple for his own endowments and to be sealed to his wife and children. In 1996, there was one temple in Australia, several thousand miles south in Sydney. When I asked him how he was going to get there, he said he had to sell his car. He also had quit his job, because he wasn't allowed time off for the trip. He said he felt there was nothing more important than to be an eternal family unit. He believed that through his faith, he would have an even better job available when he returned. "Jobs come and go," the man said, "But families can be forever."

The eternal love of a good spouse and wonderful children can provide an unshakable support structure of joy and personal fulfillment in an otherwise hectic world, especially when world events directly impact our lives in unpleasant ways.

I'd like to share the following story about one such event.

Redeeming the Dead

At the time I began to write this book, my friends Ryan and Erika Wilde, a couple in their early 30s, were expecting their second child, a daughter. In August 2002, little "Ruby Fire" Wilde was born three months early. After struggling through three weeks of intensive care, the infant slipped back into God's presence, leaving a lot of sad, profoundly disappointed people behind (there is a certain level of disappointment involved with not having the chance to see a child grow up). For both parents, the loss of Ruby will carry a bittersweet memory throughout their lives. For Ryan and Erika, however, death was not a new experience.

At the age of six, while Ryan was attending school, the car in which his parents and his other brothers were riding was struck by a locomotive. Ryan's father and a four-year-old brother were killed in the accident. With the loss of his daughter, brother, and father, Ryan had suffered three generations of death in his immediate family.

When she was two years old, Erika lost her five-year-old sister to illness. Later, about a year before Ruby was born, Erika suffered a miscarriage. In both of their cases, the Wildes had experienced difficult, unexpected losses while still early in their individual and married lives.

> **Words of Wisdom**
>
> Oh death, where is thy sting? O grave, where is thy victory? ... But Thanks be to God, which giveth us the victory through our Lord Jesus Christ.
>
> —1 Corinthians 15: 55, 57

However, both know that since they were married in the temple, as were their parents on both sides, those covenants they shared on their wedding day assures them that Ruby will be theirs again in the world to come. As well, Erika knows her sister will be part of her eternal family unit, and Ryan's, likewise. It may not completely remove the sting of death—the pain that those who are left behind must experience—but the knowledge that their spirits live on and their family can remain intact throughout all eternity gives them great comfort.

Mormonism is the only Christian religion that practices such beliefs as eternal families and redemption for the dead. A key LDS Church philosophy is that everyone gets an invitation to God's Kingdom; whether they show up is up to them.

Mormonology

Temple garments refer to special underwear that temple-worthy Latter-day Saint adults wear. These undergarments serve to remind LDS members of the sacred nature of not only their bodies, but also of those covenants that they made while in the temple. Garments must be worn with all clothing, with the exception of sporting events, swimming, and bathing. Naturally, because temple garments are somewhat more conservative than traditional boxers, briefs, and bikinis, Latter-day Saints who wear them dress to cover them.

To better see how temple work affects those who have died, let's go back to the time of Christ's crucifixion. The scriptures note that when he gave up his life, the spirit of Christ went to visit those spirits who were in prison, where he taught them until his resurrection three days later.

Latter-day doctrine, which coincides with the account of Christ visiting the spirits in prison, is that after death, people are confined to a state of detention or paradise, depending on their actions in mortality. It's a sort of holding pattern until we are all resurrected, judged, and delivered to our eternal justice. For those generations of people who did not have the chance to learn about the Gospel of Jesus Christ, they will have that opportunity to learn it then. Latter-day Saints believe that their own departed family members are in the spirit world, as well as angels directed by God, teaching those confined souls about Christ's plan of Salvation.

Latter-day Laughter

Priest to dying man: "Will you denounce Satan and his servants?" Dying man to priest: "I'd better not. I'm about to go into new territory and I don't want to anger the locals."

—Anonymous

However, without someone on *this* side of the veil (still alive), to perform those temple ordinances, those uninformed spirits cannot make the decision to accept or reject the Gospel of Christ. (See Chapter 6 for more details on the whole post-mortal life experience.)

Latter-day Saints believe that the true and living Gospel of Jesus Christ was restored to Joseph Smith in 1820. That leaves a gap of almost 20 centuries where the principles and ordinations of God's kingdom were not allowed on the earth (because there was nobody here with the authority to perform these ordinances, which included baptism, administering the Holy Ghost, and performing eternal marriages).

Billions of people have been born, lived, and died from the time of Christ to the time of Joseph Smith. These people were not able to experience the Gospel, and thus, were not allowed to make the decision on whether to accept it or not. For this purpose, members of the Church actively participate in temple work and family history research.

After a person goes through the temple for his or her own endowment, each subsequent time for the rest of that person's life, he or she attends and participates in behalf of a named individual who has died. Many Latter-day Saints, after researching their family histories, participate in behalf of their own deceased ancestors. However, others who attend the temple receive a random name that was extracted from genealogical records. Although it's important for us to look after our own ancestors, the objective is to provide the temple ordinances for as many people as possible.

> **Words of Wisdom**
>
> … The dead shall hear the voice of the Son of God: and they that hear shall live. … Marvel not at this: for the hour is coming, in the which all that are in the graves shall hear his voice, and shall come forth. …
>
> —John 5:25, 28, 29

After all, we are all related and we are our brother's keepers.

The Least You Need to Know

♦ God has always required his children to build temples.

♦ Holy temples are sanctuaries to provide spiritual instruction to the world.

♦ Modern-day temples provide temporary safe haven from worldly affairs, while also offering eternal peace of mind.

♦ Marriage and families are sealed together forever in sacred temple ordinances.

♦ The dead still get a chance at hearing the Gospel of Christ.

Chapter 27

Early Mormon Prophets

In This Chapter

- ◆ Prophets of different ages and backgrounds
- ◆ God is choosy about who he picks to lead
- ◆ Jesus Christ: the role model for all humanity
- ◆ Six early prophets of the Restoration

Of the sacred fraternity of men called to be apostles over the past 160-plus years, only 15 have served as Prophet of the Church of Jesus Christ of Latter-day Saints. These men have throughout history entertained royalty, presidents, and other celebrated people from around the world. Aside from Prophet Joseph Smith, who was only 38 at the time of his murder in 1844, the men who have led the LDS Church have been seasoned veterans in age, experience, and worldly challenge.

Latter-day Saints worldwide enjoy the blessing of knowing that their prophets are the only men who have been ordained as the authorized mouthpiece of God. They find their lives are blessed when they heed the prophets' council, and although they know these men will never mislead the Church, they also realize that the prophets are called to do the handi-work of Christ, who stands at the head of the Church.

Prophets of the Restoration

We have already spent some time discussing the role of a prophet in the LDS Church (see Chapter 20). Now let's look at the six men who followed Prophets Joseph Smith and Brigham Young during the first century of the Restored Gospel (we'll look at the modern-day prophets in the next chapter). All of the prophets from Joseph Smith to the present have lengthy backgrounds in service, leadership, and spiritual magnitude, identifying each of them as unique in the world of holy men. They include a former Methodist preacher, a lawyer, and presidential Cabinet member. Their combined time in service to the Lord spans more than 1,200 years!

When discussing LDS prophets, Brigham Young, immortalized in this statue, seems to be the most popular. However, there have been 15 leaders of the Church of Jesus Christ of Latter-day Saints over the past 170 years.

©Drew Williams (2002)

Here is a list of LDS prophets from Joseph Smith Jr. to the present, with their ages and dates when called, and how many years served.

Age and Tenure of LDS Prophets

Prophet	Age When Called	Year Called	Years Served
Joseph Smith Jr.	24	1830	14
Brigham Young	46	1847	30
John Taylor	71	1880	7
Wilford Woodruff	82	1889	9
Lorenzo Snow	84	1898	3
Joseph F. Smith	62	1901	18
Heber J. Grant	62	1918	22
George Albert Smith	75	1945	6
David O. McKay	77	1951	19
Joseph Fielding Smith	93	1970	2
Harold B. Lee	73	1972	1.5
Spencer W. Kimball	78	1973	12
Ezra Taft Benson	86	1985	8.5
Howard W. Hunter	87	1994	9 months
Gordon B. Hinckley	84	1995	Still serving

Choosing a New Prophet

Upon the death of a current prophet of the Church, that prophet's counselors return to their respective ranks within the "Quorum of the Twelve Apostles," based on seniority in the group. Until a new prophet is selected, the leadership of the Church rests with the Twelve as a group. Each member of the Twelve, when called to the Quorum, was given all of the rights and keys as prophets, seers, and revelators, but not the authority to use those keys in behalf of the entire Church. That decision depends on worthiness, seniority in the Quorum, and the unanimous decision of all members of the Twelve.

The appointment of a new Church leader usually takes place within a few days after the death of a prophet. However, for more than three years, between the death of Joseph Smith Jr. in 1844 and Christmas 1847, the LDS Church did not have a prophet ordained to the position of president of the Church. This was one of only two times in the history of the Church when a man was not immediately called to serve as the leader of the entire Church; the second time was after the death of John Taylor, when the Church waited two years for its fourth prophet, Wilford Woodruff. In the case of Joseph Smith, the Church depended upon the Quorum of the Twelve for more than four years, before Brigham Young was finally called and set apart as the second president of the Church (although he was serving as the president of the Quorum during that time).

There were several within the leadership who had felt that the Church should ordain an interim trustee. But the majority of the leadership disagreed. As a result, several key leaders who were with Joseph Smith in the beginning (along with Joseph's widow, Emma) fell away from the Church and created what became the "Reorganized" LDS Church, which is now called the "Community of Christ." This independent organization, which is completely separate from the LDS Church, believes that rightful leadership is based on a direct bloodline from Prophet Joseph Smith.

After an absence of a named prophet-leader for nearly five years, the First Presidency of the Church (which includes the prophet/president of the LDS Church and two counselors), was reestablished, and God's work was underway again. Once the First Presidency is appointed, the Quorum of the Twelve Apostles fall under direct direction of the new Church president.

In many cases, stories from the lives of these men who have been called "prophet" are replete with poverty, personal harm, and loss of loved ones. But one common theme that further binds these men is their endless pursuit of the human soul, as admonished by Jesus Christ. Each of the men who has served as prophets of the Church were also missionaries; several times over, in many cases. They also held various Church callings that would hone their leadership skills, and all of the men have been temple-worthy husbands and fathers.

The Savior as the Model

Prophet David O. McKay said of the Savior, "The highest of all ideals are the teachings and life of Jesus." Christ demonstrated to perfection the spiritual ideals of all things that are good and worthwhile in the world. He still stands as the role model to all humanity.

Those who have been called to lead the LDS Church exemplify Christ's teachings and mannerisms in their efforts to help draw LDS people closer to him. Jesus Christ possessed a great level of responsibility—even at a young age. Jesus knew at a very early age what his responsibilities to the world would be, as pointed out in the account in Luke. Jesus was found in the temple, lecturing to the learned men of Jerusalem. So it has been with each of the prophets who have led the Church. In each case, these men have chosen to live righteously even at an early age, and have done nothing to tarnish their spiritual integrity throughout their lives.

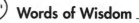 **Words of Wisdom**

For he whom God hath sent speaketh the words of God: for God giveth not the Spirit by measure unto him. The Father loveth the Son, and hath given all things into his hand.

—John 3:34–35

John Taylor: Defender of Faith

During the early 1800s, New England and eastern Canada weren't short on revivalists and religious factions. Heeding a personal intuition to travel to the New World, English minister John Taylor led a Methodist faction in Toronto, which believed the church described in the New Testament no longer existed on the earth.

In 1836 Taylor met Parley P. Pratt, an early LDS leader and missionary to Canada. Pratt taught Taylor of Joseph Smith's efforts in restoring God's one true Church. As a result, Taylor and most of his congregation converted to Mormonism.

Taylor was called to lead the LDS missionary movement throughout Canada. Later he served as a missionary in England. His focus regarded family as a high priority. He wrote, "I love the Lord and His people and all men, and my desire is to promote the happiness and well-being of the human family."

Taylor was a man of great faith throughout his life. Without any funding while in England, he relied on his faith in God to provide the means necessary to complete his mission. Stories record that he boarded the ship to England with only a single penny in his pocket, exactly the same amount he returned with.

John Taylor was one of the three men who were with Joseph Smith on that fateful June day in 1844. Taylor took four bullets during the attack on the Carthage Jail, which led to the death of Joseph and his brother, Hyrum (see Chapter 15). A pocket watch that Taylor wore on a chain in a breast pocket saved his life, deflecting the fifth bullet, which would have been fatal.

Words of Wisdom

We are here to build up the church of God, the Zion of God and the kingdom of God, and to be on hand to do whatever God requires.

—Prophet John Taylor

John Taylor has been referred to in Church history as the "Living Martyr." He would have been a dead martyr, were it not for his friend and fellow survivor, Willard Richards. Richards, who went unscathed in the attack, dragged Taylor out of the bedroom and into a cell, telling Taylor, "If your wounds are not fatal, I want you to live to tell the story." Taylor did live to tell the story, and spent the rest of his life defending the integrity of the Church.

Taylor later served as a counselor to Brigham Young until Young's death in 1877, when Taylor himself was called to lead the Church. John Taylor died in Salt Lake City in 1887.

Wilford Woodruff: Trusted Servant

As a boy in the early American Midwest, Wilford Woodruff lived a life to rival the toughest of circumstances. His youth was riddled with accidents, any one of which could have killed him. When he was three, he fell into a boiling pot of water. Before age 20, Woodruff was kicked by an ox, broke both arms from a fall in his father's barn, was involved in at least three serious horse-drawn wagon accidents, and almost drowned in 30 feet of water. He also suffered from hypothermia, was bitten by a rabid dog, and almost severed his own foot with an axe.

Aside from additional broken bones and a near-fatal bout with a grain mill wheel, Woodruff rose to become one of Joseph Smith's apostles. He served missions throughout Arkansas and Tennessee, along the coast of Maine, and in the United Kingdom.

In England, Woodruff served what has become one of the ultimate missionary conversion experiences in the Church. Woodruff had the inclination to visit a farm where a man named John Benbow was attending a congregational service of more than 600 people. They had been combined in prayer, asking the Lord to send them his messenger. Within eight months, under the teachings of Elder Woodruff, more than 1,500 people were converted to Mormonism, including the original 600 at Benbow's farm.

On one of the most memorable occasions in Church history, Woodruff recounted his experiences with Joseph Smith and the early years of the Church into one of the first voice recorders made. He said, "I bear testimony that Joseph Smith was the author of the endowments as received by the Latter-day Saints. I received my own endowments under his hands and direction, and I know they are true principles. … In all his testimonies to us, the power of God was visibly manifest in the Prophet Joseph. This is my testimony, spoken by myself into a talking machine on this the nineteenth day of March 1897, in the ninety-first year of my age."

The recording is a cherished piece of early LDS history, and stands as the only recording of a man who was actually present when Joseph Smith organized the Church in 1830. The recording is still available today, through audiotapes offered by the Church (check the official Church website at www.lds.org for details).

Wilford Woodruff died in September 1898.

Lorenzo Snow: Blessings of Tithing

Born in 1814 in Ohio, Lorenzo Snow experienced his higher education at a Presbyterian college in Ohio, and was baptized into the Church after meeting Prophet Joseph Smith. Snow was one of the few military veterans in the ranks of the prophets. However, he eventually gave up his Army commission for church service.

President Snow was well known for two major experiences in Church history, the first being one of the only documented accounts of raising the dead in modern times.

While speaking at a local Church conference north of Salt Lake City, President Snow learned that a 15-year-old girl had succumbed to scarlet fever after a week of struggling. When he received word of the girl's death, Snow and a companion left the conference to visit the girl's family. According to the reports, she had been dead for several hours. At the urging of the girl's parents, and feeling prompted by the Spirit that this child's work was not yet finished in this life, the LDS prophet placed his hands on the girl's head in the method of a priesthood blessing and commanded her to come back to the living. More than an hour later, after Snow had left the family, the girl opened her eyes and asked where the man was who called her back.

> **Words of Wisdom**
>
> The time has now come for every Latter-day Saint, who calculates to be prepared for the future and to hold his feet strong upon a proper foundation, to do the will of the Lord and to pay his tithing in full.
>
> —Prophet Lorenzo Snow

On another occasion, during the summer of 1899, the LDS Church was in significant debt. Southern Utah was also suffering from a severe drought, which threatened to destroy the year's crops. The potential for mass starvation during the coming winter was at the forefront of the prophet's mind, while visiting the southern Utah town of St. George.

Snow spoke at a conference in St. George and to the area congregations along the road back to Salt Lake City, and said that he had the distinct feeling that the local Church members were neglecting the law of tithing. Conversely, he noted that if the Saints paid their tithing, the full 10 percent of their increases, God would bless them with full crops and financial security throughout the Church.

His sermon was successful and the Saints of southern Utah did reap a full harvest. By the following year, tithing and additional donations had doubled. By 1907, only eight years following a period of serious financial difficulties, the Church was financially solvent, owing nothing to anyone. The Church has been "in the black" ever since, thanks to President Snow, who died in 1901.

Today, in part because of the prompting of this late nineteenth-century prophet for the cause of tithing, the Church of Jesus Christ of Latter-day Saints enjoys billions of dollars in financial assets.

Joseph F. Smith: Teenage Missionary

Joseph F. Smith was the son of Hyrum and nephew of Prophet Joseph Smith Jr. Joseph F. was the second of three prophets who shared a bloodline with the founder of the LDS Church. (To avoid confusion, I've referred to them as Joseph Jr., Joseph F., and Joseph Fielding.)

Joseph F. was only a boy of seven when his widowed mother, Mary Fielding, set out for Salt Lake City after the LDS expulsion from Nauvoo, Illinois, in 1846. After his family arrived in the Salt Lake Valley in the fall of 1848, the Smiths settled south of Salt Lake City.

> **Words of Wisdom**
>
> No man can preach God and godliness and the truth as it is in Christ Jesus except he be inspired by the Holy Ghost.
>
> —Prophet Joseph F. Smith

By the age of 13, Joseph F. had lost both parents, and was left to struggle with his early teens, "like a comet or fiery meteor, without attraction or gravitation to keep me balanced or guide me within reasonable bounds." But Prophet Brigham Young stepped in to help guide the young man's spiritual future, calling Joseph F. to more than 10 years of missionary service.

Joseph F. Smith's first call to serve was in the Sandwich (Hawaiian) Islands. The story goes that after his mission to Hawaii and return to Utah, 19-year-old Joseph F. and his traveling party were making camp one evening when a group of thugs rode into the camp, shooting, cursing, and shouting of what they were going to do with the Mormons. Overhearing, Joseph F. walked back into the camp, deciding not to back down from the troublemakers.

A short conversation ensued:

Tough guy: "Are you a Mormon?"

Joseph F.: "Yes, siree; dyed in the wool; true blue, through and through."

The man grabbed Joseph F.'s hand and said, "Well, you are the [expletives deleted] pleasantest man I ever met! I am glad to see a man that stands up for his convictions!"

After serving four years in the Pacific, Joseph F. was sent to serve a three-year mission in England. Brigham Young was determined to keep this missionary's mind focused on God's work during those young formidable years, and sent him back to Hawaii for another year.

Eventually, at the ripe young age of 27, Joseph F. was ordained to the office of apostle and served as one of Brigham Young's counselors. Joseph F. Smith served as an apostle until his placement as president and prophet of the Church in October 1901. When he died in 1918, Church membership had doubled to almost a half-million members worldwide.

Heber J. Grant: Never Give Up!

Heber Grant represented the epitome of the School of Hard Knocks. He never knew his father, who died when Grant was only nine days old in 1856. Raised by his mother, Grant experienced a boyhood in Utah full of challenges and responsibilities far senior to his youth. He wanted to play baseball, but couldn't, due to extended duties at home.

Neighborhood boys his age called him a sissy and taunted him so much he decided to focus some of his free time mastering the Great American Pastime. "I kept practicing, and finally succeeded in getting into the second nine of our club." Eventually, Grant and his teammates won three state-wide baseball championships in California, Wyoming, and Colorado.

 **Words of Wisdom**

Every principle of the Gospel has been revealed to us for our individual advancement and for our individual perfection.

—Prophet Heber J. Grant

Grant was also taunted by his peers for his bad handwriting and terrible singing voice. On a trip with several other apostles, over a 60-mile journey he told his traveling companions that he hoped they would not be offended if he sang songs from the Church hymn book. There was no objection at first. However, his intent was to sing all 100 songs in the Church hymnbook over the course of the journey. "After I had sung about 40 times, they assured me that if I sang the remaining 60 they would be sure to have nervous prostration." Grant paid no attention to their pleas for him to stop, and continued through the full 100 (with 15 self-requested encores!).

Elder Grant served as a mission leader in Japan, throughout the British Isles, and in most of western Europe. On an occasion in 1906, he was the guest of King Oscar II of Sweden. The king had sent representatives to all of the states in America to see how his former subjects had fared in the New World. The king told Grant that of all the settlements of his people, the people most content, "more prosperous and happier" lived in Utah.

Under the leadership of Heber J. Grant, which ended with his death in 1945, Church membership had reached more than one million worldwide.

George Albert Smith: Compassionate Servant

George Albert Smith ("G.A.") was born in 1870, 1 of 15 children. Although not a direct descendant of Prophet Joseph Smith Jr., the two men shared the same ancestry of Asael Smith, the grandfather of the first LDS prophet.

G.A. grew up in Utah on the family farm along the Jordan River. At the age of 12, he began working in the nation's first department store, Zion's Cooperative Mercantile Institution (ZCMI). Later, his work in the Boy Scout program was highly acclaimed. He served on the National Executive Board as part of his Church calling of superintendent over the youth programs. In 1932, G.A. was awarded the Silver Buffalo—scouting's highest honor—alongside Colonel Theodore Roosevelt Jr.

George Albert Smith was called to the position of prophet and president of the Church in May 1945. During his administration, the LDS movement expanded to great capacities, thanks to his efforts with the missionary program. Following World War II, seeing pairs of missionaries was not as common, mainly because of the war and subsequent draft of young men. During G.A.'s administration, there were more than 5,000 missionaries called to the task.

Words of Wisdom

Knowing that the Redeemer of mankind has offered the world the only plan that will fully develop us and make us really happy here and hereafter, I feel it not only a duty but a blessed privilege to disseminate the truth.

—Prophet George Albert Smith

At the time of his death in April 1951, George Albert Smith had seen the Church grow 10 times larger than it was when he was born, with more than one million Latter-day Saints in the world. At his funeral, a man named Fitzgerald, who was not LDS, was asked to speak. Of President Smith he said, "He was a man without guile, a religious man and spiritual leader, not only in his own Church—in any group."

Latter-day Laughter

I have known George Albert Smith all the days of my life. ... It was he who set me apart for my first mission. He married me to my good wife. ... It seems all the difficulties that have ever encountered me in my life he is responsible for.

—Apostle Matthew Cowley

The Least You Need to Know

- The calling of prophet is unique in the world, as directed by God.

- There's no smoke and mirrors when choosing a new prophet, just prayer and divine inspiration.

- Jesus sets the standard for "Ultimate Man of God."

- Many great leaders have been called, but only a few have been chosen as God's mouthpiece.

Chapter 28

Modern-Day Messengers of Christ

In This Chapter

- ◆ How modern prophets stand ready to help with today's challenges
- ◆ A profile of the modern prophets
- ◆ Thomas Monson, a man of promise
- ◆ God's plans are made known through his messengers

By the end of the nineteenth-century LDS pioneers had helped settle the western United States. Much of the effort was due to the leadership of men such as Joseph Smith, Brigham Young, and Heber J. Grant. Mass media exposure to Mormonism and its leaders has grown to even greater levels over the past 50 years. On the occasion of the Pioneer Centennial celebration of 1947, *Time Magazine* commemorated the event with a full story and cover photograph of LDS President George Albert Smith.

LDS leaders continue to embrace the world's communications resources, as in the recent popularity of LDS President Gordon B. Hinckley on such programs as *Larry King Live*, which is broadcast around the world. This suggests even greater influence of LDS thought and also of the men who are called "prophets." It makes sense, since the television itself was patented by a modern LDS "pioneer" who attended Brigham Young University.

In this chapter, we'll take a look at the prophets for modern times.

Prophets for Modern Times

With the exception of Harold B. Lee, all of the prophets listed in this chapter were Utah natives, and most were direct descendants of the earliest members of the LDS Church. Each of the men who were called during the last half of the twentieth century were uniquely geared for the tasks that would follow with the *next* generation of LDS people.

For example, during his presidency in the 1950s, David O. McKay spent a great deal of time counseling Church members on how to become closer as husband and wife—just prior to the era of "free love." Ezra Taft Benson, who was the leader of the LDS Church in the later part of the 1980s, warned the Saints to avoid R-rated movies, and spoke of the risk of a degradation in social structure. I wonder if he somehow knew that within a few years, something called the Internet would forever simplify how people communicated, learned—and became exposed to pornography in epidemic proportions.

These modern-day messengers of Christ have consistently demonstrated an ability to foresee the challenges of the human race, and to offer specific ways in which the LDS community could respond to those challenges.

David O. McKay: Defender of Family

David O. McKay was called to be the prophet of the Church in 1951 and was well known for his love and dedication to the family unit. Many LDS families have inscribed, cross-stitched, or framed quotes from President McKay in their homes. Here are three of my favorites:

◆ "I know that a home in which unity, mutual helpfulness, and love abide is just a bit of heaven on earth."

◆ "No other success can compensate for failure in the home."

◆ "The problems of these difficult times cannot be better solved in any other place … than by love and righteousness, precept and example, and devotion to duty in the home."

President McKay was remembered for much of the Church's growth during the first half of the twentieth century. However, the courtship between McKay and Emma Ray Robbins was known throughout the Church as a model to follow.

In his book, *My Father, David O. McKay*, his son Lawrence writes: "... There was a kind of magic in my parents' marriage. ... As children, we accepted our parents' world as the norm. Looking back, we can see more clearly how devoted they were to each other and the gospel. It was quite clear that their worlds revolved around each other, and it made a happy, peaceful world for us."

Also, President McKay's encouragement for the Church's missionary program led to more than 13,000 callings to serve full-time missions during his administration.

President McKay's leadership heralded high technology into the Church. During his administration LDS people would forever have worldwide access to annual Church conferences and other broadcasts following the installation of a new short-wave radio system.

While in his late 80s and early 90s, President McKay traveled throughout the world's population of LDS culture. From the small island community of Suva near Fiji, where he met with a handful of Saints in a member's small home, to Switzerland, where he dedicated the Mormon Temple, President McKay was, at the time, the most globe-trotting of God's prophets.

On January 18, 1970, the 96-year-old prophet passed away, his loving wife and children beside him.

> **Words of Wisdom**
>
> The home is the basis of a righteous life, and no other instrumentality can take its place nor fulfill its essential functions.
> —Prophet David O. McKay

> **Latter-day Laughter**
>
> Young boy to David O. McKay: "How does it feel to be 94?"
> President McKay: "It feels great, when you consider the alternative."

Joseph Fielding Smith: Third-Generation Prophet

The son of Prophet Joseph F. Smith and grandson of Hyrum Smith (Joseph Smith Jr.'s brother), Joseph Fielding Smith led the LDS Church for only two years. His birth was foreseen by his father: According to one account by Apostle Bruce R. McConkie, Joseph Fielding's mother was promised that her first son would be named after his father and would one day serve in the Quorum of the Twelve Apostles. McConkie wrote, "Julina had three daughters but no sons." However, after a plea to God, Julina eventually did deliver a boy, and he was called to the position of apostle in 1910 at age 34.

Joseph Fielding Smith spent more than 60 years as a church leader, prior to being called to prophet of the Church in 1970. In a blessing he received at 37, he was told he had the gift and obligation to defend the early teachings of Prophet Joseph Smith Jr. It was part of a lifelong mission for Joseph Fielding to defend Joseph Smith, his grandfather's brother. In fact, he wrote 25 books on the history of the Church, including several acclaimed volumes on the teachings of the first LDS prophet.

Joseph Fielding Smith was the last prophet to personally know the other 13 prophets who have followed Joseph Smith. Although he was only just more than a year old when invited to travel with Brigham Young to dedicate the St. George Temple in Southern Utah, Joseph Fielding wrote later that he nonetheless enjoyed knowing he was with Brigham for the occasion.

Joseph Fielding was a serious man and strong church leader, but he had a zeal for life and adventure. On one such adventure, as companion to his friend, the general of the Utah National Guard, Joseph Fielding piloted an Air Force jet over Church head-quarters in Salt Lake City while members of his staff and other workers watched in amazement. He was in his 80s at the time.

As recounted in one of the Church's many course manuals on religious history, "Joseph Fielding Smith's life span covered the period from the covered wagon to the jet and space age." He died in 1972 at the age of 95.

Harold B. Lee: Welfare Reformer

Harold Bingham Lee was born in Idaho in the spring of 1899. With a simple, country upbringing in the small town of Clifton, President Lee knew well the joys of youth that money could not buy. Gordon B. Hinckley, the Church's fifteenth leader, wrote, "The air was clean and clear, with something almost sweet in the taste of it. The water was like rippling glass. ... Here, [in Clifton] barefoot, overall-clad Harold grew, a boy among country boys."

During the Great Depression, Lee served as a 31-year-old president of the "Utah Pioneer Stake," one of the early Church stakes in Utah. He was the youngest Stake president in the Church. In a region where more than half of his congregations was left without jobs, Lee worked to build the Church's new welfare program. He established the first Bishop's Storehouse, a resource designed to provide food and supplies to LDS families in need.

"Education" and "service" were watchwords during President Lee's Church leadership. He visited many countries, helping to establish the LDS Church in such places as Jerusalem, South Korea, and throughout Europe. President Lee was fond of the young men and women of the military, and directed the Church's Servicemen's Program during World War II, Korea, and Vietnam.

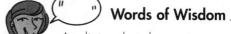

Words of Wisdom

A religion that does not require the sacrifice of all things never has power sufficient to produce the faith necessary unto life and salvation.

—Prophet Harold B. Lee

Although his leadership as prophet, which began in 1971, lasted only about 17 months—ending with his death in 1973—President Lee's influence in the welfare of LDS people worldwide can still be seen in the Church's programs for the needy.

Spencer W. Kimball: Every Member a Missionary

Spencer Wolley Kimball was born in Salt Lake City, but raised in Arizona. He spent his youth on his family farm, milking cows and gathering hay at the harvest. As a boy, Kimball was devoted to his attendance at Sunday school, and spent much of his free time studying scriptures.

This rare photo shows LDS Prophet Spencer W. Kimball (sitting at left), with two apostles who would later become prophets themselves. Ezra Taft Benson (standing), became the thirteenth prophet of the Church after President Kimball's death. Gordon B. Hinckley, the fifteenth prophet of the Church, is seated in back.

©Paul Soutar (1985)

President Kimball served as a missionary in Missouri. Because missionaries and their families are required to pay all expenses for their missions, so it was when young Spencer Kimball was called to serve in the Central States mission in 1914. To help pay his way, the young Elder Kimball sold his favorite horse for $175—enough for six months of service at a whopping $24 and change per month!

Kimball became an apostle in 1943 and prophet of the Church in 1973. As a member of the leadership of the Church, he played an important role in his service to the Native American people, and in growing the missionary efforts worldwide.

> **Words of Wisdom**
>
> In spite of all the gods that men make for themselves and the confusion incident thereto, the living and true God is in his heaven and is available to his children. If there is estrangement, it is men who have cut themselves off from God.

One of the most notable events in Church history took place while President Kimball was prophet of the Church. Much debate had ensued over the matter of the priesthood of God being made available to more than just a select few men, based on racial background. Until this time, men of color could not hold the priesthood. Prophets and members of the Quorum of the Twelve Apostles had struggled with the matter of people of color not being allowed to hold the priesthood. In response to the matter, President Kimball spent time in the temple, praying for guidance.

He wanted to be sure of the direction God planned, and on June 1, 1978, President Kimball and the Twelve Apostles met privately in the Salt Lake Temple for prayer and discussion on the matter. "The Spirit of the Lord rested mightily upon us all," wrote Apostle Bruce R. McConkie. "We all heard the same voice, received the same message." The message rang clear that no man should be prohibited from the joy of holding the priesthood because of race. The response from LDS people worldwide was illuminated by the dramatic increase in mission calls, the placement of new leaders in their respective lands—particularly in Ghana and Nigeria, throughout the Caribbean Islands, and in Brazil.

> **Mormon Myths**
>
> *Myth: The LDS Church fell to peer pressure to allow people of color to hold the priesthood.* While there was much debate and contemplation over the matter of whether the priesthood should go to all worthy men, it was ultimately a decision made by an inspired prophet of God, sitting in the temple along with his counselors and the Quorum of the Twelve Apostles. The time was right for the change, but more importantly, the spirit bore witness that it was God's desire to allow the change.

Also under the direction of President Spencer W. Kimball came the most recent canonized writing in the LDS Church. Sections 137 and 138 of the Doctrine and Covenants record revelations given earlier to Joseph Smith Jr. and Joseph F. Smith, respectively. These additions addressed temple work for the deceased and the exaltation of little children who die before the age of accountability. Also, events pertaining to the Savior's visit to the dead between the time he was crucified and the time of his resurrection were revealed.

During President Kimball's tenure, the Church's scriptures were reprinted with more detailed concordances and glossaries. In 1982, the Church was recognized by the Layman's National Bible Committee for its efforts in detailing the scriptures contained in the King James Version of the Holy Bible—which is part of the Church's Standard Works.

Later in his life President Kimball suffered several critical physical maladies. One of the most difficult challenges was the dramatic change in his voice after a partial removal of his vocal cords due to cancer. Following the surgery, President Kimball spoke to his friends at a regional conference in Arizona. He noted his experience with this often-repeated quote: "I went away to the East … and fell among thieves and cutthroats. They cut my throat and stole my voice." President Kimball loved to sing and play the piano, and the change from his pleasant voice to a lower pitch and gruff tone made him fear a negative reaction from Church members—which never came.

It was President Kimball's voice that I first heard as my introduction to Church activity back in 1980, in a radio broadcast of an LDS General Conference. I was immediately captivated by this powerful, deep resonating voice. After joining the Church in 1982, I always watched and listened to the semiannual conference events, hoping just to hear that great man speak again.

President Kimball's missionary efforts were also of great note. When he became prophet of the Church in 1973, there were slightly more than three million members worldwide. At the time of his death in 1985, the LDS population had doubled.

Today, according to national accounts, the LDS Church is still the fastest-growing Christian religion in the United States, with almost 12 million members worldwide.

(And by the way, although they might look alike George Lucas did *not* model the character "Yoda" after President Kimball!)

Ezra Taft Benson: Strong on Morality

With more than 40 years of experience as an apostle and a stint as President Eisenhower's Secretary of Agriculture, Ezra Taft Benson was ordained "Prophet, Seer, and Revelator" for the LDS Church in November 1985.

A major move under President Benson's leadership came in 1989, when the Church opened the BYU Jerusalem Center in Israel—an extension of Brigham Young University. Traditional Jews around the world protested that the center would be used for proselytizing and the conversion of Jews to Mormonism. However, from the time it was built the Jerusalem Center was dedicated as a sacred place of learning, and has not been used for missionary work.

Words of Wisdom

Great nations are never conquered from outside unless they are rotten from inside. Our greatest national problem today is erosion, not erosion of the soil but erosion of the national morality.

—Prophet Ezra Taft Benson

Like many of his predecessors, President Benson has been remembered for his efforts to focus on the family. In his address to the women of the Church in 1986, the prophet said, "Give me a young woman who is virtuous ... who will not settle for less than a temple marriage, and I will give you a young woman who will perform miracles for our Lord now and throughout eternity."

Ezra Taft Benson, the oldest of 11 children and the father of six, died May 30, 1994.

And It Came to Pass

Most memorable for many Latter-day Saints was President Benson's love and dedication to reading the Book of Mormon. He was firm in his conviction for the scriptures and admonished LDS people worldwide to make sure the Book of Mormon was the "center of our personal study, family teaching, preaching, and missionary work." Within one year of the prophet's remarks, almost three million more copies were distributed throughout the Church's missionary program—many with personal photos and testimonies inscribed from local contributors.

Howard W. Hunter: Brief, Quiet Leadership

Although he served as prophet and president of the Church for just nine months, Howard W. Hunter's influence as a church leader spanned 35 years, after being called to the apostleship in 1959, through his appointment and service as prophet in 1994.

President Hunter was a strong businessman, attorney, and even a professional musician during the late 1920s. However his resolve to serve the Lord won out over the various lucrative occupations of his time.

When called by then President McKay to the role of apostle, Hunter said, "I am willing to devote my life and all that I have in this service." During his time in Church leadership, Hunter expanded Church efforts in California, Nevada, the Midwest, North Carolina, and along the Pacific Rim nations.

President Hunter's brief position as prophet demonstrated great example in the face of adversity. Two incidents come to mind. Throughout the mid-1980s, he suffered a series of physical maladies, including tumors in his lymph nodes, a bleeding ulcer, and extensive back difficulties. President Hunter's doctors told him that it would be unlikely for him to ever walk again because of his serious health problems. Challenging adversity, President Hunter walked into a session at the Salt Lake Temple with the help of a security guard. The apostles who were present applauded as President Hunter entered the room. It was, he later noted, the first time he had ever heard clapping in a temple. Of those critics forecasting his life in a wheelchair, he wrote, "They have failed to take in consideration the power of prayer."

On another occasion, which was reported in the world press, President Hunter faced an uncertain outcome at the hands of a would-be assailant. On February 7, 1993, as president of the Quorum of Twelve Apostles, Hunter was invited to address the students at Brigham Young University. With almost 20,000 people in attendance, President Hunter was preparing to address the group when a man from the audience rushed onto the stage carrying a briefcase in one hand and an object he claimed to be a detonator in the other.

The stage was cleared except for the man, President Hunter, and two guards who refused to leave. After some confusion and heightened tension throughout the massive crowd, several students began to sing the LDS hymn, "We Thank Thee, Oh God, for a Prophet." The singing of the thousands in attendance brought a particular calming effect to the odd standoff taking place. Within a few minutes, the man was distracted and subdued, and President Hunter was able to continue his talk. Perhaps timely and not so coincidentally, the talk he prepared was titled, "Life Has a Fair Number of Challenges."

The challenge of prostate cancer took President Hunter's life on a Friday morning in March 1995.

Words of Wisdom

Please remember this one thing. If our lives and our faith are centered upon Jesus Christ and his restored gospel, nothing can ever go permanently wrong.

—Prophet Howard W. Hunter

Latter-day Laughter

Confined to a wheelchair at the Church's General Conference in October 1987, President Hunter was one of the selected speakers. His opening remarks: "Forgive me if I remain seated while I present these few remarks. It is not by choice that I speak from a wheelchair. I notice that the rest of you seem to enjoy the conference sitting down, so I will follow your example."

Gordon B. Hinckley: Temple Advocate

At 84, Gordon B. Hinckley was called to the position of prophet and president of the Church in March 1995. President Hinckley, by all accounts, has been the most traveled and most interviewed prophet in modern times. Under his direction, the Church has enjoyed more media attention than at any other time in history.

A goal of President Hinckley's was to see more than 100 temples built and dedicated, which occurred in 2001, with the dedication of the Boston Temple. President Hinckley has represented the Church on national news programs such as *60 Minutes* and *Larry King Live*. Veteran news legend Mike Wallace has said of Hinckley: "My *60 Minutes* colleagues and I learned, from the time we spent with Gordon Hinckley and his wife … this thoughtful and optimistic leader of the Mormon Church fully deserves the almost universal admiration that he gets."

Almost immediately after the terrorist attacks on September 11, 2001, President George W. Bush invited top religious leaders from around the country to a special White House meeting. President Hinckley participated in the event. And when all of the sporting world's eyes were on Salt Lake City for the 2002 Winter Olympics, President Hinckley was frequently involved in press interviews and participated in a special message to visitors.

Now in his nineties, Gordon B. Hinckley still conducts media interviews, meets with heads of state, travels throughout the world, and presides over a congregation of almost 12 million members.

> **Words of Wisdom**
>
> Our only desire is to cultivate a spirit of mercy and kindness, of understanding and healing. We seek to follow the practice of our Lord, who "went about doing good."
>
> —Prophet Gordon B. Hinckley

Thomas S. Monson: Man of Promise

While at the time of this writing President Hinckley serves as head of the LDS Church, it is worth noting the next senior ranking apostle who works with him.

Thomas Monson, a counselor to President Hinckley, is also the current president of the Quorum of Twelve Apostles, based on his seniority in the Quorum. President Monson was ordained to the office of apostle when only 36 years old, in October 1963, the youngest apostle in more than a century. Since the mid-1980s, President Monson has served as a counselor in the First Presidency of the Church, for Presidents Benson and Hunter, prior to President Hinckley.

A Navy veteran, President Monson began his leadership serving as a bishop in Salt Lake City at the age of 22, and as a mission president in Canada. His stories of a lively childhood in Utah are famous among Church members, especially the young men.

Just as a reminder, the LDS Church uses the term "president" to denote not only the leaders of each quorum or priesthood office, but also for the counselors of stake presidents and the president of the Church. Check out Chapter 20 for more information on the priesthood hierarchy of the LDS Church.

One thing is for certain, there will always be great men who walk among us, leading God's work. I hope that this book has provided you with a fundamental understanding of LDS philosophy, which I believe to be God's philosophy as well.

May you enjoy the choicest of God's blessings for yourselves and your families, as you study his words of inspiration and guidance. This is my prayer and hope, in the name of Jesus Christ, Amen.

The Least You Need to Know

- Modern-day messengers lead the Lord's congregation through troubled times.
- Physical obstacles do not slow the Lord's work; several leaders in the LDS Church were called well into their senior years.
- Thomas Monson, who works with President Hinckley, is the next senior ranking apostle.
- Latter-day Saints believe that modern-day prophets are true messengers of God.

Appendix A

Twenty Favorite Websites

If you'd like a more in-depth look at the Church of Jesus Christ of Latter-day Saints, its philosophies, and the culture of the LDS people, check out this list of 20 recommended websites.

Ancient Research (www.farmsresearch.com). The Foundation for Ancient Research and Mormon Studies is a Brigham Young University-sponsored consortium of "thinkers" who research and pontificate on the Old and New Testaments, Book of Mormon, Book of Abraham, and any other books that might interest themselves or the LDS audience.

Book of Mormon Online (www.hti.umich.edu/m/mormon). The complete Book of Mormon fully indexed with a search engine, thanks to the people at the University of Michigan.

Book of Mormon Translations (www.xmission.com/~health/mormon/language.html). Provides free access to a copy of the Book of Mormon in nearly 80 languages.

BYU (www.byu.edu/index.html). The official website of Brigham Young University, the largest church-owned college in the United States.

Family Research (www.familysearch.org). One of three official sites of the Church of Jesus Christ of Latter-day Saints. Family Search provides anyone with the resources to track down his or her family heritage. The LDS Church has the world's largest collection of family names and genealogical records, and this site provides a window into most of the available records.

Genealogy Work (www.onegreatfamily.com). A comprehensive, subscription-based online service and resource site dedicated to family research.

International Mormon Resources (www.gatheringofisrael.com). The online resource for International Members of the Church of Jesus Christ of Latter-day Saints, including a complete atlas and directory index of LDS temples and missions.

LDS Apologetics (www.mormonfortress.com). An online resource for information to defend the Mormon faith.

LDS Handicraft (www.mormonhandicraft.com). An online store dedicated to selling LDS handicrafts.

LDS History Association (www.mhahome.org). Dedicated to the research, appreciation, and critical analysis of the LDS past.

LDS Lifestyle (www.ldsliving.com). A comprehensive resource for materials used by LDS people in their day-to-day lives.

LDS Literature (http://humanities.byu.edu/MLDB/mlithome.htm#amlinfo). The Association for Mormon Letters, which provides an online resource dedicated to LDS writers, and critical analysis of the literature they publish.

LDS-Related News (www.ldstoday.com). An independent website dedicated to LDS activity in the world.

LDS Resource Directory (http://ldsfrontpage.homestead.com/Directory.html). The most comprehensive directory to LDS interests on the web.

LDS Singles (www.ldsplanet.com). One of several popular sites for the LDS dating crowd.

Mormon.org (www.mormon.org). A fundamental look at LDS principles on faith, families, and the nature of God.

MormonZone (www.mormonzone.com). The site for LDS humor, discussion boards, and yes, even the recipe for funeral potatoes and a treatise on the value of green Jell-O in the LDS household.

Official Church Site (www.lds.org). The most comprehensive site the Church offers. It provides links into the online Church publication, Church doctrine, and an excellent search engine on matters concerning Church activities.

Pioneer Historic Trail (www.nps.gov/mopi). An online guide to the official Mormon Trail, as designated by the National Park Service.

Polygamy (www.pbs.org/weta/thewest/program/episodes/five/womansexponent.htm). Although there are many sites dedicated to arguing over the matter of plural marriage, this website provides a well-documented, objective review of the outdated (and now taboo) practice.

Further Reading

General

Aspen Books. *The LDS Speaker's Sourcebook*   A great resource for people who want to find out what LDS Church leaders have said regarding specific topics about Mormonism.

Ballard, M. Russell. *Our Search for Happiness*   Written by one of the Church's apostles, a valuable book that offers an easy-to-read "pocket version" of the history of the LDS Church and the role of man and his relationship with God.

Barlow, Brent A. *What Wives Expect of Husbands*   One of the most straight-forward professors of family science at Brigham Young University, Brent Barlow offers an easy read on "marriage basics" that will appeal to couples both inside and outside the boundaries of the LDS Church.

Berrett, William Edwin. *The Restored Church*   A timeless volume of the history of the LDS people, including an account of their trials, successes, and revealed doctrines.

Dollahite, David C. *Strengthening Our Families*   A comprehensive collection of studies and writings from some of the world's most acclaimed family scientists, this book provides detailed insight into the family value system, and the challenges faced by those who want to keep their families intact in a troubled world.

Grant, George, and Karen Grant. *Letters Home*   A short anthology of words of advice from people throughout the ages.

Hartshorn, Leon R. *Remarkable Stories from the Lives of Latter-day Saint Women*, Volume II   Dr. Hartshorn, a professor of religion at Brigham Young University, has collected a second volume of stories of encouragement and trials from LDS women throughout the world.

Hawkes, Laura M. *Quotes from Prophets on Mothers and Families*   This short collection of quotes offers the reader a direct point of view from virtually every LDS prophet, regarding family unity, motherhood and the home.

Hinckley, Gordon B. *Standing for Something*   This is an excellent book on matters concerning what the author calls "10 neglected virtues that will heal our hearts and homes."

Holzapfel, Richard Neitzel. *Brigham Young: Images of a Mormon Prophet*   This is a good book that offers a visual representation of Brigham Young's time. The book is a collection of great anecdotes from the Church's pioneer era.

LDS Church Publications

When you want to know about a culture, go to the source. This collection of manuals and handbooks provides the best coverage of the LDS Church, its doctrines and history. For more information, go to the Church's website at www.lds.org.

Kimball, Edward L., and Andrew E. Kimball Jr. *Spencer W. Kimball*   This biography of the twelfth president of the LDS Church provides good insight into the modern-day Church and its leadership.

Kimball, Spencer W. *Faith Precedes the Miracle* and *The Miracle of Forgiveness*   President Kimball's two books listed here are almost always part of the LDS family library. This book offers a detailed level of understanding the principle of faith, and how, by exercising this ancient virtue, the individual can experience significant improvements in his or her life.

Knight, Hal. *111 Days to Zion*   There have been many books written about the LDS pioneer trek across America. I selected this book because of the actual journal entries that are included from the people who lived each moment of the journey.

Lewis, C. S. *A Grief Observed*   One of the most respected authors of the early twentieth century, C. S. Lewis suffered greatly at the loss of his beloved wife, Joy Davidman. This book serves as a testament to his struggle to regain a faith in God.

Ludlow, Victor L. *Isaiah: Prophet, Seer, and Poet*   If you want to dive into a comprehensive review of the most thought-provoking book in the Old Testament, this book is a must. Dr. Ludlow provides a detailed review of Prophet Isaiah, his work, and an understanding of traditional Jewish literary form.

McConkie, Bruce R. *Mormon Doctrine*   This is the lexicon of Mormon theology, and almost every LDS family has a copy of it as a reference guide. If you have any question about general Church practice or philosophy about a particular subject, it's most likely listed in *Mormon Doctrine*.

Monson, Thomas S. *Be Your Best Self*   Thomas S. Monson is the prophet of stories. He is skilled in the ability to tell the modern-day parable, and this book is full of them.

Richards, LeGrand. *A Marvelous Work and a Wonder*   The late presiding bishop of the LDS Church and member of the Twelve Apostles, Elder Richards offered the world this book, which contains the most fundamental explanation of Mormonism available. It is one of the most important books published on LDS theology, and is a must-read for anyone interested in the LDS Church.

Ririe Gundry, Linda. *Best-Loved Humor of the LDS People*   This collection of humorous quotes and incidents includes plenty of easy-going moments in the lives of Church leaders.

Smith, Joseph Fielding. *Essentials in Church History*   The late Prophet Joseph Fielding Smith was an authority on LDS Church history. He personally knew almost every one of the 15 prophets of the Church, and wrote numerous volumes on the history of the Church.

Talmage, James E. *Jesus the Christ*   This book stands out as the most comprehensive study on the life of Jesus Christ, with the exception of the scriptures themselves. Written while in the upper rooms of the Salt Lake Temple, Elder Richards' timeless profile of the Savior offers detailed views into his life and ministry.

The following publications are produced by the LDS Church with no authorship:

Achieving a Celestial Marriage

Church History in the Fullness of Times

Duties and Blessings of the Priesthood (A & B)

Teachings of Presidents of the Church: Harold B. Lee

Teachings of Presidents of the Church: Brigham Young

Teachings of Presidents of the Church: Joseph F. Smith

Marriage and Family Relations

Answers to Frequently Asked Questions

I hope this book has addressed most of the issues and fundamental concepts behind the Church of Jesus Christ of Latter-day Saints. This appendix provides additional information and answers—last words, if you will!—to some frequently asked questions about Latter-day Saints and the LDS Church. Of course, the information provided here is only a partial review of matters and interests concerning the Church.

If you have further questions or comments about Mormonism or this book, I'd love to hear from you. Feel free to e-mail me at mormoncig@yahoo.com or contact me through my website, www.drewinutah.com.

How can the LDS Church call itself "Christian" when it believes in such oddities as Jesus being the elder brother of the human race, or that he and God the Father are not the same person, or that God could possibly have anything to say to the modern world?

Because every major Christian religion can trace its roots to the Catholic Church, the minor differences between many of today's sects have been bandied about for hundreds of years. But to most Christian believers, there is no room for such concepts as modern-day revelation, a holy priesthood, mandatory 10 percent tithing, and a separation between God, Jesus, and the Holy Ghost. Ironically, all of these principles were part of the early Christian Church.

After nearly two centuries of harassment that ranged from petty to fatal, and thousands of cases of compassion toward the less fortunate, the people of the LDS Church are still often misunderstood as a passing fad or "cult." However, to those "Christians" who would exert so much effort and time to sit in judgment of Mormonism and those who follow it, Latter-day Saints would remind them that the Church is named after its leader.

Jesus stands at the head of the nearly 12-million membership of the Church of *Jesus Christ* of Latter-day Saints. The ministry and leadership of the LDS Church are offered through voluntary service, and the Church's compassionate service efforts in the world are offered without asking anything in return, and following an example that was taught by Jesus himself—to love one another. (See Chapter 25 for more on how the LDS Church conducts its business.)

What's the LDS position on God speaking through Jesus? How can God accomplish this? How many gods are there?

In Matthew 10:19–20, it says, "When they hand you over, do not worry about how you are to speak or what you are to say. You will be given at that moment what you are to say. For it will not be you who speak but the spirit of your father speaking through you." This is only one reference to a separation of leadership between God and Christ. The Bible is full of quotes, many from Jesus himself, in which God ("the Father"), is recognized not only as separate from Jesus, but also *above* him in the spiritual pecking order.

Let's use the analogy of a president versus a CEO, versus the chairman of the board. All three have different duties for running an organization, and all are frequently different entities; yet each has his own distinct and individual voice, while all share the same purpose.

As in this analogy, the LDS position is that God, Jesus Christ, and the Holy Ghost are three separate and distinct beings, with very specific responsibilities in the "Godhead." (See Chapter 2 for more information.)

Did God tease the inhabitants of the world by taking his kingdom from it, leaving the human race to wander around for hundreds of generations? If the commandments and the Word of God were not restored until the 1820s, how was it possible for people during the previous time to obey God?

Mormonism claims that there was a time on the earth when God's church was not established among men. But Mormonism also teaches that the commandments of God have always been present—either partially or in their completeness, since Adam. However, a complete restoration of God's government could not come to pass until the world (the so-called "civilized" society of mankind), was in the right frame of mind to allow such a philosophy to come forth.

Hence, it took more than 18 centuries for a society to be developed and established, which would offer the necessary freedoms to restore even the notion of complete Godliness to the world. (Learn more about the "Great Apostasy" in Chapter 9.)

Why was any reference to the restoration of the LDS Church left out of the Bible? If he is so important to salvation, why is Joseph Smith and his work never mentioned in the scriptures?

At a casual glance, readers of the Bible would probably overlook any reference to a "restoration" of the church of God.

Actually, there are several references in both the Old and New Testaments that imply the restoration of the church of Christ, including the fall of his church. I won't quote all of them, but here are a few examples and references for you to look up:

◆ On the Apostasy (falling away): Isaiah 29:13, Matthew 24:9–12, and Acts 20:28–30:

Of your own selves shall men arise, speaking perverse things, to draw my disciples after them. (Acts 20:30)

◆ On the restoration of Christ's church: Ephesians 4:4–15:

… He gave some apostles; and some, prophets; and some, evangelists; and some, pastors and teachers; For the perfecting of the saints … that we henceforth be no more children, tossed to and fro, and carried about with every wind of doctrine, by the sleight of men …

◆ On Joseph Smith Jr. and the Apostasy: Isaiah 29:10–14:

For the Lord has poured out upon you the spirit of deep sleep, and hath closed your eyes: the prophets and your rulers, the seers hath he covered. And the vision of all is become unto you as the words of a book that is sealed.… I will proceed to do a marvelous work among this people, even a marvelous work and a wonder ….

(You'll find more information about the restoration of God's Church in Chapter 11.)

Is salvation in the Latter-day concept of heaven contingent upon believing in the Book of Mormon as holy writ?

Many Christians suppose that the plan of salvation or its failure as either a kingdom in the clouds or a lake of fire, and the mere acceptance of Christ as one's personal Savior is all they need to make it into God's presence.

"Salvation" implies being saved from an eternal death—or spiritual unrest. All Christians share in the understanding that Christ died atoning for man's sins. By doing so, he provided us our salvation to be glorified to some degree, and guaranteed salvation from the grave.

However, for Latter-day Saints, the saving of one's soul to the point of eternal peace and happiness, which includes being able to live in eternity in the presence of God, requires following God's commandments as they were given by Christ and restored to Joseph Smith. And since Latter-day Saints believe that Joseph, an uneducated teenage boy, could in no way author the Book of Mormon, the LDS community considers the book the cornerstone of the LDS faith. (Check out Chapters 11, 12, and 13 for more information on Joseph Smith and the restoration of the church.)

Why do Latter-day Saints wear odd-looking undergarments? Why must they be told what to do all the way down to the type of underclothing they should wear?

When a worthy Latter-day Saint enters the temple for the first time, he or she partakes in special proceedings that require spiritual commitments be made between the individual and God—and to spouses, parents, and children.

As a reminder of those commitments, called "covenants," Latter-day Saints wear special undergarments, which provide a symbolic reminder of their temple agreements. (See Chapter 26 for more information.)

Why do Latter-day Saints get to have more than one wife, but nobody else does? Do the members of the LDS Church still practice polygamy as part of a right to religious freedom?

During the early days of the LDS Church, less than two percent of the men practiced plural marriage. The practice was eliminated more than 100 years ago, but many people still believe the LDS Church endorses polygamy.

Nobody who is currently a member of the Church of Jesus Christ of Latter-day Saints practices polygamy. The Church banned plural marriage in 1892, five years before Utah became a state. Although there might be some people who live in the state or other areas of the country who openly practice polygamy, they are in no way affiliated with the LDS Church. (See Chapter 18 for more information on the unique LDS characteristic of "Plural Marriage.")

Why all the fuss about a cup of java and a good movie? Most people understand abstinence from illegal drugs and alcohol, but does the drinking of coffee, tea, or caffeinated soft drinks mean a person can't get into heaven?

Latter-day Saints are commanded to keep the Word of Wisdom, as outlined in the Doctrine and Covenants—part of what Church members consider to be holy writ—which provide the governing set of rules and guidelines for good Latter-day Saint living.

Partaking of harmful drugs, alcohol, or "hot drinks" such as tea and coffee are mentioned as things to avoid. Latter-day Saints often follow what they believe to be the will of God, without always seeking a logical reason—it's a principle they call "faith." As for the other beverages, the LDS community considers the spirit of the law, and follows the guidelines, which are called the "Word of Wisdom," based on prayerful consideration. In many cases, Latter-day Saints abstain from all beverages that contain caffeine.

As for watching movies, LDS leaders have publicly stated that church members should not watch R-rated movies, listen to music of questionable moral value, or participate in any immoral activity such as pornography, "cybersex," or premarital intimacy.

The Church believes that there's no place in God's kingdom for unholy behavior. (You can learn more about the Word of Wisdom in Chapter 21.)

When we die, can we really be just like God? Isn't it a little absurd to think that puny mortals could become like the creator of the universe?

Mormonism teaches that the human race now exists as God once did, and that through God's own personal obedience, he became a glorified being, and so can man.

The concept of achieving a state of glory that is equal to that of the Almighty himself might sound odd to many people. However, Latter-day Saints believe that, just as Jesus Christ has obtained his own glory and sits at his father's right hand, the most righteous, obedient of God's children will inherit all that he has.

It's a relationship similar to a father raising up his son to not just be a voice in his father's family, but to *have his own family*. His father is still his father, but the son can eventually become a father as well. (Check out Chapters 2 and 6 for more information on God and his plan for the human race.)

What's the difference between an LDS temple and a normal church? Why can't just anyone go into an LDS temple? If I'm not a member of the LDS Church, does that mean I can't attend LDS meetings on Sunday?

The LDS Church has built more than 110 temples throughout the world. However, there are thousands of meeting houses, called chapels, throughout the world. On average, about one new LDS congregation is formed each week.

The temples of the Church are used to perform sacred ordinances for Latter-day Saints who have been interviewed and considered worthy to enter to participate. These sacred functions have to do with spiritual lessons required to return into God's presence. Also, worthy Church members marry in the temples for time and eternity, rather than for the duration of their mortal lives.

The many chapels that Latter-day Saints attend on Sunday are open to anyone who wishes to attend. Services that take place in the chapels include Sacrament, Sunday school, and other LDS auxiliary meetings for adults and children of all ages. (You can learn more about LDS temples and Sabbath day services in Chapters 22 and 26.)

Index

X-Y-Z

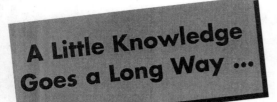
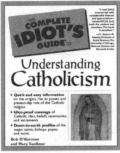

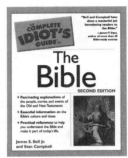

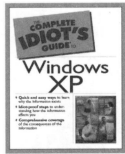